Peacemaking, peacekeeping –
international relations 1918–36

Andy Dailey and David G. Williamson

HODDER
EDUCATION
AN HACHETTE UK COMPANY

Dedication (from Andy Dailey)

To my grandparents Walter Daily (1905–94), Henry (1915–2011) and Clara Rainey Burress (1919–2001), and great aunt Elizabeth Scott (1915–2011) who made me love history.

The material in this title has been developed independently of the International Baccalaureate®, which in no way endorses it.

The Publishers would like to thank the following for permission to reproduce copyright material:

Photo credits: p10 Mary Evans Picture Library; **p72** Mary Evans Picture Library/Weimar Archive; **p75** Mary Evans Picture Library; **p76** British Cartoon Archive/Solo Syndication; **p78** Mary Evans Picture Library/Weimar Archive; **p79** Mary Evans Picture Library/Weimar Archive; **p82** British Cartoon Archive/Solo Syndication; **p84** Mary Evans Picture Library; **p92** Mary Evans Picture Library; **p93** Mary Evans/John Massey Stewart Russian Collection; **p109** Photos 12/Alamy; **p114** Mary Evans Picture Library; **p119** British Cartoon Archive/Solo Syndication; **p152** Mary Evans Picture Library; **p160** Mary Evans Picture Library/Onslow Auctions Limited; **p161** Mary Evans Picture Library; **p164** Mary Evans/Classic Stock/H. Armstrong Roberts; **p186** Bettmann/Corbis; **p202** British Cartoon Archive/Express Syndication; **p203** Hulton-Deutsch Collection/Corbis; **p205** Bettmann/Corbis; **p213** British Cartoon Archive/Express Syndication.

Acknowledgements are listed on page 244.

Every effort has been made to trace all copyright holders, but if any have been inadvertently overlooked the Publishers will be pleased to make the necessary arrangements at the first opportunity.

Although every effort has been made to ensure that website addresses are correct at time of going to press, Hodder Education cannot be held responsible for the content of any website mentioned in this book. It is sometimes possible to find a relocated web page by typing in the address of the home page for a website in the URL window of your browser.

Hachette UK's policy is to use papers that are natural, renewable and recyclable products and made from wood grown in sustainable forests. The logging and manufacturing processes are expected to conform to the environmental regulations of the country of origin.

Orders: please contact Bookpoint Ltd, 130 Milton Park, Abingdon, Oxon OX14 4SB. Telephone: (44) 01235 827827. Fax: (44) 01235 400401. Lines are open 9.00–5.00, Monday to Saturday, with a 24-hour message answering service. Visit our website at www.hoddereducation.co.uk

© Andy Dailey and David G. Williamson 2012

First published in 2012 by
Hodder Education,
An Hachette UK Company
338 Euston Road
London NW1 3BH

Impression number	5 4 3 2
Year	2016 2015 2014 2013

Cover photo. A German cartoon dated 1931: The League of Nations is dead and buried', © 2010 Mary Evans Picture Library
Illustrations by Gray Publishing
Typeset in 10/13pt Palatino and produced by Gray Publishing, Tunbridge Wells
Printed in Dubai

A catalogue record for this title is available from the British Library

ISBN: 978 1444 156324

Contents

Dedication

Keith Randell (1943–2002)

The original *Access to History* series was conceived and developed by Keith, who created a series to 'cater for students as they are, not as we might wish them to be'. He leaves a living legacy of a series that for over 20 years has provided a trusted, stimulating and well-loved accompaniment to post-16 study. Our aim with these new editions for the IB is to continue to offer students the best possible support for their studies.

Introduction

This book has been written to support your study of prescribed subject 1:
Peacemaking, peacekeeping – international relations 1918–36 of the IB History
Diploma Route 2. This first chapter gives you an overview of:

✪ the content you will study for Peacemaking, peacekeeping – international relations
1918–36

✪ how you will be assessed for Paper 1

✪ the different features of this book and how these will aid your learning.

What you will study

The period from 1918 to 1936 is a fascinating era of history. It includes the
concluding months of the First World War and the Peace of Paris treaties that
attempted to make a fairer, more peaceful and prosperous world. While the
treaties created new countries, disposed of old ones and reduced others, they
also created the League of Nations and encouraged new political systems.
The enforcement of these treaties and the impact they had on Europe were
major challenges that affected most Europeans and therefore the world in
the early twentieth century. The successes and failures of the League of
Nations were important in demonstrating the limitations of international
diplomacy and, perhaps, also show the importance of the Great Depression
on history. This significant event caused economic and therefore political
change across the world, contributing to the rise of regimes hostile to the
order established in Paris in 1919.

The Paris Peace Treaties and their impact

Your study will include the following areas:

● The participants and their goals at the Peace of Paris in 1919 in Chapter 1.
● Detailed review of the five treaties that resulted from the Peace of Paris in
1919 and 1920 in Chapter 2.
● Reaction to the decisions of the Peace of Paris in Germany and the USA in
Chapter 2.
● Effects of the treaties on central and eastern Europe in Chapter 3.

The enforcement of the treaties

Your study will include the following:

- Problems with German reparations including the Ruhr Crisis in Chapter 3.
- Impact of US isolation on international diplomacy in Chapter 4.
- Conferences and treaties regarding peace, disarmament and co-operation in Chapter 4.
- Conflicting foreign policy goals of Britain, France and other nations in Chapter 4.

League of Nations

Your study will include the following:

- The goals and structure of the League of Nations in Chapter 5.
- The successes of the League of Nations in Chapter 5.
- Mandates of the League of Nations in Chapter 5.
- Weaknesses and failures of the League of Nations in Chapters 5 and 6.

The Great Depression and threats to peace and collective security

Your study will include the following areas in Chapter 6:

- The economic and political effects of the Great Depression on governments and their policies.
- Significance of the Manchurian Crisis in international relations.
- Failure of collective security and the League of Nations during the Abyssinian Crisis.
- The importance of international agreements and diplomacy 1934–6.

 # How you will be assessed

The IB History Diploma can either be studied at Standard or Higher Level. It has three papers in total: Papers 1 and 2 for Standard Level and a further Paper 3 for Higher Level. It also has an internal assessment which all students must do.

- For Paper 1 you need to answer four source-based questions on a prescribed subject. This counts for 20 per cent of your overall marks at Higher Level, or 30 per cent of your overall marks at Standard Level.
- For Paper 2 you need to answer two essay questions on two different topics. This counts for 25 per cent of your overall marks at Higher Level, or 45 per cent of your overall marks at Standard Level.

- For Paper 3 you need to answer three essay questions on two or three sections. This counts for 35 per cent of your overall marks at Higher Level.
- For the Internal Assessment you need to carry out a historical investigation. This counts for 20 per cent of your overall marks at Higher Level, or 25 per cent of your overall marks at Standard Level.

Prescribed subject 1: Peacemaking, peacekeeping – international relations 1918–36 is assessed through Paper 1. Paper 1 of the IB History Diploma examination has five sources and four questions. The sources are from primary and secondary sources and while the majority are written, visual sources are almost always present. The visual source could be a chart, graph, table, map, cartoon, poster, stamp or photograph.

Examination questions

The four questions on Paper 1 assess different skills and knowledge. You must answer all four and have one hour to do so. The question types are as follows.

Question 1: direct questions

Question 1 is worth 5 marks and has two parts, both of which test your reading comprehension abilities on two different sources. You need to answer both parts of the question by reviewing the source material and paraphrasing information from the sources. There is a detailed guidance on how to answer question 1 on page 29. Examples of this type of question might be:

Example 1
What, according to Source A, was the importance of the New Economic Policy of the Soviet Union?

Example 2
Why, according to Source B, did Germany sign the Treaty of Versailles in 1919?

Question 2: comparing and contrasting sources

Question 2 is worth 6 marks and asks you to compare and contrast two sources. Comparing means that you explain the similarities between the sources, while contrasting explains how they are different. You should aim to have about three similarities and three differences. There is a detailed guidance on how to answer question 2 on page 65. Examples of this type of question might be:

Example 1
Compare and contrast the views of Sources A and C regarding the Bulgarian reaction to the Treaty of Neuilly.

Example 2

Compare and contrast the reasons for the failure of the USA to ratify the Treaty of Versailles as expressed by Sources B and D.

Question 3: origins, purpose, value, limitations

Question 3 is worth 6 marks and asks you to explain the value and limitations of two sources with reference to their origin and purpose.

* The origins of a source are its author or creator. This should also include the date, publisher and type of delivery which could be a book, speech, propaganda poster or diary entry.
* The purpose of the source explains what the author was trying to do, such as explaining the impact of an event or conveying a certain type of information.

The values and limitations will vary according to each source. A value could be that the author of the source witnessed the event or is an acknowledged scholar. An example of a limitation could be that an author was involved in events and therefore may be less objective. You should try to explain at least two values and two limitations per source, although this may not always be possible. There is a detailed guidance on how to answer question 3 on page 170. Examples of this type of question might be:

Example 1

With reference to their origin and purpose, assess the value and limitations of Source B and Source E for historians studying the first Five-Year Plan of the Soviet Union.

Example 2

With reference to their origin and purpose, assess the value and limitations of Source A and Source C for historians studying the Abyssinian Crisis.

Question 4: Essays integrating knowledge and sources

Question 4 is worth 8 marks and requires you to use all the sources in the examination and to integrate them into an essay that also contains your own knowledge. There is a detailed guidance on how to answer question 4 on page 218. Examples of this type of question might be:

Example 1

Using these sources and your own knowledge, discuss the extent to which you agree that the Ruhr Crisis was a failure for France.

Example 2

Using these sources and your own knowledge, explain why the League of Nations failed to intervene in the Manchurian Crisis.

The appearance of the examination paper

Cover

The cover of the examination paper states the date of the examination and the length of time you have to complete it: one hour. Please note that there are two routes in history. Make sure your paper says Route 2 on it. Instructions are limited and simply state that you should not open it until told to do so and that all questions must be answered.

Sources

Once you are allowed to open your examination paper, you will note that there are five sources, each labelled with a letter. There is no particular order to the sources, so Source A could potentially be a map, a speech, a photograph or an extract from a book. Source A is no more or less important than Source B and so on. If you see square brackets, [ ], then this is an explanation or addition to the source by the creators of the examination and not part of the original source. Sometimes sources are shortened and you will see an ellipsis, three full stops (…), when this happens.

Questions

After the five sources the four questions will appear. You need to answer all of them. It is better to answer the questions in order, as this will familiarize you with all the sources to be used in the final essay on question 4, but this is not required. Be sure to number your questions correctly. Do not use bullet points to answer questions, but instead write in full sentences when possible. Each question indicates how many marks it is worth.

 # 3 About this book

Coverage of course content

This book addresses the key areas listed in the IB History Guide for Route 2: Twentieth century world history prescribed subject 1: Peacemaking, peacekeeping – international relations 1918–36. The chapters start with an introduction outlining the key questions they address. They are then divided into a series of sections and topics covering the course content. Throughout the chapters you will find the following features to aid your study of the course content.

Key and leading questions

Each section heading in the chapter has a related key question which gives a focus to your reading and understanding of the section. These are also listed in the chapter introduction. You should be able to answer the questions after completing the relevant section.

Topics within the sections have leading questions which are designed to help you focus on the key points within a topic and give you more practice in answering questions.

Key terms

Key terms are the important terms you need to know to gain an understanding of the period. These are emboldened in the text the first time they appear in the book and are defined in the margin. They also appear in the glossary at the end of the book.

Sources

Each chapter contains several sources. These sources follow the labelling format of a Paper 1 examination. The sources have accompanying questions and are also used with the exam-style questions at the end of the chapters. The range of sources used will expose you to many different types of sources that you may find in the examination.

Key debates

Historians often disagree on historical events and this historical debate is referred to as historiography. Knowledge of historiography is helpful in reaching the upper mark bands when you take your IB History examinations. There are a number of debates throughout the book to develop your understanding of historiography.

Theory of Knowledge (TOK) questions

Understanding that different historians see history differently is an important element in understanding the connection between the IB History Diploma and Theory of Knowledge. Alongside most key debates is a Theory of Knowledge style question which makes that link.

Summary diagrams

At the end of each section is a summary diagram which gives a visual summary of the content of the section. It is intended as an aid for revision.

Chapter summary

At the end of each chapter is a short summary of the content of that chapter. This is intended to help you revise and consolidate your knowledge and understanding of the content.

Skills development

At the end of each chapter are the following:

- Examination guidance on how to answer different question types, accompanied by a sample answer and commentary designed to help you focus on specific details.
- Examination practice in the form of Paper 1-style questions.

- Suggestions for learning activities, including ideas for debate, essays, displays and research which will help you develop Paper 1 skills and a deeper understanding of the content.

These are all intended to help you develop the following skills development in order to achieve examination success:

- *Source analysis*. This book allows you to become familiar with the works of many historians and primary source material. It teaches you to analyse all types of sources and gives you the opportunity to review their strengths, weaknesses, origins, purpose, values and limitations.
- *Integrating sources into essays*. Integrating sources into essays requires that you know how to write a good essay. This book gives guidance on writing good essays that integrate sources.

End of the book

The book concludes with the following sections:

Timeline
This gives a timeline of the major events covered in the book which is helpful for quick reference or as a revision tool.

Glossary
All key terms in the book are defined in the glossary.

Further reading
This contains a list of books, websites, films and other resources which may help you with further independent research and presentations. It may also be helpful when further information is required for internal assessments and extended essays in history. You may wish to share the contents of this area with your school or local librarian.

Internal assessment
All IB History diploma students are required to write a historical investigation which is internally assessed. The investigation is an opportunity for you to dig more deeply into a subject that interests you. There is a list of possible topics at the end of the book that could warrant further investigation to form part of your historical investigation.

CHAPTER 1

The Paris Peace Conference: the aims of the participants

This chapter investigates conditions in Europe when the Paris Peace Conference meetings were held in 1919 and the aims of the participating governments. Throughout the chapter you need to consider the following questions:

✪ What contemporary events affected the Paris Peace Conference discussions?

✪ What were the main aims of the US government for the Paris Peace Conference?

✪ To what extent had Britain achieved its war aims by December 1918?

✪ Were French aims directed at making France more secure or more about punishing Germany for the First World War?

✪ To what extent did Italy's goals differ from those of other Allied Powers?

✪ How far was the new German government willing to co-operate with the victorious Allied Powers at the Paris Peace Conference and how successful was its strategy?

① Conditions in Europe in 1919

▶ *Key question: What contemporary events affected the Paris Peace Conference discussions?*

In January 1919, leaders and diplomats of the 29 countries which had emerged victorious from the First World War began a year-long series of meetings to establish world order and peace.

Each victorious nation had particular goals and concerns, although these were sometimes shared between several of them. What was clear was the need for urgent action as there were many problems throughout Europe as a result of the First World War.

Hardship in Europe

The statesmen of the victorious Allied Powers were confronted by Europe in turmoil. Soldiers were returning to towns, farms and villages which had been destroyed in battles across much of eastern Europe, France, Belgium and northern Italy. With the disintegration of the Austrian, Turkish and Russian empires there was no stable government anywhere east of the Rhine. As new nations formed, such as Poland, Yugoslavia and Czechoslovakia, people were no longer living in countries they had fought for.

← **What problems faced Europeans in early 1919?**

The peoples of Germany, Austria-Hungary and other parts of Europe were starving. The British naval blockade of Germany during the war had meant imported food, on which Germany relied, could not get through. This blockade continued until June 1919, meaning that Germans continued to starve in the early months of the Paris Peace Conference, a situation exacerbated by the fact that there were fewer farmers to grow food as they had been conscripted into the army. Chemicals that would normally have been used to make fertilizers and even manure from animals that would help the soil replenish nutrients were used instead by the warring states to make explosives and other war goods. The soil simply grew less food and there were fewer people farming.

The problems facing the statesmen in Paris were thus not only the negotiation of peace and the drawing up of new frontiers, but also the pressing need to avert economic chaos and famine.

What conditions in Europe at the end of the First World War created revolutions?

Revolution

The sudden and complete defeat of the **Central Powers** had made Europe vulnerable to the spread of **communism** from Russia.

The Russian Revolution

In October 1917 a radical political group, the **Bolsheviks**, overthrew the Russian government and began a violent take-over of the entire nation. The Bolsheviks ended Russia's war with Germany and fighting broke out between the Bolsheviks and many other groups for control of the country. This civil war, which lasted for more than three years, was still taking place

SOURCE A

'Bolshevik atrocities', Latvia, 1919.

What information is contained in Source A (both the photo and caption) that is important for historians?

during the Paris Peace Conference. During the civil war, many national groups fought for independence from Russia with varying degrees of success and with much bloodshed. Some of these states were Estonia, Latvia, Lithuania, Georgia, Armenia and Azerbaijan. Estonia, Latvia and Lithuania were successful, while Georgia, Armenia and Azerbaijan were not.

Revolution in Germany

SOURCE B

German Chancellor Friedrich Ebert's announcement of 10 November 1918. *New York Times*, 11 November 1918, vol. LXVIII, no. 22,206. The *New York Times* had been published since 1851 in New York, USA and has had one of the largest circulations of any newspaper in the world for over 100 years.

Citizens:

The ex-Chancellor, Prince Max of Baden, in agreement with all the Secretaries of State, has handed over to me the task of liquidating his affairs as Chancellor.

I am on the point of forming a new Government in accord with the various parties, and will keep public opinion freely informed of the course of events.

The new Government will be a Government of the people. It must make every effort to secure in the quickest possible time peace for the German people and consolidate the liberty which they have won.

The new Government has taken charge of the administration, to preserve the German people from civil war and famine and to accomplish their legitimate claim to autonomy. The Government can solve this problem only if all the officials in town and country will help.

I know it will be difficult for some to work with the new men who have taken charge of the empire, but I appeal to their love of the people. Lack of organization would in this heavy time mean anarchy in Germany and the surrender of the country to tremendous misery. Therefore, help your native country with fearless, indefatigable work for the future, everyone at his post.

I demand every one's support in the hard task awaiting us. You know how seriously the war has menaced the provisioning [supplying food] of the people, which is the first condition of the people's existence.

The political transformation should not trouble the people. The food supply is the first duty of all, whether in town or country, and they should not embarrass, but rather aid, the production of food supplies and their transport to the towns.

Food shortage signifies pillage and robbery, with great misery. The poorest will suffer the most, and the industrial worker will be affected hardest. All who illicitly lay hands on food supplies or other supplies of prime necessity or the means of transport necessary for their distribution will be guilty in the highest degree toward the community.

I ask you immediately to leave the streets and remain orderly and calm.

What is the importance of Source B in understanding the conditions in Germany in November 1918?

KEY TERM

Kaiser Emperor of Germany. Wilhelm II, 1888–1918, was the last German Emperor.

Parliamentary government A government responsible to and elected by parliament.

Armistice Agreement to stop fighting.

Fourteen Points A list of points drawn up by Woodrow Wilson on which the peace settlement at the end of the First World War was based.

Socialist One who believes that a society should be as equitable as possible with few, if any, differences between society members in terms of economic or social standing.

Republic A form of government in which representatives are elected by a population to rule, usually in a parliamentary method of government.

Chancellor Head of the German parliament and equivalent to prime minister.

Pariah state A nation with no friendly relations with other states.

On 28 September 1918, the German Generals Ludendorff and Hindenburg conceded defeat in the First World War and advised the **Kaiser** to form a new **parliamentary government**. This was intended to impress US President Wilson with its democratic credentials and receive more lenient treatment at the war's end.

On 4 October the new German government asked Wilson for an **armistice** on the basis of the **Fourteen Points** (see page 15). Wilson, however, asked France and Britain to draft the details of the armistice agreements. They produced tough terms that were not wholly consistent with the Fourteen Points, but which anticipated their key aims at the coming peace conference. The terms were too harsh for the German government to accept.

Once news of the armistice negotiations became public, the demand for peace by the German people, after the years of deprivation caused by the Allied blockade and false hopes of victory, became unstoppable.

Rashly, on 28 October, the German Admiralty ordered the fleet out on a suicide mission against the British. In protest, the sailors at the Wilhelmshaven base mutinied. When the ringleaders were arrested, their colleagues organized mass protest meetings and formed councils, as **socialist** revolutionaries had done in Russia in 1917. By early November, sailors took control of all naval facilities and ports and were soon joined by socialist political parties which were in the majority in the German parliament, the *Reichstag*. Socialist revolutionaries soon controlled most German cities.

On 9 November the Kaiser was forced to abdicate and Germany became a **republic**. The German government had little option but to accept the armistice on 11 November. The new German **chancellor**, Friedrich Ebert, worked with great urgency to prevent the revolution from becoming violent and overthrowing the social and economic order of Germany as had happened in Russia with the Bolsheviks. By forming a republic, it was hoped Germany would be treated more leniently because the Allied Powers were also republics. For the army, it had the benefit of creating a new government which could sign any surrender documents rather than the army having to do so; this would preserve the army's honour.

SOURCE C

General Erich Ludendorff, General of the Infantry of the German Empire, quoted in My War Memories 1914–1918, first published in 1919. Currently published by Naval & Military Press, UK, 2005. Ludendorff was overall commander of German military forces in the final years of the First World War.

By the Revolution the Germans have made themselves pariahs among the nations, incapable of winning Allies, helots [slaves] in the service of foreigners and foreign capital, and deprived of all self-respect. In twenty years' time, the German people will curse the parties who now boast of having made the Revolution.

According to Source C, what will happen to Germans as a result of the 1918 revolution?

The Spartacist uprising

In January 1919, just as the delegates were arriving in Paris, a group of German communists, called the Spartacists, attempted to overthrow the newly created German republic. The Spartacists were aggressively suppressed, partly because the world had witnessed the violence of the Bolsheviks in Russia. In May 1919, the German government was also able to crush the short-lived Bavarian Soviet Republic, another Marxist-inspired rebellion against Germany and the old political and social order (see page 71).

Fear of communist revolution

In March 1919, much of Hungary, a state forming out of the old **Austro-Hungarian Empire**, became the Hungarian Soviet Republic when communists seized power. It survived until August, when defeated by anti-communist Romanian and Hungarian troops, but at the time it seemed to the Allied leaders that the door to central Europe was now open to communism.

In 1918 and early 1919, there were workers' strikes in France, Britain, Italy and other countries, all demanding better wages and working conditions. The fear of communist revolution was felt throughout much of Europe, including among the victorious Allies. This fear of revolution was intensified by the **Spanish influenza pandemic** which, by the spring of 1919, had caused the deaths of millions of people, and by the near famine conditions in central and eastern Europe.

So, the context in which the Paris Peace Conference met was one of political turmoil in a Europe which was starving and where millions were infected with influenza. As one Allied official observed, 'There was a veritable race between peace and anarchy.'

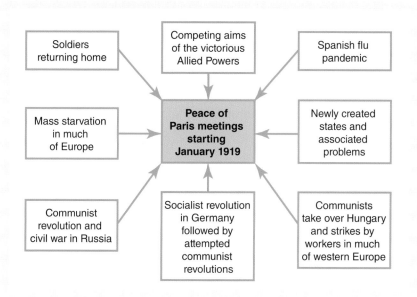

Conditions in Europe in 1919

KEY TERM

Austro-Hungarian Empire A multinational empire which was administrated in two separate parts: Austria and the Kingdom of Hungary, with the Habsburg Emperor of Austria also being the King of Hungary. Its territory compromised all of modern-day Austria, Hungary, Czech Republic, Slovakia, Slovenia, Croatia, Bosnia-Herzegovina and parts of Poland, Romania, Italy, Serbia, Montenegro and Ukraine. It was formed in 1867 from the Austrian Empire and lasted until 1918.

Spanish influenza pandemic This disease killed between 50 million and 100 million people worldwide from 1918 to 1920.

Aims of the USA in Paris 1919

▶ **Key question:** *What were the main aims of the US government for the Paris Peace Conference?*

? What is the importance of Source D in understanding the aims of the USA in the Paris meetings of 1919?

SOURCE D

Excerpt from a speech about the Fourteen Points given on 8 January 1918 by Woodrow Wilson, President of the USA.

What we demand in this war, therefore, is nothing peculiar to ourselves. It is that the world be made fit and safe to live in; and particularly that it be made safe for every peace-loving nation which, like our own, wishes to live its own life, determine its own institutions, be assured of justice and fair dealing by the other peoples of the world as against force and selfish aggression. All the peoples of the world are in effect partners in this interest, and for our own part we see very clearly that unless justice be done to others it will not be done to us.

How did the USA's experience of war influence its aims for peace?

The USA in the First World War

The USA officially entered the war in 1917 but was unable to participate in the fighting in a significant way until 1918. The USA had to build ships, an army and war equipment, while also supplying Britain, France and Italy with food and munitions. The USA did not suffer the great loss of life and property of the other **Allied Powers** because of their late entry into the conflict. They lost only about 117,000 soldiers, according to the US Department of Justice, with 43,000 of these from the Spanish influenza. Russia and France had over a million deaths of soldiers each, while the British Empire had just over 900,000 war-dead.

KEY TERM

Allied Powers Britain, France, the USA, Italy and other countries which fought against Germany, Austria-Hungary, Bulgaria and the Ottoman Empire.

Many in the USA believed that no country should benefit from such a tremendous catastrophe as the First World War and were suspicious of their Allies, believing, correctly, that they hoped to reward themselves with land and financial compensation. Many Americans believed that taking colonies and provinces from defeated powers would simply lead to future conflicts.

Which US aims were meant to create lasting conditions for world peace?

General aims

US President Wilson issued his Fourteen Points in a speech in January 1918. According to Wilson, these points were not only to be the basis of a German surrender, but also for creating a lasting world peace. Throughout 1918, the USA worked successfully to get other Allied Powers to agree to the points as a basis for post-war peace treaties. Italy, France and Britain all eventually agreed, but with significant reservations.

A summary of the Fourteen Points

1. Secret treaties between nations will end.
2. All ships of all countries have the right to use the sea at all times.
3. All nations must accept free trade.
4. All nations must work towards **disarmament**.
5. Colonial issues must be resolved, but in co-operation with the people living in the colonies.
6. Foreign troops must leave Russia and the new government there must be welcomed by other nations.
7. All foreign troops must leave Belgium and its independence restored.
8. German troops must leave all French territory and Alsace-Lorraine, part of Germany since 1871, must return to France.
9. Italy should be expanded to include areas where Italian-language speakers live.
10. The various groups living within the Austro-Hungarian Empire should be allowed to form **nation states**.
11. Foreign troops should leave the Balkan peninsula and all states there should be restored; Serbia should have access to the sea.
12. Turks in the **Ottoman Empire** should continue to rule themselves, but other nationalities in the Empire should be free to form their own states; the **Dardenelles** should be a free international waterway.
13. An independent Poland should be created and also have access to the sea.
14. An international body of states [League of Nations] should be formed to work towards resolving conflicts.

 **KEY TERM**

Disarmament Limiting weapons and militaries in order to reduce the possibility of war.

Nation state A state consisting of a culturally united population.

Ottoman Empire Large, nationally and religiously diverse empire ruled by Turks that included most of the Middle East and a small part of Europe, including the Dardenelles and Bosphorus straits that linked the Aegean and Mediterranean Seas with the Black Sea.

Dardenelles Strait connecting the Mediterranean and Aegean Seas with the Black Sea, separating Europe from Asia Minor.

Covenant Rules and constitution of the League of Nations.

Although Wilson believed that Germany should be punished and, according to historian Margaret MacMillan, treated like a convict for starting the First World War, he was determined to ensure that the Fourteen Points served as a basis for the peace negotiations and to anchor the **Covenant** of the League of Nations in the text of the peace treaties. He was convinced that this was the key to creating a just and lasting peace.

The Fourteen Points very obviously demonstrate Wilson's belief that free trade, self-rule for the various nationalities of Europe and the Middle East, and disarmament would lead to world peace. Like many others at the time, Wilson also believed that military alliances with secret clauses and the lack of an international body to discuss problems also produced war.

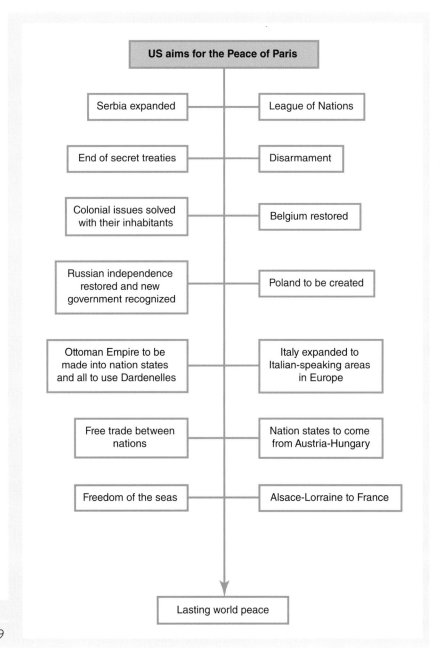

British aims for the Paris Peace Conference 1919

> ▶ **Key question:** *To what extent had Britain achieved its war aims by December 1918?*

SOURCE E

Statement by David Lloyd George, British Prime Minister, 5 January 1918, regarding British war aims. From *Encyclopedia of International Affairs*, **edited by J.C. Johari, Ammol Publications Pvt. Ltd., New Delhi, India, 1997. Johari has published numerous books on politics.**

… The first requirement … [is the] independence of Belgium, and such reparation as can be made for the devastation of its towns and provinces. This is no demand for war indemnity, such as that imposed on France by Germany in 1871. It is not an attempt to shift the cost of warlike operations from one belligerent [warring nation] to another, which may or may not be defensible. It is no more and no less than an insistence that, before there can be any hope for a stable peace, this great breach of the public law of Europe must be repudiated [rejected] and, so far as possible, repaired.

… We believe, however, that an independent Poland comprising all those genuinely Polish elements who desire to form part of it, is an urgent necessity for the stability of Western Europe …

… Finally, there must be reparation for injuries done in violation of international law. The Peace Conference must not forget our seamen and the services they have rendered to, and the outrages they have suffered for the common cause of freedom.

> What reasons does Lloyd George give in Source E for the specific aims of independence of Belgium, the independence of Poland and reparations?

Britain in the First World War

> ← **Why did Britain join the First World War and what was the impact of its participation?**

Britain declared war on Germany in 1914 when the German army crossed into neutral Belgium. The neutrality of Belgium was guaranteed by the Convention of 1839 which prohibited any alliances for Belgium and its invasion by any country. This treaty had been signed by Britain and France, among others, and the British government believed it had a legal and moral obligation to fulfil its pledge to defend Belgium in case of attack by another country.

There was also fear of the powerful German navy. If Belgium and France fell, the German navy and its submarines, U-boats, would be within very easy striking distance of Britain. Britain imported the vast majority of its food and much of its raw materials for industry, so security of the sea was vital for its independence. Many in the British government also felt obligated to assist France, which Germany had declared war on, due to several military arrangements between them, although there was no formal alliance such as the one France had with Russia.

The British Empire lost over 900,000 soldiers fighting primarily against Germany and the Ottoman Empire in the First World War. There were also over two million wounded. Many ships had been sunk, complete with valuable cargoes, and Britain ended the war with tremendous debt, owed mostly to the USA.

By the end of the war, the British Empire was in possession of most German colonies and huge areas of the Ottoman Empire. Most German merchant ships had been either been seized or destroyed and with the November 1918 armistice, the entire German navy was turned over to Britain. By the end of the First World War, many British aims had been achieved.

How were most British demands for naval superiority already accomplished before the Paris Peace Conference?

Naval supremacy

As an island and a world-spanning empire, Britain was most concerned with maintaining a navy superior to all others. As such, one of the main aims of the British government was the elimination of the German naval threat that had existed before and during the First World War.

This aim was largely achieved by the time the Allied Powers met in Paris as the German fleet had surrendered in order to secure the armistice in November 1918.

Britain did, however, reject Wilson's second point of the Fourteen Points which stated that all nations should have free use of the seas during peace and war. Wilson had to drop the issue during the subsequent negotiations.

To what extent did Britain intend to reward itself for victory in the First World War?

Colonial and territorial considerations

The British wished to divest Germany of its colonies. This had already been accomplished during the war, when Britain and its **Dominions**, as well as Japan, took over these territories. Part of this concern over colonies was driven by British desire to take over some of Germany's trade, but there were also security concerns. By depriving Germany of colonies, Britain could guarantee that no bases or ports for a future German navy would exist. Colonies were seen as a form of reward for Britain and the Dominions.

Britain's territorial ambitions lay primarily in the Middle East, due to its oil. It wanted colonial expansion there at the expense of the Ottoman Empire and, in 1916, it had made an agreement with France to divide Ottoman territory between them at the war's conclusion in the Sykes–Picot Agreement (see page 157). The British wanted to confirm this agreement in the discussions in Paris and thereby expand their control over a potentially mineral-rich area.

KEY TERM

Dominions Self-ruling parts of the British Empire such as Australia, Canada, New Zealand, Newfoundland and South Africa.

Preservation of Germany

Britain believed that Germany should be made to pay for the war through **reparations**. At the same time, they believed that Germany should be rehabilitated as soon as possible to stabilize international trade. Germany was one of the most industrialized nations in the world and, as such, was not only an exporter, but a great importer of British materials and goods. Britain needed German trade for both economic and political reasons. Many of its overseas markets were lost to the USA during the war years. In addition, many colonies and dominions became more economically independent when British industries switched to military from consumer production. Moreover, an economically revitalized Germany would be better able to make reparations to the Allied Powers.

Britain was also concerned with the emerging Soviet Union. Britain, like most industrialized countries, not only wanted to prevent the Bolsheviks from being successful in Russia but also from spreading their philosophy to other nations. Bringing a peaceful Germany back into the world system of international trade would prevent revolution from spreading and serve as a barrier against the emerging Soviet Union.

Why did Britain want the German economy to recover as soon as possible?

🔑 **KEY TERM**

Reparations Payments made by a defeated country to the victor in order to pay for the victor's war expenses, damages, and as a penalty for losing.

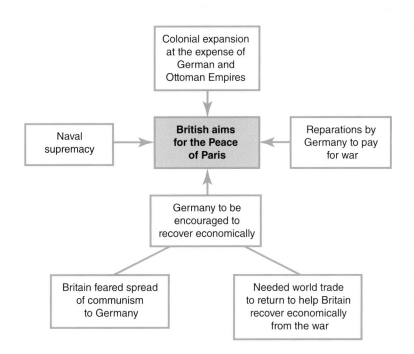

SUMMARY DIAGRAM

British aims for the Paris Peace Conference 1919

French aims for the Paris Peace Conference 1919

> ▶ *Key question:* Were French aims directed at making France more secure or more about punishing Germany for the First World War?

? According to Source F, what was one French goal for the end of the First World War?

SOURCE F

Excerpt from a letter from Aristide Briand to Jules Cambon dated 12 January 1917, published in *The Foreign Policy of France from 1914 to 1945* by Jacques Néré, Routledge Publishers, 2002, p. 267. Briand was Prime Minister of France eleven times and often Foreign Minister at the same time. Cambon was French Ambassador to Germany at the outbreak of the First World War, subsequently serving as head of the Political Section of the French Foreign Ministry. Néré is a French historian who has published numerous books on the modern history of France.

In our eyes, Germany must no longer have a foot beyond the Rhine; the organisation of these territories, their neutrality and their temporary occupation must be considered in exchanges of opinion between the Allies. It is, however, important that France, being the most directly concerned with the territorial status of this region, should have the casting vote in examining the solution of this serious question.

How was France affected by the German invasion?

France in the First World War

On 28 July 1914 the Russian government ordered **mobilization** of its forces in reaction to Austria-Hungary's declaration of war on Serbia. Germany believed that war between Russia and its ally Austria-Hungary was possible. This led to Germany putting the **Schlieffen Plan** into action (see Source G) and duly declaring war on France. The plan depended on defeating the French, an ally of Russia, before the Russian army was fully prepared for war. This unprovoked attack led to the death of over 1.3 million French soldiers and the wounding of millions more. It also meant the destruction of most of northern France and massive war debt. Losses and damage were tremendous and as a result France wanted to guarantee that Germany could never attack again.

 **KEY TERM**

Mobilization Preparing armed forces for war.

Schlieffen Plan German plan for war against France and Russia. The plan was to defeat France within weeks, moving through Belgium and Luxembourg, avoiding the fortified border between France and Germany. After the defeat of France, the mass of the German army would move quickly east by rail to invade Russia.

SOURCE G

Map of the Schlieffen Plan with movements of troops and anticipated conquests in terms of weeks.

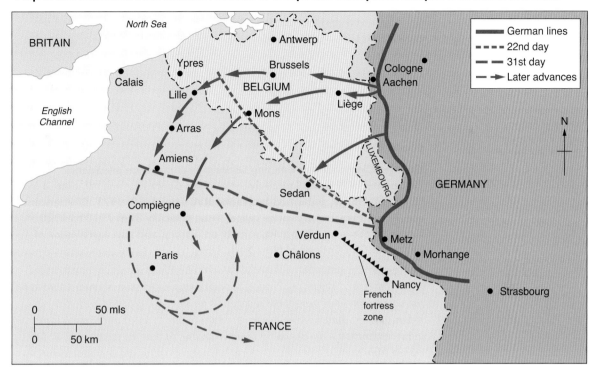

What is the importance of Source G in understanding French desire for security against Germany after the First World War?

Territorial and colonial considerations

France first and foremost demanded the return of the provinces Alsace and Lorraine. These had been annexed by the newly formed German state in 1871. They had the added benefit of coal and iron mines, as well as steel factories. In November 1918, just days after the armistice with Germany, French troops occupied the two provinces, ending a week-old Republic of Alsace-Lorraine. Wilson's Fourteen Points called for the return of Alsace and Lorraine to France and this was very agreeable to the French.

France desired the creation of the state of Poland, as well as other states in central Europe, such as Czechoslovakia and Yugoslavia, to balance German power. If Poland could be created with German territory, then the French government would be even more satisfied. France also wanted to create an independent Rhineland state which would weaken Germany economically; major resources and industry were located there. This would also create a **buffer state** between Germany and Belgium and Germany and France in case of future conflicts.

What territorial adjustments did France desire in Europe?

 **KEY TERM**

Buffer state A country separating two other nations who are enemies.

21

The Saar was one of the most industrialized and coal-rich areas of Germany and bordered France. France wanted the Saar as compensation for the war.

France believed that Germany should not be allowed to retain any of its overseas territories for reasons similar to those of Britain. France desired parts of the defeated Ottoman Empire, specifically access to the Mosul oil fields, and already had a long-term relationship with the territory known as Lebanon during the Ottoman era.

Why did France expect Germany to pay for the entire war?

Reparations

SOURCE H

Georges Clemenceau's opening address as conference president, 18 January 1919 from *Source Records of the Great War, vol. VII*, edited by Charles F. Horne, published by National Alumni, USA, 1923. Clemenceau was Prime Minister of France twice, most critically from 1917 to 1920. Horne wrote over 100 books, mostly on history, and was a professor of English at City College of New York, USA.

The greater the sanguinary [bloody] catastrophe which devastated and ruined one of the richest regions of France, the more ample and more splendid should be the reparation – not merely the reparation for material acts, the ordinary reparation, if I may venture to say so, which is due to us – but the nobler and loftier reparation – we are going to try to secure, so that the people may at last escape from this fatal embrace, which, heaping up ruins and sorrows, terrorizes the populations and prevents them from devoting themselves freely to their work for fear of the enemies who may spring up at any moment.

According to Source H, what was the purpose of German reparations?

France owed approximately $3.5 billion to Britain and the USA as a result of the First World War. In addition, France had lent 12 billion francs to Russia, but this was repudiated by the Bolshevik government and these funds would never be repaid. During the war, thousands of businesses, factories, mines and homes had been destroyed in northern France. The severely damaged economy and massive debt meant that France would have difficulty recovering economically. France believed that Germany should receive a massive **indemnity** to pay for the war and also serve as a punishment. It is important to remember that in the Franco-Prussian War of 1870–1 France was defeated, the German states formed the German Empire, and France was given a massive war indemnity to pay for the war and to punish it for starting the conflict.

🔑 KEY TERM

Indemnity A financial penalty where one country owes another.

What was the main motive for the French to desire a much smaller German military?

Military considerations

France naturally wished to limit the Germany military as much as possible so that future attacks would be essentially impossible. Germany had threatened France several times since 1871, including during the Moroccan and Agadir Crises of 1905 and 1911, respectively, to achieve concessions from France. France had every reason to limit the Germany military because of the sheer number of dead and wounded from the First World War. France also desired a military alliance with Britain and the USA against any future German aggression.

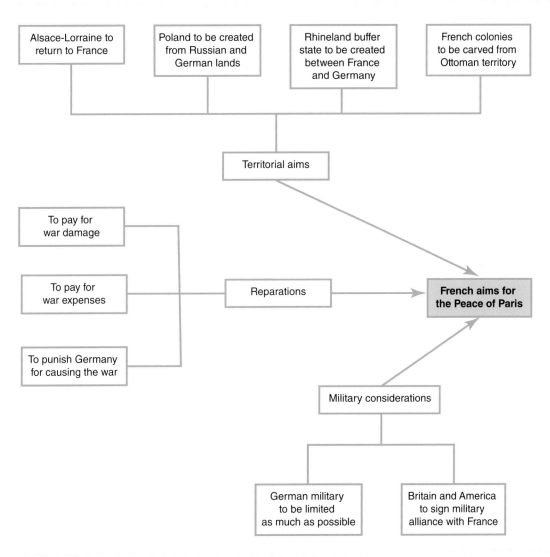

French aims for the Paris Peace Conference 1919

5 Italian aims for the Paris Peace Conference 1919

▶ **Key question:** *To what extent did Italy's goals differ from those of other Allied Powers?*

According to Source I, what are the incentives for Italy to join the First World War?

SOURCE I

Excerpt from the *Treaty of London*, 26 April 1915. This document was signed by the foreign ministers of Britain, France, Italy and Russia.

ARTICLE 4 By the future treaty of peace, Italy is to receive the district of Trentino; the entire Southern Tyrol up to its natural geographical frontier, which is the Brenner Pass; the city and district of Trieste; the County of Gorizia and Gradisca; the entire Istria [Istrian peninsula] …

ARTICLE 9 France, Great Britain and Russia admit in principle the fact of Italy's interest in the maintenance of the political balance of power in the Mediterranean, and her rights, in case of a partition of Turkey, to a share, equal to theirs, in the basin of the Mediterranean …

ARTICLE 11 Italy is to get a share in the war indemnity corresponding to the magnitude of her sacrifices and efforts.

Why did Italy join the First World War and with what success by 1918?

 **KEY TERM**

Triple Alliance Military alliance established in 1881 between Germany, Austria-Hungary and Italy.

Italian nationalists In this period, people who wanted to expand the nation state of Italy to include all Italian-language speakers.

→ Italy in the First World War

Italy had been part of the **Triple Alliance** with Austria-Hungary and Germany before the First World War. Italy left the alliance at the start of the war, pointing out that the alliance was meant to have been defensive in nature, not offensive. The possibility of joining the war was extremely unpopular in Italy, a country with few resources and little unity. There was some desire, however, by **Italian nationalists** to have the Italian-language territories in Austria-Hungary join the rest of Italy, regardless of what the residents of those areas wanted. The idea of an Italian Empire appealed to some. Italy did join the war in May 1915, but only after being promised significant territories in a secret treaty, the Treaty of London.

Italy struggled during the First World War. After initial small successes against Austria-Hungary, at the cost of tens of thousands of men, there was little military progress. Austria-Hungary and Germany launched a massive counter-attack in 1917 that almost took Italy out of the war. In 1918, French and British troops reinforced the Italian army and only at the end of 1918 was there any major success on the battle field, as Austria-Hungary began to collapse militarily and politically. Over 600,000 Italians were killed with few territorial gains to show for it.

Territorial claims

Italy's main concerns for the Paris Peace Conference were territorial in nature, perhaps because Italy specifically entered the war to gain territory, not because it was attacked by another nation. The Treaty of London promised Italy large sections of Austro-Hungarian land, mostly where there were at least some Italian-speaking people living. The territories promised were the province of Tyrol up to the Brenner Pass, the port of Trieste and the Istrian peninsula, plus most of the Dalmatian coast. Italy would also receive the Dodecanese islands in the Aegean Sea, part of German colonies in Asia and Africa, and the Albanian port of Vlorë. Italy was to be the protector of Albania, thereby giving it control over much of its foreign policy and resources. Italy expected to be granted parts of the Ottoman Empire and the deep-water port of Fiume, today's Rijeka, adjoining the Istrian peninsula, although this was not stated in the Treaty of London. These promises were made without any provision to determine the wishes of the inhabitants of the regions concerned. Italy's involvement in the war was very unpopular and there was much pressure on the government to demonstrate that the sacrifices made in the war were rewarded. Naturally, Italy expected reparations for war damage, as did all the Allied Powers.

What was the importance of the Treaty of London of 1915?

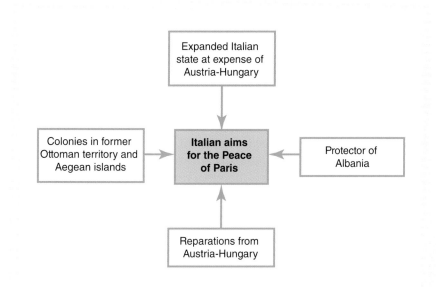

SUMMARY DIAGRAM

Italian aims for the Paris Peace Conference 1919

6 German hopes for the Paris Peace Conference 1919

▶ *Key question:* How far was the new German government willing to co-operate with the victorious Allied Powers at the Paris Peace Conference and how successful was its strategy?

SOURCE J

What, according to Source J, was the basis of German arguments against the aims of some of the Allied Powers, France in particular?

Excerpt from 'Germany Before the Peace Conference by Count von Brockdorff-Rantzau' in *The Living Age*, vol. 301, published by The Living Age Company, Boston, USA, 1919, pp. 68–9. Brockdorff-Rantzau was Foreign Minister of Germany during the Paris Peace Conference meetings. *The Living Age* was an American weekly news magazine.

We decline our enemies as judges because of their prejudice. We can inwardly submit not to the claims of the conqueror but only to the judgment of the unbiased. Therefore, I will not allow myself to be driven away from the points of the Wilson peace program as recognized by both sides … We are prepared for both limitations of our sovereignty, if our previous enemies and our future neighbors submit to the same limitation.

… Therefore, we hold fast to the Wilson principles that no costs are to be paid to the conqueror and no territory is to be ceded by the vanquished.

We are bound and prepared to make good the damage which has resulted from our attack to the civil population in the territories occupied by us, but if we again build up what has been destroyed in those territories, we wish to do that by our own free work.

… Our enemies have to thank for their victory to an overwhelming extent not the military but the economic conduct of the war. From this it follows that the peace must be not merely a political, but also essentially an economic peace. President Wilson rightly described the principle of economic freedom and equality as the main condition of a just and permanent peace.

… Germany can no more enter the League of Nations without colonies than she can without a merchant fleet. According to Wilson's programme there should be a free, generous, and absolutely equitable settlement of colonial questions …

… it would be unjust to dispose of [the people of Alsace-Lorraine] without their consent, without even respecting the language frontiers.

What actions did Germany take to reduce potential punishment at the hands of the victorious Allied Powers?

→ Self-preservation

Germany realized that victory on the Western Front against France, Britain and the USA was not possible by late September 1918. The army informed the German Emperor who then allowed the formation of a parliamentary government. This meant that the German government was now under the control of the *Reichstag,* the German parliament. It was hoped that Allied governments would grant better armistice and peace terms as a result of this democratic change.

The army and emperor also believed that in some way the new government could be blamed for Germany's surrender. In a little over a month, the emperor was removed from office and sent into exile. Germany had become a republic under the leadership of Frederich Ebert.

The new republic agreed to a harsh armistice on 11 November 1918. This was done for several reasons. First, the new government faced many internal threats from both Bolshevik-inspired socialists and those who supported the old former government. There was mass starvation in the cities and the Spanish influenza pandemic affected millions. The economy had essentially collapsed and millions of soldiers and sailors were no longer willing to fight in a lost cause.

By agreeing to an armistice, however harsh, Germany also hoped to demonstrate its willingness to co-operate with the Allies. It was hoped that this would translate into fair treatment at the Paris Peace Conference. The armistice included the surrender of the entire German fleet, including U-boats, to Britain and the removal of all German troops from occupied lands and from the western bank of the Rhine River which would then be occupied by Allied armies. Germany had to repudiate the Treaty of Brest-Livotsk (see below), which had been signed earlier in the year with Russia. Germany was not invited to Paris in January 1919 and would simply have to wait for the decision of the victorious Allied Powers to be announced.

War guilt and reparations

Why did Germany hope to avoid being blamed for the First World War?

Germany was aware of French and British demands that Germany and its ally Austria-Hungary be blamed for the war. If Germany could be forced to accept guilt for causing the war, then it would be easier to punish Germany in a legal way. Germany was anxious to avoid a declaration of war guilt. Germany was also aware of British and French demands for reparations and expected to be forced to make a substantial payment to at least those two countries. In order to mitigate an expected harsh indemnity, Germany offered to rebuild much of northern France and Belgium with its own workers and materials.

Treaty of Brest-Litovsk

What was the importance of the Treaty of Brest-Litovsk for the German government?

Many hundreds of thousands of German soldiers were killed or wounded fighting Russia between 1914 and early 1918. Russia was slowly defeated with great sacrifice and the fight against Russia drained German manpower and resources needed to fight France and Britain on the Western Front. In early 1918, Russia left the war by signing the Treaty of Brest-Litovsk. The treaty gave Germany control of Poland, the Ukraine, Lithuania, Latvia,

Estonia and Finland. This territory contained one-third of the population and farmland of Russia and over half its industry. Most Germans believed that their great sacrifice in defeating Russia should mean that the Treaty of Brest-Litovsk either remain intact or as intact as possible in the coming Paris Peace Conference although the armistice required Germany repudiate that agreement.

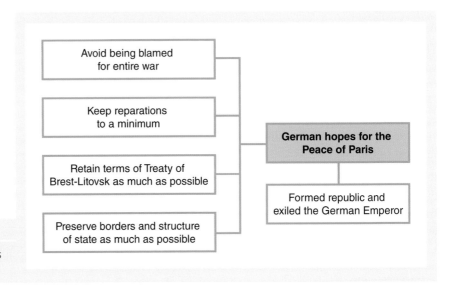

German hopes for the Paris Peace Conference 1919

Chapter summary

The Paris Peace Conference: the aims of the participants

Many nations gathered in January 1919 in Paris to settle the First World War. Each of the major participating powers, including the USA, Britain, France and Italy had different agendas. These varied partly as a result of their different experiences with Germany over the decades since its creation, but also their experiences in the war.

- The USA suffered fewer losses, but was owed billions of dollars from the others and hoped to achieve world peace forever.
- Britain had already achieved many of its major objectives during the war and through the armistice of November 1918, yet needed money to pay its war debts to the USA.

- France had more dead and wounded than the other Allied Powers in Paris and had much of its northern areas destroyed. It also owed more than the others and was set on eliminating any future threat from Germany.
- Italy had joined the war specifically to gain territory which was promised in a secret treaty,

Germany was not invited to the conference, nor were the Austro-Hungarian or Ottoman Empires. However, Germany was different from its former Central Power allies in that it was one of the most industrialized nations in the world and was a nation-state of Germans. Austria-Hungary and the Ottoman Empire contained multiple nationalities and had underdeveloped economies. This meant that Germany could not be easily destroyed like Austria-Hungary or the Ottoman Empire. It also meant that it would be a challenge to limit Germany in such a way as to prevent it from rebuilding its military and economy in a short period of time.

Examination advice

Paper 1 question 1: how to answer direct questions

Question 1 on the IB History Diploma examination is in two parts. Each part involves reading comprehension and simply asks you to tell the examiner what the sources say. Each of the questions will ask only about one source. You will often see questions that ask you to convey the message or meaning of a source. This is asking you to explain what the source is saying.

Question 1 requires no prior knowledge, just the ability to read and understand sources. When you start your examination, you will receive five minutes of 'reading time' when you cannot actually touch your pen and start writing. Use the time wisely and read question 1a to see which source it is asking about. Once you understand which source the question is about, read the source and then think of your response. When the five minutes are up, you may begin writing and you should be ready to answer the question immediately.

Question 1 is worth 5 marks out of the total of 25 for all Paper 1. This means it is worth about twenty per cent of the overall mark. Answering questions 1a and 1b should take five minutes or less of the actual examination time.

How to answer

In order to best answer the question, you first have to determine what the question is asking you about the source and what type of source it is. The vast majority of sources are fragments of speeches, quotes from various historians or historical figures, or any other type of written source. There are, however, visual sources that can be asked about as well, such as photographs, charts, maps, cartoons and diagrams.

When you start your answer it is good practice to use the wording in the question to help you focus your answer. For example:

Question	Begin your answer with ...
According to Source X, what is the significance of The Treaty of London?	The significance of the Treaty of London, according to Source X is ...
What was the importance of the Treaty of London according to Source X?	The importance of the Treaty of London according to Source X was ...
What was Clemenceau's view on war reparations according to Source X?	According to Source X, Clemenceau's view on war reparations was ...

After starting your answer, understand that you should paraphrase what the original source stated. This means you should explain what the source says, but in your own words. Sometimes this is impossible because the words used in the source may be so specific that there is no other way to say them.

If this occurs, make sure you put quotation marks around the phrases which you are copying from the source.

The total number of marks available for question 1 is 5. One part is worth 3 marks and the other 2 and this will be clearly indicated on the examination. If a question is worth 2 marks, try to have at least two specific points to your answer. If a question is worth 3 marks, have at least three points.

Example

This question uses Sources C and D found in this chapter on pages 12 and 14.

a) According to Source C, what will be the outcome of the German revolution of 1918? (3 marks)

b) What is the message conveyed in Source D? (2 marks)

It has just been announced that your reading time has begun on the IB History Paper 1 examination. Find the Paper 1 questions at the back of the examination booklet and read question 1a. It asks you to explain what Source C says will be the result of the German revolution of 1918. You cannot touch your pen for several minutes, so go to Source C in the booklet and read it. Once you are allowed to pick up your pen and start writing, do so. Below is a good sample answer to the question:

Each answer repeats part of the question, using phrases such as 'According to Source C' and 'The message conveyed in Source D is.' This helps the answer focus on the question.

Both sources are paraphrased in the answers.

Both 1a and 1b are answered in paragraph form and not bullet points.

Each answer states the origin of the source. While this is not required, it helps you build a better paragraph and may help you later when you are asked to discuss the origins of two of the sources.

1a) According to Source C the outcome of the German revolution of 1918 will be a negative one. Source C is a quote from German General Ludendorff. He believes that the Germans will become economic slaves to other nations and depend financially on others. He also believes Germany will have neither Allies nor self-respect. He states that Germans will regret the revolution in time.

1b) The message conveyed in Source D is that US President Wilson believes that all people in all nations should live in a world where they do not fear violence. Nations should have the right to be free to develop as they wish and should deal with each other justly and in fairness. The source also states that these desires are shared by all the people in the world and they are to be partners in working towards these goals.

Questions 1a and 1b are worth a combined 5 marks. Both answers indicate that the student read and understood what each source stated. Question 1a is worth 3 marks. The answer for 1a contains at least three different points to address the question. Question 1b is worth 2 marks. The answer has more than two points to answer the question. Mark: 5/5.

Examination practice

The following are exam-style questions for you to practise, using sources from the chapter. Sources can be found on the following pages:

- Source B: page 11
- Source C: page 12
- Source D: page 14
- Source E: page 17
- Source H: page 22
- Source I: page 24

1 What, according to Source B, is the purpose of the new German republican government?

2 What, according to Source B, is the most important issue facing the new German government in November 1918?

3 What is the message of Source B?

4 What message is conveyed by Source C?

5 What, according to Source D, are the aims of the United States for the Paris Peace Conference?

6 What, according to Source E, is the purpose of German reparation payments?

7 What, according to Source E, are three desires for the British in a future peace treaty with Germany?

8 Why, according to Source H, will France seek war reparations?

9 What is the message conveyed by Source H?

10 What, according to Source I, will Italy receive as a result of the Treaty of London signed in 1915?

 # Activities

I In groups, using paragraphs of this chapter as sources, create Paper 1-type questions assigning them either 2 or 3 marks. Use the paragraphs that focus on individual war aims of each of the countries discussed. Vary your questions such as in the examples above. Try to create at least two different questions per paragraph. Exchange your questions with other groups, being sure to indicate the location of the paragraphs in the chapter, and give yourselves approximately five minutes to answer the two questions. Once questions have been answered, review the answers and assign marks. Be sure to indicate what was successful and appropriate and what could have been improved.

2 As homework, create Paper 1-type questions using sources from Chapters 3 and 4. Once you have created your questions and assigned a mark value of 2 or 3, depending on the source, answer your own questions. Have your questions marked by classmates. They should give you a mark per question and comment on your answers' strengths and weaknesses. This activity can be extended to include other chapters or only speeches, only quotes from historians, and so forth.

CHAPTER 2

The terms of the Paris Peace Treaties 1919–20

This chapter will examine the five treaties that resulted from the Paris Peace Conference meetings. These treaties affected the former Central Powers of Germany, Austria-Hungary, Bulgaria and the Ottoman Empire, as well as the former Russian Empire. New states were recognized, old states abolished, financial penalties imposed and a new body, the League of Nations, was created to prevent future wars. You need to consider the following questions throughout this chapter:

✪ Which nation's goals were mostly met by the Treaty of Versailles?
✪ What was the main purpose of the Treaty of St Germain-en-Laye?
✪ What was the most significant result of the Treaty of Neuilly on Bulgaria?
✪ Why do some historians believe the Treaty of Trianon to be the harshest treaty to emerge from the Paris Peace Conference?
✪ How did the Treaty of Sèvres serve the interests of Britain and France?

 The Treaty of Versailles

▶ *Key question: Which nation's goals were mostly met by the Treaty of Versailles?*

The Treaty of Versailles is arguably the most important of the five treaties that came out of the Paris Peace Conference in 1919. Versailles dealt with Germany, the most economically, politically and militarily powerful of the Central Powers. All the peace settlements were to a greater or lesser extent the result of compromises between the Allied Powers, and Versailles was no exception. Its key clauses were the result of fiercely negotiated agreements, which were often only reached when the conference appeared to be on the brink of collapse. The clauses of the treaty can be broken down into general categories:

● the Covenant of the League of Nations
● war guilt clause
● reparations
● territorial adjustments
● disarmament.

The Covenant of the League of Nations

The League of Nations, proposed in US President Wilson's Fourteen Points speech in January 1918 (see page 15), was one of the first agreements at the Paris Peace Conference. The first 26 articles of the Treaty of Versailles (which appeared in all other treaties as well) were the Covenant of the League of Nations. The League was to be an organization composed of independent states which would work to promote peace through negotiation. All member states would be considered equal with one vote each. Germany would not be allowed to join.

Articles 8–17

The heart of the Covenant, Articles 8–17, was primarily concerned with the overriding question of the prevention of war. Members had to agree to reduce their armaments to the lowest possible point for national safety and to limit the manufacture of weapons. A process for solving disputes between countries was defined in Articles 12–17, with Article 16 being concerned with **collective security**. This concept called for the declaration of war by all members of the League on any country that declared war on a member state. It was hoped that the threat of group action against an aggressor would force countries to resort to negotiation and arbitration to settle disputes.

SOURCE A

Woodrow Wilson as I Know Him, by Joseph Patrick Tumulty, published by Doubleday, Page, & Co., Garden City, New York, USA and Toronto, Canada, 1921, p. 427. Tumulty served as Wilson's private secretary from 1911 until 1921.

Woodrow Wilson believed that the League of Nations was the first modern attempt to prevent war by discussion in the open and not behind closed doors or 'within the cloistered retreats of European diplomacy'. To him the League of Nations was the essence of Christianity.

Other articles

Other articles explained that the League would work to end slavery, human and drug trafficking, and diseases. Former colonies of Germany and parts of the Ottoman Empire were to be under League of Nations supervision while a system of **treaty registration** was also established. The League stated that there should be freedom of religion, but declined a Chinese and Japanese request that racial equality be added to the document. The USA, Britain and Australia objected to this addition, so it was not included.

SOURCE B

Excerpt from *Paris 1919: Six Months that Changed the World* by Margaret MacMillan, published by Random House, New York, USA, 2003, p. 85. MacMillan is a professor of history at University of Toronto, Canada.

In Paris, Wilson insisted on chairing the League commission, because for him the League of Nations was the centerpiece of the peace settlements. If it could be

What was the significance of the creation of the League of Nations?

KEY TERM

Collective security
An agreement between nations that an aggressive act towards one nation will be treated as an aggressive act towards all nations under the agreement.

Treaty registration
League of Nations initiative that filed and published treaties between the First and Second World Wars so that details were public.

According to Source A, what were the main reasons Wilson wanted a League of Nations?

What, according to Source B, was Wilson's goal for the League of Nations?

brought into being, then everything else would sooner or later fall into place. If the peace terms were imperfect, there would be plenty of time later for the League to correct them. Many new borders had to be drawn. If they were not quite right, the League would sort them out. German's colonies were going to be taken away; the League would make sure that they were run properly. The Ottoman Empire was defunct; the League would act as liquidator and trustee for the peoples who were not yet ready to rule themselves. And for future generations the League would oversee general prosperity and peace, encouraging the weak, chiding the wicked and, where necessary, punishing the recalcitrant. It was a pledge that humanity was making to itself, a covenant.

War guilt clause

What was the purpose of Article 231 of the Treaty of Versailles?

There was universal agreement among the victorious powers that Germany was guilty of starting the First World War. It was this principle of war guilt, or responsibility, which was to provide the moral justification for the reparations and other punishing clauses of the Treaty of Versailles, as was stressed in the so-called war guilt clause, Article 231.

SOURCE C

? Who, according to Source C, caused the First World War?

Treaty of Versailles, Part VIII [8], Section I [1], Article 231, 1919.

The Allied and associated governments affirm and Germany accepts the responsibility of Germany and her allies for causing all the loss and damage to which the Allied and associated governments and their nationals have been subjected as a consequence of the war imposed upon them by the aggression of Germany and her allies.

Reparations

Why could the Allies not agree easily on German reparations?

There was a general agreement in Paris that Germany should pay for some of the damage for the First World War. There was, however, tremendous disagreement on the amount.

SOURCE D

? According to Source D, why could the Allies not agree on German reparations in 1919?

Excerpt from *The Origins of the Second World War* by A.J.P. Taylor, published by Penguin Books, UK, 1991, p. 69. First published in 1961 by Hamish Hamilton, this book has been most recently reprinted by Penguin Books in 2001. Taylor was a British historian who wrote many books on European history and was lecturer at many British universities.

In 1919 the French wished to lay down uncompromisingly the principle that Germany must pay the full bill for war damage – an indeterminate liability [unknown amount] that would swell in the future with every step of German economic recovery. The Americans, more sensibly, proposed to state a fixed sum. Lloyd George appreciated that, in the heated atmosphere of 1919, this sum, too, would be far beyond German capacity. He hoped that in time men (himself included) would come to their senses: the Allies would make a reasonable demand, the Germans would make a reasonable offer, and the two figures would more or less coincide. He therefore swung round behind the French, though for exactly the opposite reason: they wanted to make the bill fantastically large, he wanted to scale it down. The Americans gave way. The peace treaty merely stated the principle of reparations; their amount was to be settled at some time in the future.

The USA

The USA believed a moderate, fixed amount should be levied against Germany. The US President Wilson believed that requiring Germany to pay massive reparations would lead to resentment and sow the seeds of yet another war. According to historian Margaret MacMillan, the American delegation believed that Germany should pay approximately $22 billion.

Britain

The British government was somewhat divided on the issue of reparations as it was recognized that Germany should pay for **war pensions** in the least, but also needed to become a trading partner again so that the British economy could recover from the war. Public pressure, however, demanded Germany be forced to pay for the war. There were other reasons for demanding large sums from Germany as well, including:

- The **Imperial War Cabinet** urged that the reparations for the cost of war should include soldiers' pensions in both Britain and its Dominions. It was understood that Belgium and France would receive the largest part of any reparation payments from Germany, so Britain and its Dominions wanted Germany to pay the largest amount possible in order that they, too, would receive funds.
- Britain owed the USA billions of dollars and hoped it would simply cancel the debt which the USA refused to do. In order for Britain to pay its debt, it needed France to pay its war debt to Britain. In order for France to pay its debt, huge reparations were needed from Germany.
- British Prime Minister Lloyd George believed that high war reparations would keep Germany from rebuilding its military. According to historian Margaret Macmillan, Lloyd George's government considered the overall sum of $120 billion in German reparations to be sufficient.

France

British demands for debt repayment meant that France needed a huge amount in reparations from Germany. Reparations would not only pay French and British debt, but also rebuild the northern areas of France and most of Belgium. France expected reparations to pay for the entire war and French military pensions as well. France wanted reparations to punish Germany for starting the war and to damage the German economy. The amount that the French considered demanding of Germany was approximately $220 billion; $100 billion more than Britain suggested.

 **KEY TERM**

War pensions Payments made to wounded or retired men from the military who served in war, or their families.

Imperial War Cabinet A cabinet made up of prime ministers of the Dominions of the British Empire, also called the Commonwealth, such as Canada, Australia, New Zealand and South Africa.

🔑 KEY TERM

Marks German currency.

Prussia Large German state that was primarily responsible for forming the German Empire in 1871.

Plebiscite When all eligible voters of an area vote to accept or reject a specific issue.

The Reparation Commission

It was resolved at the end of April 1919 that a Reparation Commission would be set up to assess, by 1 May 1921, what the German economy could afford. In the meantime, the Germans would make an interim payment of 20 billion gold **marks** and raise a further 60 billion through loans. France would receive just over half of this money, while Britain would receive a quarter. Belgium would receive the remaining funds. It was also agreed that Belgium, unlike Britain and France, would have all its war expenses paid in full through German reparations. Belgian territory had not only been occupied during the war by Germany, but also was heavily damaged in some of the largest battles. The final sum and conditions for reparations are addressed on page 75.

? Why, according to Source E, was the total amount of German reparations not announced in 1919?

SOURCE E

Excerpt from *Versailles and After: 1919–1933* by Ruth Henig, published by Methuen & Co., London, UK, 1984, pp. 19–20. Henig has been a history lecturer and Dean of the Faculty of Arts and Humanities at Lancaster University, UK.

The Americans had their own reasons for endeavouring to limit German reparation payments. They were owed considerable sums of money by the other Allies, and the suggestion had already been floated by some British officials that the powers should consider an all-round cancellation of war debts and reparations. The Americans wanted their money back, with interest. The repayment of war debts was likely to be financed out of German reparation payments, and therefore the United States worked to conclude a reparations settlement based on Germany's capacity to pay and yet substantial enough to satisfy the European allies. In the atmosphere of early 1919, this was asking the impossible. Clemenceau could not retreat from the astronomic sums the French public had been led to expect. In April, Lloyd George received a telegram signed by 376 Members of Parliament, much publicised in the popular press, urging him to 'present the bill in full' to the Germans. The consequence of all these conflicting pressures was that the exact total of reparations to be paid by Germany was not stated in the Treaty of Versailles.

How significant were the changes to Germany's borders as dictated by the Treaty of Versailles?

Territorial adjustments

Minor territorial changes

It was accepted, even by many Germans, that the predominantly Danish northern Schleswig, annexed by **Prussia** in 1866, should be returned to Denmark. There was therefore general agreement that a **plebiscite** should be held to determine the size of the area to be handed back.

The former German territories of Eupen and Malmedy, together with Moresnet, which before 1914 had been administered jointly by Germany and Belgium, were granted to Belgium and this was to be confirmed with a plebiscite (see page 138). The neutrality of the Grand Duchy of Luxembourg was confirmed.

SOURCE F

Map showing territorial adjustments to Germany's borders.

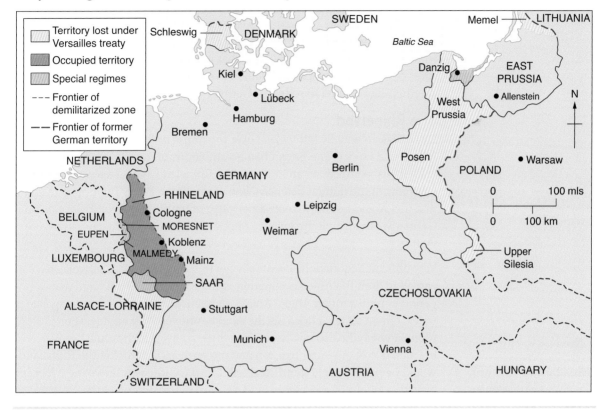

Alsace-Lorraine

All nations attending the peace conference agreed that France should receive its former province of Alsace-Lorraine. The Treaty of Versailles confirmed what had already taken place as the November armistice with Germany required that the Germany army leave the area. In mid-November 1918, the French army had occupied the provinces and they were incorporated into France.

The Saar

The French proposals for the future of the Saar proved more controversial. Clemenceau insisted on the restoration to France of that part of the Saar which was given to Prussia in 1814. He also aimed to detach the mineral and industrial basin to the north, which had never been French, and place it under an independent non-German administration. Finally he demanded full French ownership of the Saar coalmines to compensate for the destruction of the pits in northern France by the Germans.

Wilson immediately understood that here was a clash between the national interests of France and the principle of **self-determination** as enshrined in

What information is conveyed by Source F? You should be able to state at least three facts.

 **KEY TERM**

Self-determination The idea that a nation can choose its own form of government and international status such as independence.

the Fourteen Points. While he was ready to agree to French access to the coalmines until the production of their own mines had been restored, he vetoed all other demands on the Saar. To save the conference from breaking down, Lloyd George persuaded Wilson and Clemenceau to accept a compromise whereby the mines would become French for fifteen years, while the actual government of the Saar would be entrusted to the League. After fifteen years, the people would have the right to decide in a plebiscite whether they wished to return to German rule (see page 204).

The Rhineland

There was an equally bitter clash over the future of the Rhineland between Britain and France. The British had no ambitions on the Rhine, but the French wished to create an independent Rhineland state. This would deprive Germany of the natural defensive line of the Rhine River. The British feared that this would not only create a new area of tension between France and Germany, but also tilt the balance of power in Europe decisively towards France.

Very difficult negotiations eventually led to a compromise. Clemenceau agreed to limit the Allied occupation of the Rhineland to a fifteen-year period in return for an Anglo-American treaty guaranteeing France against a new German attack, known as the Anglo-American Guarantee. The Rhineland would also be divided into three zones, which would be evacuated in stages after five, ten and fifteen years. Thereafter the Rhineland would be permanently **demilitarized**. Lloyd George was unwilling to accept even this length of occupation, and right up to the signing of the Treaty he sought to evade the commitment.

KEY TERM

Demilitarized To remove all weapons and troops.

According to Source G, how did Clemenceau hope to make France secure from German attack?

SOURCE G

Excerpt from *Paris 1919: Six Months that Changed the World*, by Margaret MacMillan, published by Random House, New York, USA, 2003, p. 170. MacMillan is a professor of history at the University of Toronto, Canada.

The Rhineland, Clemenceau argued, should be removed from German control to ensure France's security. 'The Rhine was the natural boundary of Gaul and Germany.' Perhaps the Allies could create an independent state with its neutrality guaranteed, just as Belgium's had been done, by the powers. 'I can see,' reported the British ambassador, 'that he intends to press for that very strongly.' Clemenceau in fact was prepared to compromise on many of France's demands as long as the overriding goal of security was met.

Poland and eastern Europe

Germany defeated Russia in early 1918. The Treaty of Brest-Litovsk was signed by Germany and the new Bolshevik government of Russia giving Germany control of much of eastern Europe. The armistice between the Allies and Germany in November 1918 required Germany to repudiate the

Treaty of Brest-Litovsk. Article 118 of the Treaty confirmed that Germany could not claim any benefit from its victory against Russia.

Anglo-French disagreements again dominated negotiations on Germany's eastern frontiers. Poland was created out of the chaos of the end of the First World War. Poles had last had an independent country in 1815 when **Napoleonic Europe** was reorganized at the Congress of Vienna. Polish territory had been divided between Prussia, which would later form the core of Germany, Russia and the Austrian Empire, later known as the Austro-Hungarian Empire. The Treaty of Versailles granted most of the German provinces of West Prussia and Posen to the new Poland without a plebiscite. The small territory of Soldau in East Prussia also was given to Poland.

A commission recommended on 12 March that Danzig, Marienwerder and Upper Silesia should all also be included in the new Polish state. This would give it access to the sea and give it industrialized areas which would help its economy. Only the future of Allenstein would be decided by plebiscite. Lloyd George vigorously opposed the inclusion of Danzig and Marienwerder as he feared the long-term resentment of the local predominantly German-speaking population and dreaded that an embittered Germany might turn to Bolshevik Russia for help. By threatening to withdraw from the Anglo-American Guarantee pact, he forced Clemenceau to agree to a plebiscite in Marienwerder and the establishment of a free and autonomous city of Danzig. Danzig was to be ruled by a High Commissioner appointed by the League of Nations and to form a **customs union** with Poland. It was also to be linked with Poland through a narrow corridor of territory – the Danzig, or Polish, Corridor. These agreements meant that Polish territory separated the majority of Germany from the province of East Prussia. Memel was a small German territory bordering the new state of Lithuania and this was given to France to administer, but later seized by Lithuania (see page 114).

 **KEY TERM**

Napoleonic Europe Period starting about 1799 and ending in 1815 when Europe was dominated by France, ruled by Napoleon Bonaparte, with new countries formed, others abolished and still others absorbed into France.

Customs union A free-trade area.

SOURCE H

Excerpt from *Paris 1919: Six Months that Changed the World* by Margaret MacMillan, published by Random House, New York, USA, 2003, p. 216. MacMillan is a professor of history at the University of Toronto, Canada.

In the Polish commission [sic.] the British and the American experts, meeting informally as they did on most matters, agreed that Poland's boundaries should be drawn on ethnic lines as much as possible but that other factors, such as access to the Baltic, control of railways or strategic considerations also had to be taken into account. The French, who were headed by the wise old diplomat Jules Cambon, generally accepted this but, when it came to disputes, were invariably for giving Poland the benefit of the doubt. Poland, they said, must have borders that could be defended against Germany and Russia even if that meant including non-Poles. The Italians generally sided with the French. The Japanese, as usual, said little.

What does Source H indicate were the most important concerns for Allied diplomats as they created Poland?

Austria

The Austro-Hungarian Empire dissolved at the end of 1918 and new states began to form. The German Republic of Austria was created and included areas where Germans lived in the former Grand Duchy of Austria. Article 2 of Austria's draft constitution of November 1918 proclaimed that German Austria would be a part of the German Republic which had just formed in Germany. Plebiscites were held in some provinces with over 98 per cent of voters approving unification with Germany. The constitution of the German Republic, written in early 1919, stated in its Article 2 that other nations could join Germany if their people so desired.

Wilson's Fourteen Points specifically stated that the people of Austria-Hungary should be free to develop themselves as they see fit. Britain and France, however, absolutely would not agree to Germany expanding to include Austria. This would be some sort of reward for the First World War and would serve to strengthen Germany economically and possibly militarily as well. Article 80 was included in the treaty to prevent a unification of the two countries:

? According to Source I, what was the purpose of Article 80 of section VI of the Treaty of Versailles?

SOURCE I

Treaty of Versailles, Part II [2], Section VI [6], Article 80, 1919.

Germany acknowledges and will respect strictly the independence of Austria, within the frontiers which may be fixed in a Treaty between that State and the Principal Allied and Associated Powers; she agrees that this independence shall be inalienable, except with the consent of the Council of the League of Nations.

German colonies

It was agreed by all groups that Germany should not keep any of its colonies. President Wilson insisted that the League of Nations should have ultimate control over these lands. This was accepted only reluctantly by the British Dominions of New Zealand, Australia and South Africa, each arguing that the outright annexation by themselves of the South Pacific islands, Samoa and South West Africa, respectively, was vital for their security. They also saw these lands as reward for their participation in the war.

In May, agreement was reached on the division of the German colonies. Britain, France, Belgium and South Africa were made **mandatories** under League supervision over most of the former German colonial empire in Africa, while Australia, New Zealand and Japan secured the **mandates** for the scattered German possessions in the Pacific. Italy was awarded control of the Juba Valley in East Africa, and a few minor territorial adjustments were made to its Libyan frontier with Algeria. Essentially Britain, the Dominions and France rewarded themselves with colonies, pretending the League of Nations would oversee these lands as mandates.

 **KEY TERM**

Mandatories Nations that administered mandates for the League of Nations.

Mandates Lands administered by the League of Nations in theory but by Britain and France almost exclusively in reality.

A serious clash arose between Japan and the USA. The Japanese were determined to keep the former German territory of **Kiaochow** on the Shantung peninsula that Germany had leased from China. The Chinese government, however, on the strength of its declaration of war against Germany in 1917, argued that all former German rights should automatically revert to the Chinese state, despite the fact that in 1915 it had agreed to recognize Japanese rights in Shantung. Wilson was anxious to block the growth of Japanese influence in the Pacific and supported China, but Lloyd George and Clemenceau, wanting to protect their own rights in China, backed Japan. Wilson, already locked in conflict with the Italians over their claims to Fiume (see page 99) and facing Japanese threats to boycott the conference and sign a separate peace with Germany, had no option but to concede.

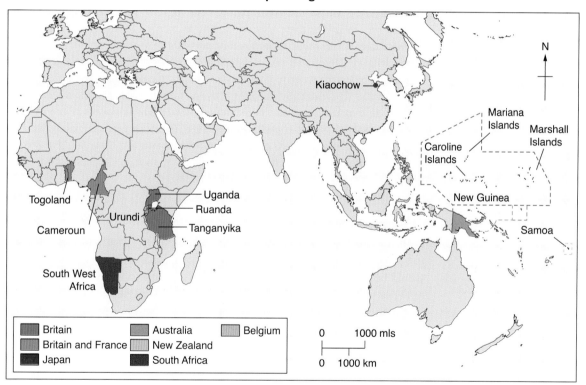

KEY TERM

Kiaochow Territory located on the Shandong peninsula in China that was leased to Germany for 99 years starting in 1898; seized by Japan in the First World War.

SOURCE J

Former German colonies as mandates with supervising nations.

What information is conveyed in Source J? You should be able to state at least five facts.

What were the main limitations on the German military as a result of the Treaty of Versailles?

KEY TERM

Conscription Compulsory military service for a certain length of time.

?

According to Source K, what was the purpose of disarming Germany?

→ Disarmament

As with reparations, the Allied and associated nations agreed on the necessity for German disarmament, but there were differences in emphasis. The British and Americans wished to destroy in Germany the tradition of **conscription**, which they regarded as 'the tap-root of militarism'. Instead they wanted a small professional army created along the lines of the British or US peacetime armies. French General Foch, more wisely as it turned out, feared that a professional German army would merely become a tightly organized nucleus of trained men which would be capable of quick expansion when the opportunity arose.

SOURCE K

Excerpt from *Paris 1919: Six Months that Changed the World* by Margaret MacMillan, published by Random House, New York, USA, 2003, p. 166. MacMillan is a professor of history at University of Toronto, Canada.

Most people agreed that militarism and huge armed forces, especially the German, were bad for the world; indeed, books arguing that the arms race had caused the Great War were already starting to appear. One of Wilson's Fourteen Points talked about reducing national armaments 'to the lowest point consistent with domestic safety,' and one of the selling points of the League was that it would provide such security that nations would willingly cut back on their armed forces … Disarming the most powerful nation on the continent was clearly an important first step to the more general disarmament to be carried out by the League. Although it mattered much less, the Allies intended to impose stringent military conditions on the other defeated nations. They would also try, unsuccessfully, to persuade their friends in Europe, such as Czechoslovakia, Poland and Greece, to accept small armed forces.

Military terms

Foch was overruled and it was decided that Germany would reduce its army to a maximum of 100,000 men. No artillery, air force, poison gas or tanks would be permitted. If Germany needed to manufacture any type of weapon, bullet or shell, it had to be approved by Allied governments. Germany was prohibited from importing any type of weapons or munitions. Terms of military service were explained in the treaty and most military schools were closed.

The British insisted on ending any German naval threat and so the treaty terms were harsh. The navy was limited to six battleships, six cruisers, twelve destroyers and twelve torpedo boats. Submarines were forbidden, as were torpedoes. The navy could have only 15,000 men. All German warships held by the Allies at the time of the signing of the Treaty of Versailles, would belong to the country that held them. Germany was required to remove all mines in the Baltic and North Seas and to remove various fortifications.

SOURCE L

Excerpt from *The Independent*, vol. 97, p. 394, 22 March 1919. *The Independent* was an American journal published in Boston, USA that focused on politics, history, arts, and social and economic issues. It became part of *The Outlook* in 1928.

Naval and other provisions were taken up on March 11, and it was tentatively agreed that the personnel of the German navy should hereafter be restricted to 15,000 men. At the beginning of the war in August, 1914, the German navy contained 3,889 officers and 75,486 men, besides a Naval Reserve of about 110,000 men. At the date of the surrender of the fleet it had approximately 197,375 officers and men …

According to Source L, how would the German navy be affected by disarmament?

German reaction

While the Allies were working on the treaty, the German government could only prepare for the time when it would be summoned to Paris to receive the draft terms. Optimistically in what one German intellectual, Ernst Troeltsch, called 'the dreamland of the armistice period', Berlin hoped that it would be able to protect Germany from excessive reparation claims and so keep the way open for a rapid economic recovery. Wilson's Fourteen Points had given Germans hope that a moderate USA would mitigate British and French demands against them. Germany had become a republic in November 1918 and in elections held in January 1919 voted for a democratic **coalition government** in which the moderate Social Democrats were the largest party. Immediately the new government began work on a democratic constitution.

On 7 May the draft peace terms were at last presented to the Germans, who were given a mere fifteen days to draw up their reply. This led to a crisis in Germany where the chancellor resigned and the president of the country asked the army if it could resist an Allied invasion. The army responded that it could not, so the German government worked towards gaining some concessions while bitterly criticizing the treaty for not conforming to the Fourteen Points. Some of the concessions it demanded were:

- immediate membership of the League of Nations
- a guarantee that Austria and the ethnic Germans in the Sudetenland, which was a part of the new Czechoslovak state, should have the chance to decide whether they wished to join Germany
- plebiscites in areas that were granted to Poland to determine the desire of the inhabitants
- the setting up of a neutral commission to examine the war guilt question
- that no German territory would be occupied by foreign troops.

These demands, if met, would have strengthened Germany's position in central Europe, so they were rejected outright by the Allied and associated powers. Nevertheless some ground was conceded. It was agreed to allow a plebiscite in Upper Silesia which had earlier been granted to Poland. Lloyd George was able to get other Allied leaders to agree to a vague assurance,

Why did Germany fail to receive many concessions in the treaty after the initial draft?

 **KEY TERM**

Coalition government When two or more political parties join together to form a parliamentary majority, allowing a cabinet to operate a government.

which later became Article 431 of the treaty, 'that once Germany had given concrete evidence of her willingness to fulfil her obligations', the Allied and associated powers would consider 'an earlier termination of the period of occupation' of the Rhineland.

Why did Germany agree to the Treaty of Versailles?

The signature of the Treaty of Versailles

On 16 June the Germans were handed the final version of the treaty incorporating these minor concessions. In view of its own military weakness and the continuing Allied blockade (see page 10), the Berlin government had little option but to accept the treaty, although it made very clear that it was acting under duress.

On 28 June 1919 the treaty was signed in the Hall of Mirrors at Versailles where in 1871 the German Empire had been proclaimed. The treaty was known in Germany as the **diktat**.

? According to Source M, why did the Germans sign the Treaty of Versailles?

SOURCE M

Gustav Bauer, a member of the German coalition government, discussing German acceptance of the Treaty of Versailles, quoted in *Revolutions and Peace Treaties 1917–1921* by Gerhard Schulz, published by Methuen & Co., London, UK, 1972, p. 189. Schulz was a historian in modern German history at the University of Tübingen, Germany.

Surrendering to superior force but without retracting its opinion regarding the unheard of injustice of the peace conditions, the government of the German Republic therefore declares its readiness to accept and sign the peace conditions imposed by the Allied and associated governments.

Why did the USA fail to ratify the treaty and what were the consequences of this?

US rejection of the Treaty of Versailles

The prime ministers of Britain and France, Lloyd George and Clemenceau, represented the majorities of their parliaments and therefore negotiated with authority for their countries. Their agreements would be ratified by their governments. US President Wilson, however, was limited by the nature of the US government. While the president was allowed by law to negotiate treaties, any treaty had to be agreed upon by the Senate. The Senate was under the control of the **Republican Party**, opponents of Wilson's **Democrats**, who advocated a policy of **isolationism**.

Reasons for rejection

The Senate rejected the Treaty of Versailles and US membership in the League of Nations for several reasons:

- It did not want the USA obligated to go to war to defend other countries from aggression.
- The Republicans were displeased that Japan was allowed to keep the Shantung peninsula which would be used as a Japanese military and economic base to challenge US trade in China.

KEY TERM

Diktat Harsh penalty imposed on a defeated country.

Republican Party US political party that, in the early 1920s, emphasized free trade and complete independence in foreign policy.

Democrats US political party that, in the early 1920s, believed good government could solve national and international problems.

Isolationism Policy of avoiding alliances and international agreements.

- There was general frustration that France and Britain had expanded their empires in Africa and the Middle East and limited the creation of democratic governments in those regions.
- Many worried that participation in the League of Nations would somehow compromise the **Monroe Doctrine**, a US policy from the early 1800s that banned European interference in Central and South America; this policy allowed the USA to politically and economically dominate the region.

As a result of the treaty not being ratified by the USA, the Anglo-American Guarantee to protect France in case of future attack by Germany collapsed. The USA would sign a separate peace treaty with the former Central Powers in July 1921.

KEY TERM

Monroe Doctrine US government policy from the early nineteenth century which stated that European countries were not to interfere with nations in North and South America.

SOURCE N

Excerpt from *Woodrow Wilson as I Know Him* by Joseph Patrick Tumulty, published by Doubleday, Page, & Co., Garden City, New York, USA and Toronto, Canada, 1921, p. 425. Tumulty served as Wilson's private secretary from 1911 until 1921.

It is plain now, and will become plainer as the years elapse, that the Republican opposition to the League was primarily partisan politics and a rooted personal dislike of the chief proponent of the League, Mr. Wilson. His reelection in 1916, the first reelection of an incumbent Democratic President since Andrew Jackson [president 1829–37], had greatly disturbed the Republican leaders. The prestige of the Republican Party was threatened by this Democratic leader. His reception in Europe added to their distress. For the sake of the sacred cause of Republicanism, this menace of Democratic leadership must be destroyed, even though in destroying it the leaders should swallow their own words and reverse their own former positions on world adjustment.

Why, according to Source N, did the Republican Party of the USA oppose the treaty of Versailles?

SOURCE O

Excerpt from a speech by Henry Cabot Lodge, Republican leader of the US Senate, 28 February 1919. *The League of Nations*, published by The Old Colony Trust Company, Boston, USA, 1919, pp. 20–1.

In this draft prepared for a constitution of a League of Nations, which is now before the world, there is hardly a clause about the interpretation of which men do not already differ. As it stands there is serious danger that the very nations which sign the constitution of the league will quarrel about the meaning of the various articles before a [year] has passed. It seems to have been very hastily drafted, and the result is crudeness and looseness of expression, unintentional, I hope. There are certainly many doubtful passages and open questions obvious in the articles which cannot be settled by individual inference, but which must be made so clear and so distinct that we may all understand the exact meaning of the instrument to which we are asked to set our hands. The language of these articles does not appear to me to have the precision and unmistakable character which a constitution, a treaty, or a law ought to present. The language only too frequently is not the language of laws or statues. The article concerning

Why, according to Source O, was there opposition to the Treaty of Versailles in the USA?

mandatories, for example, contains an argument and a statement of existing conditions. Arguments and historical facts have no place in a statute or a treaty. Statutory and legal language must assert and command, not argue and describe. I press this point because there is nothing so vital to the peace of the world as the sanctity of treaties.

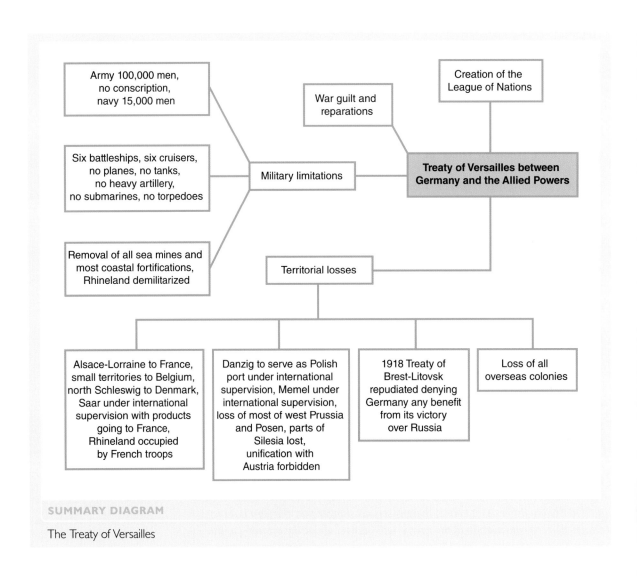

The Treaty of Versailles

The Treaty of St Germain-en-Laye

> ▶ *Key question*: *What was the main purpose of the Treaty of St Germain-en-Laye?*

Commonly referred to as the Treaty of St Germain, the Treaty of St Germain-en-Laye was signed in September 1919 and concerned the Republic of Austria. While the Treaty of Versailles was attended to by the leaders of various nations, the Treaty with Austria was primarily the work of professional diplomats. Like Versailles, St Germain included the Covenant of the League of Nations. Austria became a member of the League in 1920.

As with Versailles, the main clauses dealt with:

- war guilt
- reparations
- territorial adjustments
- disarmament.

War guilt

Austria, like Germany, had to accept responsibility as part of Austria-Hungary for dragging the rest of the world into war. Once guilt had been assigned and accepted, reparations could be demanded.

> **Why was it critical to have Austria-Hungary admit to helping start the First World War?**

SOURCE P

Treaty of St Germain-en-Laye, Article 177.

The Allied and Associated Governments affirm and Austria accepts the responsibility of Austria and her Allies for causing the loss and damage to which the Allied and Associated Governments and their nationals have been subjected as a consequence of the war imposed upon them by the aggression of Austria-Hungary and her Allies.

> According to Source P, what was the purpose of Article 177 of the Treaty of St Germain-en-Laye?

Reparations

Austria was required to make reparations to Italy and other Allied countries for the cost of the war as well as damages. A committee was established to study the economy and resources of Austria to determine a final sum it would be required to pay. It was understood, as stated in Article 178, that Austria would have limited resources as a result of losing most of its lands and population. While the committee investigated, Austria was required to give various historical and cultural treasures, including artistic works, jewels and ancient manuscripts to the lands where they originated. Austria was also required to turn over large numbers of livestock to Romania, Yugoslavia and Italy. Italy also was given undersea cables that the Austro-Hungarian government had owned in the Adriatic Sea.

> **What was the main problem with Austria and reparation requirements?**

According to Source Q, what problems did Austria face after signing the Treaty of St Germain-en-Laye?

SOURCE Q

Excerpt from 'The European war', *The New York Times Current History*, vol. 20, July 1919–October 1920, published in 1920 by the New York Times Co., New York, USA. *The New York Times Current History* was a monthly news magazine.

The conditions in the shrunken State [Austria] immediately after the signing of the treaty were worse than in any other country of Europe. A new Cabinet was formed under the leadership of Dr. Karl Renner [Austrian Chancellor], and it strove as best it could to bring order out of chaos. But the difficulties it faced were almost insuperable [not possible to overcome]. There was practically no coal, and food was extremely scarce and at prohibitive prices. Eighty-three per cent of the children were suffering from rickets, due to malnutrition. The country was on the very brink of famine, and had it not been for the aid rendered by the American and other relief commissions thousands would have starved to death. Demobilized soldiers thronged the thoroughfares, begging for alms. The temperature of the hospitals was so low from lack of coal that new-born infants and their mothers died of cold. The krone, nominally 20 cents, sold for 1 cent of American money. Conditions were made worse by the refusal of unfriendly neighboring states to trade with the bankrupt republic and send coal and food in return for almost worthless currency.

To what extent were the territorial adjustments to Austria-Hungary more severe than those imposed on Germany?

Territorial adjustments

The Treaty of St Germain officially ended the Austro-Hungarian Empire. It confirmed the creation of new states at the expense of the old empire and a new Republic of Austria. Austria would now be a small, German-speaking state of about six million people. Other parts of the former Grand Duchy of Austria were distributed to Italy, Czechoslovakia, Yugoslavia, Poland and Romania.

SOURCE R

According to Source R, how were many decisions made about the future of Austria in Paris in 1919?

Excerpt from *Paris 1919: Six Months that Changed the World*, by Margaret MacMillan, published by Random House, New York, USA, 2003, p. 250. MacMillan is a professor of history at the University of Toronto, Canada.

Enough was leaking out about the peace terms [of the Treaty of St Germain-en-Laye], mainly from the Italians, to make the Austrians uneasy and depressed. Austria's borders had been largely left to the specialist committees, who had heard from countries such as Czechoslovakia or Italy about what they wanted, but not of course from Austria itself. Galicia went to Poland, Bohemia to Czechoslovakia. Some three million German-speaking Austrians went with them. Otto Bauer, Austria's cleverest socialist and its foreign minister, made an impassioned speech back in Vienna. 'No less than two-fifths of our people are to be subjected to foreign dominations, without any plebiscite and against their indisputable will, being thus deprived of their right of self-determination.' He had a point, but few in Paris were prepared to listen.

Italy

Italy was awarded South Tyrol, despite it being home to 230,000 ethnic Germans. It also took the Istrian peninsula and many islands in the Adriatic Sea. Italy also received the important port of Trieste, cutting off Austria from a seaport.

SOURCE S

Excerpt from *Diplomacy* by Henry Kissinger, published by Simon & Schuster, New York, 1995, p. 231. Kissinger is a former US Secretary of State, Nobel Peace Prize winner, and author of various books on foreign relations.

The Allies had induced Italy into the war by promising it the South Tirol [Tyrol] and the Dalmatian coast in the Treaty of London of 1915. Since the South Tirol was predominantly Austro-German and the Dalmatian coast Slavic, Italy's claims were in direct conflict with the principle of self-determination. Yet Orlando [Italian prime minister] and Sonnino [Italian foreign minister] deadlocked the Conference until, in utter exasperation, South Tirol (though not Dalmatia) was turned over to Italy. This 'compromise' demonstrated that the Fourteen Points were not etched in stone, and opened the floodgates to various other adjustments which, collectively, ran counter to the prevailing principle of self-determination …

According to Source S, what was the importance of South Tyrol?

Czechoslovakia

The provinces of Bohemia and Moravia were ceded to the newly created Czechoslovakia. Any second thoughts the British or Americans had about handing over to the Czechs the three million Germans who made up nearly one-third of the population of these provinces were quickly stifled by French opposition. The French wanted a potential ally against Germany to be strengthened by a defensible frontier and the possession of the Škoda munitions works in Pilsen. This meant the forcible integration of large German minorities into Czechoslovakia.

Yugoslavia, Poland and Romania

Slovenia, Bosnia-Herzegovina and Dalmatia were granted to the expanded Serbia, now called Yugoslavia. Many Slovenes rejected incorporation into Yugoslavia. The treaty allowed a plebiscite for German-speaking Slovenes in the Austrian province of Carinthia to vote on their future; they voted in 1920 to remain part of Austria. The provinces of Galicia and Bukovina were given to Poland and Romania without plebiscites.

Relationship with Germany

The Allied Powers did not want Germany and Austria to unite, despite the desires of their governments (see page 40). Article 88 of the Treaty stated that only the Council of the League of Nations could change Austria's status as an independent state. In reality, this gave France the power, as a permanent member of the League's Council, to veto any change. Republic of German Austria was required to change its name to Austria.

? What information is conveyed by Source T? You should be able to state at least five facts.

SOURCE T

Map of the former Austro-Hungarian Empire with new national divisions indicated.

Legend:
— External boundary of Austria-Hungary in 1914
----- Territorial boundaries within Austria-Hungary in 1914

POLAND
N
GERMANY
CZECHOSLOVAKIA
AUSTRIA
HUNGARY
ROMANIA
ITALY
YUGOSLAVIA

0   100 mls
0   200 km

SOURCE U

? According to Source U, why did many desire the unification of Austria and Germany?

Excerpt from *Austria 1918–1938: A Study in Failure* by Malcolm Bullock, published in London by Macmillan & Co., UK, 1939, p. 67. Bullock was a Conservative member of the British parliament and former soldier.

The terms of the Treaty produced a feeling of complete hopelessness over the whole country. There was open advocacy for an immediate Union with Germany even among people who up to now had been opposed to the idea. It was held that the Treaty gave them the alternatives of becoming a colony of the Allies or else of being submerged in Czechoslovakia, unless they were able to find their way into the German Fatherland. The makers of the Peace Treaty had failed to realise that the breaking up of the Hapsburg Empire [Austrian-Hungarian Empire] had released races whose rivalries were a thousand years old, and who had been held together only by the traditions of the Monarchy. The boundaries had now been drawn so that thousands of people were subjected to a rule they would never recognise and, when it came to a decisive moment, these races were never likely to be willing to submit their claims to the League of Nations.

Disarmament

According to the treaty, Austria would be limited to an army of 30,000 men. There could be no conscription and all but a few military schools were abolished. Only one factory in the entire country would be allowed to make replacement weapons and munitions. Importing and exporting weapons and munitions of any kind were prohibited. Austria was not allowed an air force and its navy was abolished. Austria no longer had access to the sea as a result of territorial changes, so all ships were confiscated by the Allies.

> **What were the main terms of the Treaty of St Germain regarding arms limitations?**

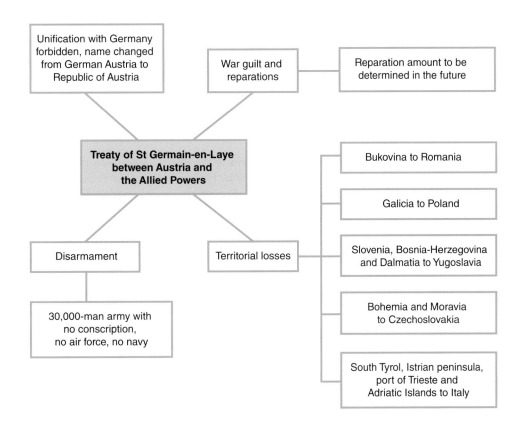

SUMMARY DIAGRAM

The Treaty of St Germain-en-Laye

3 The Treaty of Neuilly-sur-Seine

> ▶ **Key question:** *What was the most significant result of the Treaty of Neuilly on Bulgaria?*

The Treaty of Neuilly-sur-Seine, more commonly called the Treaty of Neuilly, dealt with Bulgaria and was signed in November 1919. Bulgaria was seen by Britain and France as a militarily aggressive state that reminded them of Germany, threatening the stability of the Balkan peninsula; this state needed restraining. In fact, Bulgaria had a German royal family as its rulers. The USA and Italy had reservations about treating Bulgaria harshly, but these were overcome by French and British demands. As with other Paris Peace Conference treaties, the Covenant of the League of Nations made up the first 26 articles. Bulgaria would join the League in 1920.

As with the other main treaties, the main clauses dealt with:

- war guilt
- reparations
- territorial adjustments
- disarmament.

SOURCE V

? According to Source V, what did Bulgaria hope to accomplish through negotiation that it was unable to achieve in the First World War?

Excerpt from *Some Problems of the Peace Conference* by Charles Haskins and Robert Lord, published by Harvard University Press, USA, 1920, p. 264. Haskins was a history professor at Harvard University who was one of only three personal advisers to Wilson at the Paris Peace Conference. Lord was a history professor at Harvard University and a specialist on Slavic Europe. He was part of the American delegation to the Paris Peace Conference and headed the Inter-allied Commission on Polish Affairs, among other positions.

Bulgaria escapes with far slighter losses than any other member of the defeated alliance. Nevertheless, she is quite as indignant as any of the rest of them over the peace treaty imposed upon her … But she is indignant, not so much over what she has lost, as over what she has failed to gain. There is, of course, not a little irony in the fact that at the close of a war which she entered so perfidiously [like a traitor], conducted so brutally, and ended so disastrously, Bulgaria should still be clamoring that to the vanquished belong the spoils [rewards], and should be demanding that the Entente [Allied Powers] hand over to her, at the expense of its Greek and Serbian allies, the lands which she hoped to gain by fighting throughout the War on the side of the Germans.

War guilt and reparations

In Article 121 Bulgaria was required to admit that it had caused much loss of life and damages to the Allies, but was not required to state that it was responsible for causing the war. In fact, the Treaty of Neuilly states that Germany and Austria-Hungary were only joined by Bulgaria. Nonetheless, Bulgaria was required to make reparations in the same article. The amount owed to the Allies was set at 2.25 billion gold francs, about £100 million. This would be paid in equal instalments twice per year for 37 years with a five per cent interest rate annually after 1921.

> **Why was Bulgaria treated differently from Austria in terms of war guilt and reparations?**

Territorial adjustments

Bulgaria lost the province of Western Thrace which bordered the Aegean Sea to the Allied Powers. This would later be given to Greece as a reward for the First World War. Over 2500 sq km of western Bulgaria was ceded to Yugoslavia without a plebiscite. These new territories gave Yugoslavia a strategic advantage over Bulgaria; it moved the Yugoslav–Bulgarian border closer to the Bulgarian capital of Sofia. In this way it was hoped that Bulgaria would be less aggressive in the future. The area of Southern Dobruja had been taken by Bulgaria in the war, but this was now returned to Romania. Southern Dobruja was home to 250,000 Bulgarians and 7000 Romanians.

> **Which of the territorial adjustments was most likely the most difficult for Bulgaria?**

SOURCE W

Map of Bulgarian territorial losses.

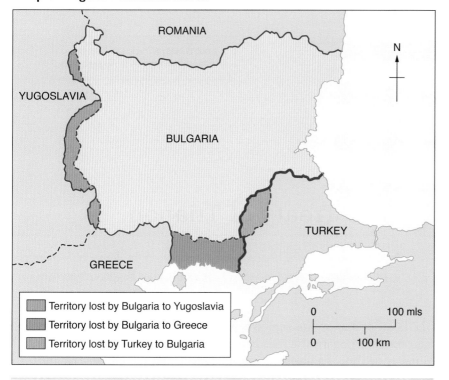

Territory lost by Bulgaria to Yugoslavia
Territory lost by Bulgaria to Greece
Territory lost by Turkey to Bulgaria

> What was the importance of territory lost to Yugoslavia according to Source W?

How similar were the terms of disarmament for Bulgaria and Austria?

→ # Disarmament

- The Bulgarian army was reduced to 20,000 men and conscription forbidden.
- They were allowed only: 33,000 rifles in the entire country for any purposes and one factory for the making of weapons and munitions.
- Most military schools were abolished.
- The Bulgarian navy was reduced to four torpedo boats and six motor boats, with no torpedoes. Submarines were forbidden, as was an air force.
- Military equipment of any type could not be exported or imported.

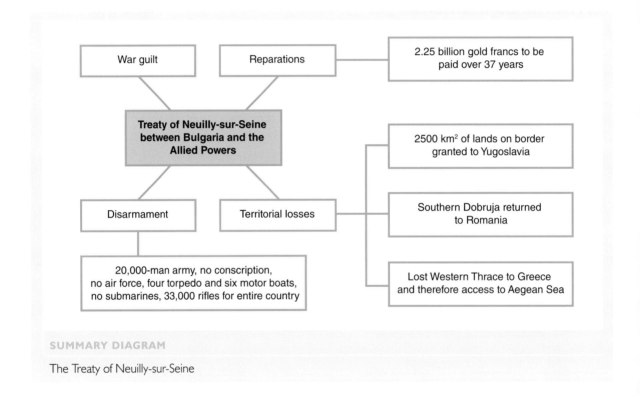

SUMMARY DIAGRAM

The Treaty of Neuilly-sur-Seine

④ The Treaty of Trianon

▶ *Key question: Why do some historians believe the Treaty of Trianon to be the harshest treaty to emerge from the Paris Peace Conference?*

The Treaty of Trianon was signed in June 1920 and dealt with the former Kingdom of Hungary. The Allied Powers delayed peace negotiations with Hungary in 1919 as a Bolshevik-inspired revolution was established and then crushed. The Kingdom of Hungary was half of the Austro-Hungarian

Empire and contained many nationalities. In many areas, it was difficult to separate these nationalities into discreet territories as the language could vary from village to village. For example, in southern Hungary it was possible for five villages in very close proximity to each speak a different language. This did not prevent Romanian and Yugoslav troops from occupying any territory they wished to annex. As with all the Paris treaties, the Covenant of the League of Nations was contained in the first 26 articles. Hungary joined the League in 1922.

As with the other main treaties, the main clauses dealt with:

- war guilt
- reparations
- territorial adjustments
- disarmament.

War guilt and reparations

As part of Austria-Hungary, in Article 161 Hungary was required to agree it was responsible for starting the war. As a result, the Allied Powers could morally and legally justify reparations and territorial adjustments. Hungary was expected to pay for the Allied war costs and damages to other countries but, as with Austria, Hungary had lost much of its territory and therefore ability to pay. A committee was established to determine what Hungary could afford.

How similar were the war guilt clauses of the Treaty of Neuilly and the Treaty of Trianon?

SOURCE X

Treaty of Trianon, Article 161, 1920.

The Allied and Associated Governments affirm and Hungary accepts the responsibility of Hungary and her allies for causing the loss and damage to which the Allied and Associated Governments and their nationals have been subjected as a consequence of the war imposed upon them by the aggression of Austria-Hungary and her allies.

What does Source X suggest the Allied Powers and Hungary agreed on?

Territorial adjustments

The Treaty of Trianon caused Hungary to lose 72 per cent of its territory and about 64 per cent of its population. Over three million ethnic Hungarians would find themselves living in new countries, about 30 per cent of all Hungarians.

The USA at first rejected the **partition** of Hungary without regard to ethnic lines. Britain and France had, however, signed a secret treaty with Romania promising it the huge province of Transylvania if it attacked Austria-Hungary during the war. This obligation by America's allies and the fact that much of the lands in question were occupied by various armies who were unlikely to give them up easily caused the Americans to give in.

How can it be argued that Hungary suffered more than any other former Central Power at the Paris Peace Conference?

 **KEY TERM**

Partition The breaking up of a larger state into smaller ones.

Western areas of Hungary were given to Austria as they contained Germans. This was insignificant compared to the loss of Slovakia and Ruthenia which went to the newly formed Czechoslovakia. This loss meant that the former Hungarian capital, Bratislava (also known as Pressburg), was in another country, as were almost one million Hungarians.

Croatia and Slavonia left the Kingdom of Hungary in October 1918 as Austria-Hungary fell apart. These provinces joined Yugoslavia in December 1918 and the treaty confirmed this. The loss of the port city of Fiume, also called Rijeka, to Yugoslavia meant that Hungary would no longer have access to the sea, limiting its ability to trade. The ethnically diverse, but strategically important province of Vojvodina was also given to Yugoslavia.

The largest prize went to Romania. Transylvania was a massive province with 1.6 million Hungarians and over 102,000 sq km of territory. It contained mines, industries and vast farmlands. Like all territories, with the exception of one small city, the treaty did not allow plebiscites to determine the desires of the inhabitants. Wherever there was a clash of interests between Hungary and its neighbours, the Allies ensured that the decision went against Hungary.

? What evidence is presented in Source Y that indicates Hungary was treated harshly in the Treaty of Trianon?

SOURCE Y

Excerpt from *The Politics of Backwardness in Hungary: 1825–1945* by Andrew C. Janos, published by Princeton University Press, Princeton, New Jersey, USA, 1982, pp. 205–6. Janos is the author of many books on European history and is a professor of history at the University of California, Berkeley, USA.

The terms of the treaty were very harsh indeed, much harsher than those imposed on Germany at Versailles. The territory of the political unit was reduced from … 128,879 square miles … to 36,311 square miles; the population of the country from … 20.8 million … to 7,980,143 … The rest of the territory and population of the old kingdom of Hungary were divided among Rumania, Czechoslovakia, Yugoslavia, and Austria, with Poland and Italy eventually acquiring a few square miles each from Czechoslovak and Yugoslav portions respectively. The detached territories included such 'historical' provinces as Transylvania – long regarded as the cradle of the Hungarian national state – a circumstance that added extra fuel to the revisionist propaganda of the forthcoming years …

To what extent were the Treaties of St Germain, Neuilly and Trianon similar in terms of disarmament?

Disarmament

The Hungarian army was limited to 35,000 men and conscription was prohibited. Most military schools were abolished and Hungary was to have no poison gas, flamethrowers or tanks. All ships that formerly belonged to Germany were to be turned over to the Allies. No air force was allowed and no weapons or munitions could be imported or exported.

SOURCE Z

The former Kingdom of Hungary showing ethnic divisions.

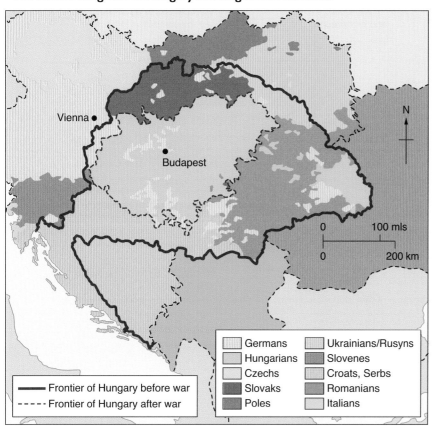

> What information is conveyed by Source Z? You should state at least five facts.

SOURCE AA

Excerpt from *A History of Modern Hungary 1867–1994*, second edition, by Jörg K. Hoensch, published by Longman, London and New York, 1996, p. 105. Hoensch was a noted German scholar on eastern European history and Head of the Institute of East European History at the University of the Saarland, Germany, from 1972 until 2001.

In an eruption of national patriotism which permeated all social classes, they argued for a revision of the peace treaty, invoking the symbol of the crown of St. Stephen to argue for the restoration of the territories lost to their despised neighbours. Although differences of opinion soon emerged regarding the extent of the desired revision, the treaty's failings were pilloried [ridiculed]. Its unrealistically high reparations demands, war-guilt clause, territorial and military terms and unjust treatment of the Magyar [Hungarian] minorities in Hungary's neighbor states all became a focus of resentment. The slogan, 'Nem, nem, soha!' (no, no, never!) summed up the attitude of every Magyar to the peace treaty.

> What was the Hungarian reaction to the Treaty of Trianon according to Source AA?

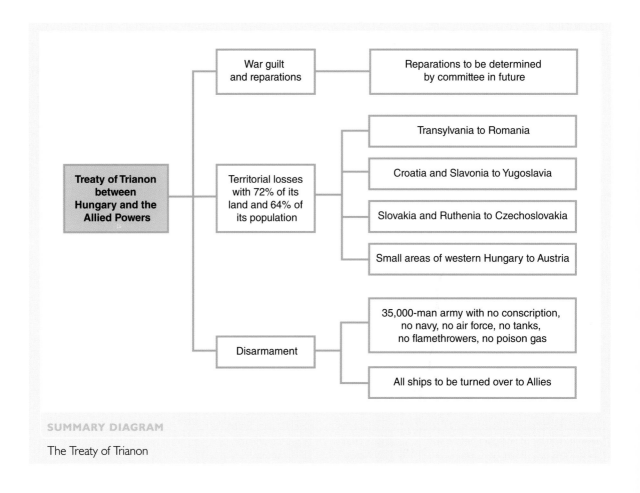

The Treaty of Trianon

5 The Treaty of Sèvres

▶ *Key question: How did the Treaty of Sèvres serve the interests of Britain and France?*

The Treaty of Sèvres was signed in August 1920 in the showroom of the famous Sèvres porcelain factory in France. This treaty was another Anglo-French compromise. British Prime Minister Lloyd George hoped drastically to weaken Turkey, not only by depriving it of Constantinople and of the control of the Bosphorus straits, but also by forcing it to surrender all territories where there was no ethnic Turkish majority. He now envisaged Greece, as a close ally of Britain, controlling the eastern Mediterranean instead of Italy. The French, on the other hand, concerned to protect their pre-war investments in Turkey, wished to preserve a viable Turkish state. Above all, they wanted the Turkish government to remain in Constantinople, known today as Istanbul, where it would be more vulnerable to French pressure. The end product of this Anglo-French compromise was a harsh and humiliating treaty, the first clauses of which contained the Covenant of the League of Nations; the others concerned:

- war guilt
- reparations
- territorial adjustments
- disarmament.

War guilt and reparations

The Treaty of Sèvres stated that the Ottoman government joined the war against the Allies to support Germany and Austria-Hungary and that this caused a great loss of life and much damage. The treaty did acknowledge, however, that the Ottoman Empire had collapsed and that the state of Turkey that had emerged from it had lost most of its resources and lands. The Allies did not require war reparations. They did, however, state that they would now control all of Turkey's finances, currency rates and banking.

> **How different were the war guilt clauses of the Treaties of Neuilly and Sèvres?**

SOURCE BB

Treaty of Sèvres, Article 231, August 1920.

Turkey recognises that by joining in the war of aggression which Germany and Austria-Hungary waged against the Allied Powers she has caused to the latter losses and sacrifices of all kinds for which she ought to make complete reparation.

On the other hand, the Allied Powers recognise that the resources of Turkey are not sufficient to enable her to make complete reparation.

In these circumstances, and inasmuch as the territorial rearrangements resulting from the present Treaty will leave to Turkey only a portion of the revenues of the former Turkish Empire, all claims against the Turkish Government for reparation are waived by the Allied Powers …

> What is the importance of Source BB for understanding the fate of the Ottoman Empire at the Paris Peace Conference?

Territorial adjustments

Before the First World War, the Ottoman Empire was one of the largest countries in the world at around 1.5 million sq km. It contained a large number of nationalities including Turks, Greeks, Armenians, Arabs, Egyptians, Kurds and others. Naturally many of these groups lived in areas where language groups were mixed. Dividing the Empire by ethnic lines proved to be a challenge.

> **What were the main reasons for the dismantling of the Ottoman Empire?**

Greece

The treaty called for Constantinople to remain Turkish, but the remaining land in Europe to go to Greece. The Dardenelles and Bosphorus straits, which connected the Aegean and Black Seas, were to be under international control for the safe passage of ships. In the area around Izmir, also called Smyrna, Greeks would be allowed to create their own parliament and administer themselves within the Turkish state. Within five years this zone could hold a plebiscite to determine whether to remain in Turkey or become part of Greece.

🔑 KEY TERM

Asia Minor Western-most peninsula of Asia.

Armenia

The new state of Armenia in the Caucasus Mountains would receive the vast majority of eastern **Asia Minor**, including the city of Trebizon on the Black Sea. This area included many Turks and Kurds who were not allowed to hold a plebiscite to determine their future. There was much discussion in Paris that the USA could be a mandatory over Armenia, but the USA declined to participate.

Kurds

Kurds were to be given a large zone of land in south-eastern Asia Minor for their own state around the city of Diyarbakir. Discussions on a Kurdish homeland were complicated by the fact that Kurds lived in areas granted to Armenia and in lands claimed by Britain and France.

Hejaz

The Arab-led Kingdom of the Hejaz was proclaimed on the Arabian peninsula, bordering the Red Sea and the Arabian or Persian Gulf in the East. The new state would span over 250,000 sq km but host a population of only around 750,000.

SOURCE CC

? What information is conveyed by Source CC? You should be able to state at least seven facts.

Map showing proposed changes to the Ottoman Empire based on the Treaty of Sèvres.

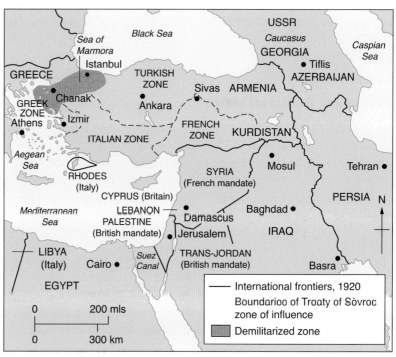

Italy

European states were also rewarded at the expense of the Ottoman Empire. The Treaty of Sèvres granted Italy the Dodecanese Islands which they had occupied since 1912. Almost the entirety of south-western and south-central Asia Minor bordering the Mediterranean Sea and extending far inland was also given to Italy.

Britain and France

British and French claims were more complicated. During the war they had already divided up much of the Middle East in a series of documents, including the Sykes–Picot Agreement of 1916 (see page 157) and the **Balfour Declaration** in 1917. While Sykes–Picot created spheres of French and British influence, the Balfour Declaration agreed that Palestine could be a national homeland for Jews as **Zionists** desired. They had also promised Arabs that there would be an Arab-led state throughout the region (see page 157).

In deference to Wilson and the Fourteen Points, the French and British agreed to exercise control over their Ottoman acquisitions under the League of Nations. The French received control of Lebanon, today's Syria and central Asia Minor. They were also granted access to oil wells in the British-held territory around Mosul in today's Iraq. The British also took Palestine, Trans-Jordan (today's Jordan and the West Bank) and oil-rich Iraq. Ostensibly these lands were to be mandates under the League of Nations but in reality were French and British colonies (see page 132).

 **KEY TERM**

Balfour Declaration A communication to the Zionists by A.J. Balfour, the British Foreign Secretary, declaring British support for establishing a national home for Jews in Palestine.

Zionists Supporters of Zionism, a group that wanted to establish a Jewish national state in Palestine.

SOURCE DD

Excerpt from *A Shattered Peace: Versailles 1919 and the Price We Pay Today*, by David A. Andelman, published by John Wiley & Sons, Hoboken, New Jersey, USA, 2008, p. 71. Andelman is a former *New York Times* reporter, editor with forbes.com online magazine, author of several history books, and current editor of *World Policy Journal*.

By the time the Peace Conference had adjourned and the delegations and their entourages headed home, the Middle East had become little more than another bargaining chip for the Americans. Self-determination was traded away in a vain effort to salvage Wilson's precious League of Nations. The British and French both realized, separately, that they could prey on the president's desire for an international body that he believed would be capable of salving any wound, correcting any injustice that diplomats had foisted on innocent people at a distant conference table. The result was a broad series of failures. The Paris Peace Conference effectively awarded 80 million new Arab subjects to Britain. But it failed to resolve the principal outstanding issues troubling the region ... The only parties who really came out winners in Paris [in regards to the Middle East] were the Zionists.

What, according to Source DD, were major failures by the USA at the Peace of Paris?

Turkey

The Turks were allowed north-central Asia Minor bordering the Black Sea which included the cities of Bursa, Ankara and Samsun.

How similar were the Treaties of St Germain and Sèvres in terms of arms limitations?

Disarmament

The Turkish army was limited to 50,000 men or fewer and conscription was forbidden. Turkey was allowed no air force, tanks, poison gas or the import or export of weapons. The navy was allowed seven sloops and six torpedo boats – but with no torpedoes. Submarines were forbidden and all fortresses guarding the Dardenelles and Bosphorus straits were to be dismantled.

Why was the Treaty of Sèvres never enacted?

Treaty complications

Of all the treaties negotiated in 1919–20, Sèvres, signed on 10 August 1920, was the most obvious failure as it was never put into effect by the Turkish government. When the Allies imposed it, they took little account of the profound changes in Turkey brought about by the rise of Mustapha Kemal, the leader of the new nationalist movement. Kemal had set up a rebel government which controlled virtually the whole of the Asia Minor except coastal areas and he was determined not to accept the treaty. The treaty's delay until August 1920 ensured that growing Turkish resentment, particularly at Greek control of Smyrna which the Allies had encouraged in May 1919, made its enforcement impossible.

Kemal settled a dispute with the Soviet Union over border issues in the east, enabling him to concentrate his forces against the Greeks without fear of Soviet intervention. By August 1922, he was poised to enter Constantinople and the **straits zone**, which were still occupied by Allied troops. Both the Italians and French rapidly withdrew from Asia Minor leaving the British isolated. Kemal, however, avoided direct confrontation with the British forces and negotiated an armistice which gave him virtually all he wanted. The Greek government withdrew from eastern Thrace and Turkey's other European territories, and the British recognized Turkish control over Constantinople and the straits. The Armenian and Kurd states promised in Sèvres were unable to form as these areas were under the control of Kemal and Turkish nationalists.

The Treaty of Lausanne

In 1923 an international conference met at Lausanne, Switzerland to revise the Treaty of Sèvres. The treaty worked to protect Christian minorities in Turkey and Muslim minorities in Greece. It required that Turkey give up all claims to Cyprus, Syria, Iraq, Egypt and Sudan. The status of oil-rich Mosul province would be decided by a special commission of the League of Nations. Turkey was recognized as a republic and the straits were to be controlled by an international commission to ensure free passage for all ships. Turkish finances would not be under the control of Allied countries and no mention was made of the First World War or disarmament.

SOURCE EE

Map of Turkey and Middle East showing British and French Mandates and other territorial boundaries by 1923.

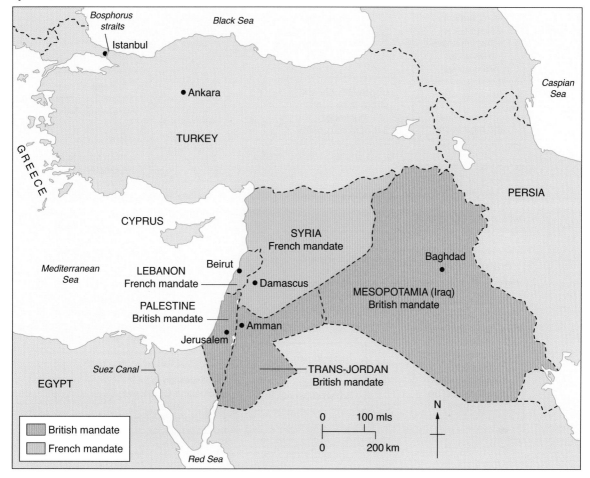

How different are Sources CC (page 60) and EE? You should be able to state at least five differences.

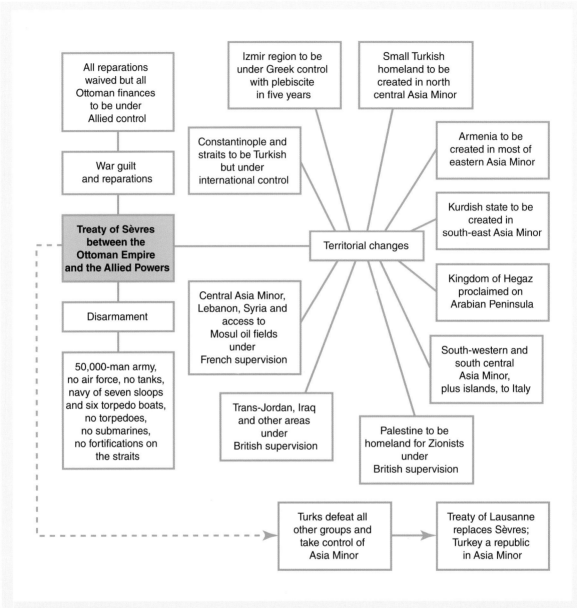

All reparations waived but all Ottoman finances to be under Allied control

War guilt and reparations

Treaty of Sèvres between the Ottoman Empire and the Allied Powers

Disarmament

50,000-man army, no air force, no tanks, navy of seven sloops and six torpedo boats, no torpedoes, no submarines, no fortifications on the straits

Izmir region to be under Greek control with plebiscite in five years

Small Turkish homeland to be created in north central Asia Minor

Constantinople and straits to be Turkish but under international control

Armenia to be created in most of eastern Asia Minor

Kurdish state to be created in south-east Asia Minor

Territorial changes

Kingdom of Hegaz proclaimed on Arabian Peninsula

Central Asia Minor, Lebanon, Syria and access to Mosul oil fields under French supervision

South-western and south central Asia Minor, plus islands, to Italy

Trans-Jordan, Iraq and other areas under British supervision

Palestine to be homeland for Zionists under British supervision

Turks defeat all other groups and take control of Asia Minor

Treaty of Lausanne replaces Sèvres; Turkey a republic in Asia Minor

SUMMARY DIAGRAM

The Treaty of Sèvres

Chapter summary

The terms of the Paris Peace Treaties 1919–20

The peacemaking process in Paris was complicated. Conflicting aims, secret treaties from the First World War, complicated questions of nationalities and borders and reparations meant that no single country could be satisfied with the results. The USA hoped to create new democratic nation states that conducted free trade and negotiated their problems instead of fighting over them. Britain wished to expand its empire, make Germany pay as much as possible, and to then use Germany to limit the spread of communism. France desired a severely weakened Germany both economically and militarily and reward for its First World War sacrifice by obtaining territory in the Middle East. Italy wanted to expand Italy and to gain colonies.

The Paris meetings created five treaties, all of which attempted to appease the USA by including the Covenant of the League of Nations. They also attempted to create nation states of distinct national groups and dismantle large armies, all part of the Fourteen Points. The treaties also went against the Fourteen Points by not often giving inhabitants of regions a say in which country they would be assigned to. Germans were particularly ignored by the treaties, finding themselves living in Austria, Czechoslovakia, Hungary, Poland and Italy.

While Wilson hoped to remove excuses for future wars, the treaties created many. Reparations from Germany would obviously be high since they would be used to rebuild Belgium and northern France, pay French debts to the USA and Britain, pay British war pensions and debts to the USA.

Austria and Hungary were left with fragments of their former lands and there were millions of Hungarians living in newly created states.

Bulgaria lost access to the Aegean Sea and Yugoslavia was given land which made the Bulgarian capital vulnerable in future conflicts.

The vast Ottoman Empire was destroyed by war and nationalism, so there was little left for the Europeans to punish.

Britain and France, however, helped themselves to much of the Middle East although they had promised self-rule to the Arabs and land for Zionists.

 # Examination advice

Paper 1 question 2: comparing and contrasting sources

Question 2 on the IB History Diploma examination requires you to compare and contrast two sources. This means you will discuss the similarities and differences between them. The most commonly used form of the question will ask you to compare and contrast two sources and how they view a certain historical event, document or person. Usually the similarities and differences are fairly clear and can be easily answered in a few minutes.

Question 2 requires no own knowledge, just the ability to read and understand the sources. It is possible that one of the sources will have been used in question 1. If this is the case, read the source again.

Question 2 is worth 6 marks out of the 25 total for Paper 1. This means it is worth 24 per cent of the overall mark. Answering question 2 should take ten minutes or less of your examination time.

How to answer

Read question 2 carefully. Determine which sources you need to read and what exactly you are being asked to compare and contrast. You will not be asked to just compare and contrast the two sources, but the two sources' view on something specific. Do not discuss the origins or purpose of the sources; focus only on the demands of the question. You should make notes on your paper from the source regarding the question's focus. Do this for both sources. There is no need to record or use any information which does not specifically address the question. Once you have completed answering your question, you should draw a line through any notes you made so they will not be reviewed by the examiner.

- First paragraph: explain how the sources compare, or are similar, on whatever is being asked in the question.
- Second paragraph: explain how the sources contrast, or are different, on whatever is being asked in the question.

You should not treat each source separately, but integrate them in the same sentences as much as possible. Use quotes from the sources to strengthen your answer and help you obtain more marks, but you should also paraphrase and summarize the sources.

Remember, the total marks available for this question is 6. A general rule to follow would be to have at least three points of comparison and three of contrast. This is not always possible, so in certain circumstances it may be possible to have four compares or contrasts and two of the other. Again, this is a general rule and it is always better to have as many of each as possible, making sure that all points are completely relevant and focused on the question. There may be minor similarities and differences between the sources. Do not let these take the place of the more significant points.

Example

This question uses Sources D and E found in this chapter on pages 34 and 36.

> Compare and contrast the views expressed in Sources D and E about why German reparation amounts were not stated in the Treaty of Versailles.

You will immediately make a note on your examination paper 'Why German reparations not in treaty?' and then 'Source D'. You will go to Source D in the examination booklet and start reading it, making notes on the Allied debate. You will probably write 'USA' and make quick, small points about US views and then the same for Britain and France. You will repeat this for Source E. Use these notes to determine how the sources are similar and different. Your notes may appear something like this:

Source D	Source E
USA: 1. Wanted fixed sum unlike Britain and France 2. Gave in to France and Britain	USA: 1. Wanted to limit German reparations 2. Would not agree with Britain and France
Britain: 1. Germany cannot afford to pay anything now 2. Wanted to negotiate with Germany in the future 3. Joined France in not stating amount so they could negotiate the amount lower	Britain: 1. Not satisfied with US plan 2. British Parliament and press demanded 'bill in full' for Germany 3. Position similar to France and opposite of USA
France: 1. Wanted massive reparation bill	France: 1. Pressured by French public for 'astronomic' reparations from Germany
General: 1. USA and Britain joined France in not stating amount so France could be convinced to lower demands later	General: 1. No sum stated because Allies couldn't agree

Hopefully, your answer will read something like the one on page 68.

There is running comparison in both paragraphs, with both sources usually mentioned together in the same sentence.

There is an appropriate use of quotations as supporting evidence.

Comparisons and contrasts have been separated into two paragraphs.

The comparisons and contrasts are the most significant ones. Minor points have not been used, keeping the paragraphs focused and strong. Examples of minor points could be that the USA, Britain and France are mentioned in both sources or both sources discuss the issue of reparations.

There is an appropriate use of language, especially in connecting sources or points. Examples of words that help build linkage include 'both', 'whereas', 'while' and 'however'.

Both Sources D and E agree that the USA wanted to have a limited amount of reparations stated in the Treaty of Versailles, but that both Britain and France were successful in their desire to not have an amount placed in the document. Sources D and E both agree that France wanted Germany to 'pay the full bill for war damage' and that the French public wanted 'astronomic sums'. Both Sources D and E indicate that negotiations were difficult with statements such as the one in Source D that negotiations were 'heated' while in Source E that compromise in 1919 'was asking the impossible'.

Sources D and E contrast strikingly. Source D indicates that Lloyd George wanted to negotiate a 'reasonable offer' with Germany on reparations, whereas Source E clearly states that he was under major pressure from the press and public to 'present the bill in full' to Germany. Source D states that Lloyd George sided with the French to not state a reparation total in the Treaty of Versailles so that he could convince them later to limit their demands: 'they wanted to make the bill fantastically large, he wanted to scale it down'. Source E, however, implies it was the British and French both who wanted 'astronomic sums' from Germany. The USA, however, did not so that the Allied Powers could not agree between these two positions. This led to reparations not being stated in the treaty.

The answer indicates that the question was understood. There are at least three comparisons and three contrasts between the two sources. There is running comparison and contrast in each paragraph with both sources often treated in the same sentence. Appropriate quotations used from the sources to reinforce the answer. The answer addresses all criteria. Mark: 6/6.

Examination practice

The following are exam-style questions for you to practise, using sources from the chapter. Sources can be found on the following pages:

- Source A: page 33
- Source B: page 33
- Source H: page 39
- Source N: page 45
- Source O: page 45

- Source R: page 48
- Source U: page 50
- Source Y: page 56
- Source AA: page 57

1 Compare and contrast the views expressed in Sources A and B about Wilson's thoughts on the creation of the League of Nations.

2 Compare and contrast the views expressed in Sources N and O regarding reasons the Treaty of Versailles and the League of Nations were opposed by the US Senate.

3 Compare and contrast the views expressed in Sources H and R regarding the creation of new states in Europe after the First World War.

4 Compare and contrast the views expressed in Sources R and U regarding the effect of the Treaty of St Germain-en-Laye on Austria.

5 Compare and contrast the views expressed in Sources Y and AA about the impact of the Treaty of Trianon on Hungary.

Activities

1 Compare each of the treaties mentioned in this chapter in terms of war guilt, territorial adjustment, reparations, disarmament and League of Nations issues. Do this in the form of a chart. Remember that comparing means to demonstrate the similarities. Once you have completed your chart, convert your chart into a narrative paragraph.

2 Repeat activity 1 but contrasting the various treaties. Remember to focus on major points instead of minor ones. An example of a minor point might be to state that all the treaties deal with different countries or the Treaty of Trianon mentions Ruthenia, while the other treaties do not.

3 Create five Paper 1 question 2-type questions using sources and paragraphs from Chapters 2 and 3 of this book:

- create five different questions
- discuss the wording of each of your questions with your classmates, making sure that your compare and contrast questions are worded with precision and are not too general
- select your best question and exchange it with a partner so that everyone has one to answer
- answer your question in 30 minutes
- give the question and answer back to the person who wrote the question who should then read the answer, make suggestions for improvement, and give it a mark out of 6.

Repeat this activity several times, reducing the amount of time allowed to answer the question gradually from 30 minutes down to ten.

CHAPTER 3

The geopolitical and economic impact of the Paris Peace Treaties on Europe

The treaties flowed out of the Paris Peace Conference for over a year and a half, affecting economic and political systems across Europe. Dismantling parts of Germany and most of the Austro-Hungarian Empire were traumatic experiences for tens of millions of people, many of whom had no desire to be in new states. Former economic systems collapsed and had to be reformed, along with currencies. Political systems transformed throughout the 1920s as well, with some states becoming more democratic, but with most establishing various forms of dictatorship. While central and eastern Europe transformed, the Soviet Union emerged out of the chaos of the Russian Civil War establishing a new form of state that many saw as a great threat. You need to consider the following questions throughout this chapter:

✪ To what extent were economics the main concern of post-war Germany?

✪ Was Germany strengthened or weakened as a result of the Paris Peace Conference?

✪ What factors allowed the Soviet Union success by 1933?

✪ How successful was Italy in overcoming political, economic and foreign policy difficulties after the First World War?

✪ How functional were the newly created and expanded states of central, eastern and south-eastern Europe after the Paris Peace Conference?

① Germany 1919–29

▶ *Key question: To what extent were economics the main concern of post-war Germany?*

The new German republic faced tremendous difficulties after the First World War, partly as a result of the Treaty of Versailles. An unpopular government agreed to relinquish German lands, organize reparations which were announced in 1921 and attempt to re-enter normal foreign relations. These foreign policy efforts occurred while the government faced multiple rebellions in the early 1920s and suffered assassinations of political figures. **Hyperinflation** brought the entire nation to the brink of collapse in 1923. By the late 1920s, however, Germany had achieved major foreign policy and economic gains, as well as political stability.

 **KEY TERM**

Hyperinflation Rapid reduction in the value of a currency.

Political unrest and territorial adjustments 1919–25

What were the main political challenges to the German government in the early 1920s?

On 11 February 1919, Friederich Ebert was elected as the first President of Germany. He had earlier served as chancellor after the collapse of the German Empire at the end of the First World War. Ebert was head of the Social Democratic Party, a **moderate socialist** group who advocated working with a parliament to improve the conditions of workers and create a democratic society where all were treated equally. Other socialist and communist groups were more radical, including the Spartacists (see page 13), who in January 1919 attempted to overthrow the new government to establish a communist one. This and other attempts at insurrection were crushed by the Free Corps, or *Freikorps*. Ebert was able to obtain their support by supplying them with food, equipment, uniforms and money.

Berlin and Bavaria 1919

Major disturbances continued to plague the first years of the German Republic. In March 1919, the Free Corps put down a communist rebellion, led by a companion of the dead Spartacist leader Rosa Luxemburg, in Berlin that lasted only seven days. The rebellion was crushed using 42,000 heavily armed troops, damaging much of the city, killing approximately 1500 people.

The southern province of Bavaria was taken over by the Independent Socialists in November 1918. Independent Socialists were much more aggressive than Social Democrats and believed that only by opposing the established government could real reforms be enacted to improve worker conditions and to achieve real democracy. By March, communists had taken control of Bavaria and proclaimed it a Soviet Republic, using Bolshevik Russia as their model. A Bavarian Red Army was formed, forcing the German government to take action. Munich, the Bavarian capital, was placed under siege and by April there was starvation. On 1 May, the Free Corps entered the starving city, executing all communists they found and ending the Soviet Republic of Bavaria.

Signing the Treaty of Versailles 1919

Another major crisis occurred on 7 May 1919 when the Treaty of Versailles terms were announced. Government ministers resigned in protest and to avoid placing their names on the document that most Germans found humiliating and undeserved. The army drew up plans to counter an invasion of Germany and Ebert prepared to step down as president. Field Marshall Von Hindenburg, leader of the German army, informed Ebert that although he would prefer to fight instead of accepting the treaty, the army would not be able to withstand a major attack from the west. Government officials were found and sent to Paris to sign the Treaty of Versailles. Many Germans blamed socialists, Jews and others for Germany's defeat in the First World War. The socialist-led government signed the Treaty of Versailles, making them criminals in the eyes of many **ultra-nationalist** Germans.

 **KEY TERM**

Moderate socialists Political groups who were influenced by Marxist thought, did not believe in the use of violence and wanted to work within parliamentary government to improve living conditions and standards through legislation.

Freikorps Heavily armed paramilitary units of ex-soldiers who were generally German nationalists, hated communism and were willing to use extreme brutality to crush dissent.

Ultra-nationalist Extreme nationalist usually opposed to all forms of socialism or communism, believing their nationality superior to that of others.

Kapp *Putsch* 1920

On 13 March 1920, some units of the Free Corps attempted to overthrow the German government by marching into Berlin and seizing the city. Ebert and his government fled and the Free Corps believed they had won. The Free Corp leader, Wolfgang Kapp, detested the government for agreeing to the Treaty of Versailles. His agenda was to make the German army strong, make Germans proud of being German again, and to seize parts of Poland that had recently been German provinces. Members of the army and the Berlin police supported him, but the workers did not. A general strike was called, cutting off the city's water, gas and coal supplies. Trains and buses came to a halt and government workers refused to supply Kapp and his men with money. In less than a week, the Kapp *Putsch* collapsed and Kapp fled to Sweden. Ebert returned to Berlin with the government just in time to deal with another crisis with the help of other Free Corps units.

Ruhr communist revolt 1920

Workers in the Ruhr Valley, the most industrialized area of Germany, went on strike and by the end of March 1920 had formed a communist army of about 50,000 people. The Free Corps were sent in to restore order. Two thousand workers were shot and order was established.

🔑 **KEY TERM**

Putsch A German word used to describe a revolt.

❓ What does Source A inform you about the Ruhr Red Army?

SOURCE A

The 'Red Army' of the Ruhr. Communist workers are given weapons in Dortmund.

Assassination of Rathenau 1922

Most Germans feared communism and perhaps even socialism. The German Republic was essentially created by the German army so that better terms could be negotiated with the Allied Powers. While there was obviously some support for a German Republic, the level and depth of support are impossible to know. Many conservative, nationalist Germans, however, were unhappy with the end of the old government which was seen as orderly, prosperous and dignified. Some decided to take the law into their own hands and at least 356 murders of various politicians, mostly socialists and communists, took place between 1919 and 1922. One of these was of Walter Rathenau.

On 24 June 1922, the German Foreign Minister, Walther Rathenau, was assassinated as he rode to work. Four men, who used pistols and a grenade, were captured and interrogated. One of the assassins explained that Rathenau had to be killed because he supported the Treaty of Versailles. Many Germans believed that he had been killed because he was Jewish and therefore unable to truly represent German interests.

Over a million people marched through Berlin protesting his assassination. There were major divisions between elected government officials, many of whom were socialists, and its civil servants, mostly conservatives who had served under the German emperor. This is most clearly seen when conservative judges gave prison sentences to the assassins that averaged only four years.

Munich *Putsch* 1923

The Munich *Putsch* against the German government was attempted in the Bavarian capital in November 1923. The ultra-nationalist National Socialist German Workers' Party (Nazis), had gained some support for their views as a result of the signing of the Treaty of Versailles and during the period of hyperinflation (see page 79).

The Nazis were led by Adolf Hitler who was an Austrian who had fought for Germany on the Western Front in France during the First World War. He was supported by General Ludendorff, the main German war leader in the final years of the war, which gave him legitimacy in the eyes of some. They captured three main Bavarian leaders in a beer hall and seized control of government offices on 8 November. The German army, however, ended the revolt on 9 November, killing 16 Nazis and arresting Hitler and Ludendorff. Ludendorff was released, but Hitler was sentenced to five years in prison. Hitler's trial gave him the largest audience he had ever had for his nationalist speeches and much coverage in most German newspapers. Hitler served nine months of his sentence in a prison where he could have unlimited visitors. He wrote *Mein Kampf (My Struggle)*, which presented his political ideas. The Nazi Party was reduced to insignificance for the remainder of the 1920s.

Return of stability

Gustav Stresemann served as German Foreign Minister starting in 1924 and helped negotiate the Dawes Plan that year (see page 81). The result of the American-led plan was massive foreign investment in Germany which resurrected the economy in a short period of time. Twenty-five billion gold marks were invested in Germany allowing new factories to be established, new machinery to be created and installed and new houses to be built. Unemployment was no longer a problem and prosperity returned to the country. With economic success, internal political tensions were reduced.

Although communists and Nazis fought each other in occasional street battles, this did not translate into election success for either group. The Communist Party won only 54 seats in the 1928 election for the *Reichstag*; the Nazis won only 12. The Social Democratic Party, the group that signed the Treaty of Versailles, continued to dominate with 153 seats as a result of economic success and stability.

Territorial adjustments with Poland

The main territorial concern for Germany was the creation of Poland. While there was some desire for the return of mineral-rich Alsace-Lorraine, even by some people living there, and other minor border regions with Denmark and Belgium, these concerns paled in contrast to those border disputes in the east. While some territories were granted to Poland outright, such as Posen, the Treaty of Versailles required plebiscites to be held in Allenstein, Marienwerder and Upper Silesia. In July 1920, Allenstein and Marienwerder voted overwhelmingly to remain part of Germany. Upper Silesia, however, proved difficult.

KEY TERM

Ruhr A heavily industrialized area in western Germany.

Upper Silesia had a population of some 2,280,000 Germans and Poles, who were divided along ethnic lines. It also had a massive concentration of coal mines and industries that were second only in size to the **Ruhr**, meaning that whichever country ruled this area would benefit economically.

The plebiscite on 17 March 1921 produced a result in which 60 per cent voted to remain part of Germany, but much of the eastern areas voted overwhelmingly to join Poland. This further complicated British and French disagreement over Poland (see page 39). The British argued that the plebiscite result justified keeping the key industrial regions as part of Germany, while the French insisted that they should be awarded to Poland. Fearing that once again British wishes would prevail, the Poles seized control of the industrial area, and an uprising broke out in May 1921. Order was eventually restored by British and French troops in July 1921 and the whole question was handed over to the League of Nations in August. In 1922 the League, bowing to French pressure, decided to hand over most of the industrial areas to Poland (see page 114).

Danzig, a major German port on the Baltic Sea, was to be governed by the League of Nations after November 1920. This would guarantee Poland access to the sea so that its economy could develop, although practically the entire population was German. East Prussia was a large German province that was now disconnected from the rest of the country by the Polish Corridor, a narrow strip of land adjoining Danzig and annexed to Poland which gave Poland further access to the sea (see the map on page 37).

SOURCE B

Photograph taken after plebiscite results in Silesia 1921. After a plebiscite which splits the region into German and Polish districts, people make their way to whichever district they want to live in.

What is the message of Source B? **?**

Reparations

← What were the problems with reparations and how were they solved?

The Treaty of Versailles required Germany to make reparations, but the Allied Powers could not agree on the amount. A commission was formed to study the issue and set an amount to be announced at a later date.

Reparations begin

At the end of April 1921 the Reparation Commission at last fixed a global total for reparations of 132 billion gold marks to be paid over a period of 42 years. German reaction was one of shock and dismay. When this sum was rejected by Germany, on the grounds that it was too high, Britain and France gave it an ultimatum: accept the new payment schedule within a week, or the heavily industrialized and populated Ruhr region would be occupied.

Walther Rathenau, the German Minister for Reconstruction in 1921, was determined to pursue a policy of negotiation rather than confrontation. The first instalment was paid, and Rathenau made some progress in persuading the French to accept the payment of a proportion of reparations in the form of the delivery of industrial goods and coal. However, by the end of the year the German government dropped a bombshell by announcing that, as a consequence of escalating inflation, it could not raise sufficient hard currency to meet the next instalment of reparation payments.

SOURCE C

Cartoon by David Low, *The Star*, 3 May 1921. Low was a cartoonist
from New Zealand who worked for many British newspapers from 1919
to 1953. *The Star* was a British newspaper that published from 1788
until 1960.

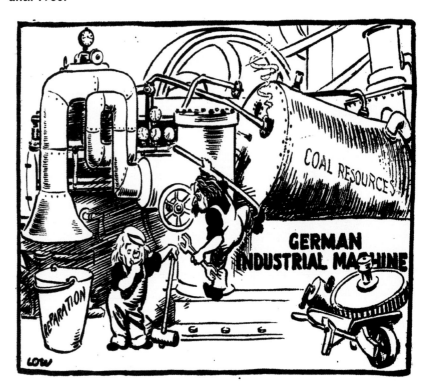

The Efficiency Experts. 'Half a
minute! I wonder if removing bits
of the machine really does speed
up production.'

KEY TERM

Moratorium A pause in
activity.

The Geneva Conference, April 1922

Lloyd George was convinced that Germany needed a temporary
moratorium to put its economy in order. He believed that in the longer term
the key to the payment of reparations and a European economic revival lay
in creating a European group of industrial nations, including Germany, to
rebuild Russia which had suffered major destruction in unending conflict
since 1914. Lloyd George may have been convinced that the Bolsheviks
would fail to win the civil war, or he was hopeful that the Bolsheviks would
welcome rebuilding and investment despite their stated beliefs and
propaganda. It was not yet fully understood by world governments that the
Soviet Union represented a new type of state, one which would not
necessarily welcome foreign investment or even co-operation with other
non-communist governments. He hoped that the rebuilding of Russia, the
world's largest nation, would generate an international trade boom, which
would also benefit Germany, and enable it to pay reparations without
damaging the commerce of the other European nations.

Raymond Poincaré had just become both French Prime Minister and Foreign
Minister and grudgingly consented to holding an international conference in

Geneva in 1922, to which both the Soviet Union and Germany would be invited to discuss these plans. He vetoed, however, the idea that any concession would be made on reparations. The Soviets agreed to attend, but were highly suspicious of Lloyd George's plans for opening up their economy to foreign capital.

During the conference, Germany and the Soviet Union pulled off a major diplomatic triumph by secretly negotiating the Rapallo Agreement. Both countries agreed to write off any financial claims on each other dating from the First World War. Germany also pledged to consult with Moscow before participating in any international plans for exploiting the Soviet economy. This meant that both countries would work together enough that neither would truly be diplomatically isolated as they had been before.

SOURCE D

Excerpt from *The Origins of the Second World War in Europe*, second edition, by P.M.H. Bell, published by Pearson, London, UK, 1997, p. 134. The book is currently in its third edition, published in 2007. Bell is an honorary senior fellow in the Department of History at the University of Liverpool, UK, and has published several books.

According to Source D, what was the result of the Treaty of Rapallo?

After the Treaty of Rapallo, over 2,000 German engineers and technicians went to work in Soviet industry. Junkers, the German aircraft firm, had a factory in Fili, near Moscow; and Krupps [a German company] were making guns in factories in central Asia … As Lenin predicted, the capitalist search for profits caused firms to contribute to building up the Soviet economy; and the Soviet authorities were willing to allow them to do so.

Rapallo effectively killed Lloyd George's plan. While it helped Germany to escape from isolation, it did so at the cost of intensifying French suspicions of its motives. In many ways these were justified, as a **secret annex** to Rapallo was signed in July allowing Germany to secretly train its soldiers in Soviet territory, thereby violating the terms of the Treaty of Versailles.

 **KEY TERM**

Secret annex Parts of an agreement that are not made public.

SOURCE E

Excerpt from *The Origins of the Second World War* by A.J.P. Taylor, published by Penguin Books, UK, 1991, pp. 76–7. First published in 1961 by Hamish Hamilton, this book has been most recently reprinted by Penguin Books in 2001. Taylor was a British historian who wrote many books on European history and was lecturer at many British universities.

According to Source E, what was the importance of the Treaty of Rapallo?

In fact the treaty of Rapallo was a modest, negative affair. It is true that it prevented a European coalition for a new war of intervention against Russia; it is also true that it prevented any revival of the old Triple Entente [Allied Powers]. Neither of these was a practical proposition in any case; and the treaty did no more than record the fact. But there was equally little chance of active cooperation between the two signatories. Neither was in a position to challenge the peace-settlement; both asked no more than to be left alone. The Germans thereafter provided Soviet Russia with a certain amount of economic assistance, though – absurdly enough – the Americans, who did not recognise Soviet Russia at all, provided more. The Russians enabled the Germans to evade the restrictions of the treaty of Versailles (to which after all the Russians were not a party) by setting up [poison] gas schools and flying schools on Soviet territory. These were trivialities. There was no sincerity in German–Soviet friendship; and both sides knew it. The German generals and conservatives, who promoted the friendship, despised the Bolsheviks; and they in their turn were friendly with Germany only according to the Leninist [principle] of taking a man by the hand, preparatory to taking him by the throat [that is fighting Germany in the future].

The Ruhr Crisis

In July 1922 a major confrontation between France and Germany seemed inevitable when the German government requested a three-year moratorium on reparation payments. At the same time Britain announced

SOURCE F

'No – You Cannot Force Me!' German poster in 1923 about passive resistance to the Ruhr occupation by France and Belgium.

? What is the message of Source F?

that, as the USA was demanding the repayment of British wartime debts, it must in turn insist on the repayment of money loaned to former allies, particularly France. To the French, Britain's demand for these repayments contrasted painfully with the concessions Lloyd George was ready to offer the Germans, causing further diplomatic stress in their relationship.

On 27 November 1922, the French Prime Minister Poincaré decided finally that the occupation of the Ruhr was the only means of forcing Germany to pay reparations. French and Belgian troops moved into the Ruhr region on 11 January 1923. Significantly, Britain did not join in but adopted a policy of **benevolent neutrality** towards France.

Passive resistance

For nine months the French occupation of the Ruhr was met by **passive resistance** and strikes financed by the German government. Germany continued to pay wages and benefits to striking workers while the massive industrial output of the Ruhr slowed almost to a halt. This denied the French German goods and raw materials, but at the same time meant that Germany was also not making money through exports and taxes.

Hyperinflation 1923

The government needed to support its citizens although it had little money and it did so by printing huge quantities of paper money, causing hyperinflation. The price of a loaf of bread in Berlin in January 1923 was

> **KEY TERM**
>
> **Benevolent neutrality**
> Not willing to be involved but also not criticizing.
>
> **Passive resistance**
> Resisting by not participating in any way, usually by refusing to work, shop or be provoked.

SOURCE G

Germany 1923: men are selling money as scrap paper. By weight, it is worth more than old bones, but less than rags.

In what ways does Source G demonstrate the value of German paper money in 1923?

250 marks, but by November the price had reached 201 billion marks. The bag or basket that people used to carry money in was worth more than the money being carried. Workers had to be paid twice per day because the value of their wages fell almost hourly. Older people on pensions which granted them fixed amounts of money per month faced starvation as prices rose beyond their ability to buy even bread. People could not afford clothing, transportation or to heat their homes. Money saved in bank accounts became worthless.

Hyperinflation also wiped out debt since people could pay off whatever they owed with just a few of the now worthless paper marks. A million mark debt in early 1923 was an enormous amount, but by the end of the year this could be paid off with a single banknote that could not even buy bread. By the end of 1923, people used million mark banknotes to start fires or wallpaper their bedrooms. In August 1923, the crisis caused the German government to be replaced and Gustav Stresemann was appointed chancellor.

? What is the value of Source H to a historian?

SOURCE H

The price of a loaf of bread in Germany. From *Years of Weimar and the Third Reich* by David Evans and Jane Jenkins, published in 1999.

Date	Price in marks
1918	0.63
January 1923	250
July 1923	3465
September 1923	1,500,000,000
November 1923	201,000,000,000

? According to Source I what was Stresemann's method of revising the Treaty of Versailles?

SOURCE I

The Origins of the Second World War by A.J.P. Taylor, published by Penguin Books, UK, 1991, p. 78. First published in 1961 by Hamish Hamilton, this book has been most recently reprinted by Penguin Books in 2001. Taylor was a British historian who wrote many books on European history and was lecturer at many British universities.

Stresemann came to power with the avowed policy of fulfilling the treaty [of Versailles]. Of course this did not mean that he accepted the French interpretation of the treaty or that he would acquiesce in the French demands. It meant only that he would defend German interests by negotiations, not by resistance. Stresemann was as determined as the most extreme nationalist to get rid of the whole treaty lock, stock, and barrel: reparations, German disarmament, the occupation of the Rhineland, and the frontier with Poland. But he intended to do this by persistent pressure of events, not by threats, still less by war. Where other Germans insisted that revision of the treaty was necessary for the revival of German power, Stresemann believed that the revival of German power would inevitably lead to revision of the treaty.

Effect on France

France, too, had exhausted itself financially and politically in the prolonged Ruhr Crisis:

- French currency had been seriously weakened.
- Massive expenditure had been made in occupying part of Germany with next to nothing to show for it.
- Relations between Britain and France became strained.

France's attempts to create an independent Rhineland state to weaken German and separate Rhineland currency were unsuccessful. Rhineland separatist leaders were assassinated by German nationalist agents from unoccupied Germany or lynched by angry crowds. Poincaré had little option but to co-operate with an Anglo-American initiative for setting up a commission chaired by the US financier Charles G. Dawes. The commission began work in early 1924 and studied Germany's ability to pay and how it could best balance its budget and restore its currency. The Ruhr Crisis marked the end of the attempts to carry out the Treaty of Versailles by force and the beginning of the gradual revision of the treaty itself.

The Dawes Plan

The Dawes Plan developed out of the commission's work. Some of the recommendations included:

- Not modifying the reparation requirement of 132 billion gold marks.
- US banks to loan Germany 800 million gold marks to help restore the Germany economy.
- Reparations payments to be lower in the beginning, but rise to the maximum amount in five years.
- Reparations payments to be guaranteed using the revenues made from German railroads and other specific industries.
- A committee chaired by a US government official would be established in Germany to oversee reparation payments and their distribution to Belgium, France and Britain. This committee would ensure that reparation payments were made in such a way that the German economy was not damaged.
- Plan would be reviewed and renegotiated in ten years.

Reaction to Dawes Plan

The British

The Dawes Plan was welcomed enthusiastically in April 1924 by the British Treasury as 'the only constructive suggestion for escape from the present position, which if left must inevitably lead to war, open or concealed, between Germany and France'. It also had the advantage of involving the USA in the whole process of extracting reparations from Germany. Britain wanted the USA to participate in European affairs in order to reassure France and to counter any future threats by the Soviet Union.

SOURCE J

Cartoon by David Low, *The Star*, 15 August 1924. Low was a cartoonist from New Zealand who worked for many British newspapers from 1919 to 1953. *The Star* was a British newspaper that published from 1788 until 1960.

FREE AT LAST!

The French

There was much that the French disliked about the plan. For instance, it was not clear to them how the Germans could be compelled to pay if they again defaulted and refused to pay, as they had in 1922. However, with the defeat of Poincaré in the elections of June 1924, their willingness to co-operate markedly increased. Essentially, if the French were ever to receive any reparation payments and to avoid isolation, they had little option but to go along with the Dawes Plan.

The Germans

The Germans also disliked the plan as it placed their railways and some of their industry under international control and did nothing about scaling down their reparation debts. Stresemann, who after the fall of his cabinet in November 1923 was now foreign minister, realized that Germany had no alternative but to accept the plan if the French were to be persuaded to evacuate the Ruhr sooner rather than later.

The London Conference 1924

At the London Conference in August 1924, it was agreed to implement the Dawes Plan and to withdraw French and Belgian forces from the Ruhr within twelve months. The new balance of power in Europe was clearly revealed when Britain and the USA devised a formula for effectively blocking France's ability to act alone against Germany in the event of another default in reparation payments. If Germany again refused to pay, it was agreed that:

- Britain as a member of the Reparation Commission would have the right to appeal to the **Permanent Court of International Justice** at The Hague (see page 135).
- A US representative would immediately join the Reparation Commission.

Joint Anglo-American pressure would then be more than enough to restrain France from reoccupying the Ruhr. Deprived of much of their influence on the Reparation Commission, the French suffered a major diplomatic defeat at the London Conference.

New German currency

In November 1924, Germany replaced the devalued German currency with the temporary *Rentenmark* which was itself replaced soon afterwards with the *Reichsmark*. The *Reichsmark* was placed on the **gold standard**, which, coupled with the Dawes Plan that brought the Ruhr Crisis to an end, made Germany an attractive prospect for investment from US banks and individuals. Germany quickly restored its economy and experienced significant economic growth.

France continued to worry about security and continued to insist, in as far as it still could, on the literal implementation of the Treaty of Versailles. France refused, for instance, to agree to the evacuation of the Cologne zone, which was due in January 1925 (see page 84), on the grounds that Germany had not yet carried out the military clauses of the treaty.

The Young Plan and the evacuation of the Rhineland

The Young Plan was formulated at the Hague Conference in 1929. The plan reduced German reparations by about seventeen per cent, from 132 billion gold marks to 112 billion, and allowed this to be paid over 59 years. Britain and France also agreed to evacuate the Rhineland in 1930 instead of 1935, removing the humiliation of occupation and making the Young Plan acceptable to many in Germany. In December, however, the government faced a referendum forced on them by the National Socialist German

 **KEY TERM**

Permanent Court of International Justice
Court established by League of Nations in 1922 to rule on aspects of international law.

Gold standard When a specific amount of paper currency can be exchanged for a set amount of gold.

 **KEY TERM**

Treason Working against one's country.

Workers' Party (Nazi Party, see page 73) and other nationalists, declaring that its signature would be an act of high **treason** on the grounds that the Young Plan committed Germany to making reparations which they believed should be ended. This was easily defeated and the Young Plan was officially implemented on 20 January 1930.

Why did much of Europe celebrate the decisions made at Locarno in October 1925?

The Locarno Conference 1925

There was an urgent need to reassure the French of Germany's peaceful intentions after the London Conference in 1924, in light of the recovering German economy, and as a result of France's lack of a military guarantee against a German attack in the future. Germany also wanted France to evacuate Cologne. A conference was organized in Locarno, Switzerland, in October 1925 between British Foreign Minister Austen Chamberlain, French Foreign Minister Aristide Briand and German Foreign Minister Stresemann.

According to Source K, what is Germany's status at the start of the Locarno Conference?

SOURCE K

A German cartoon about the Locarno Conference 1925. Germany, represented by Stresemann, in debtor's chains being led by Briand with Chamberlain standing behind.

The Locarno Treaties

Stresemann put forward a scheme that would have Britain, France and Germany recognize permanent borders on Germany's western border with France and Belgium, agreeing that the territories taken by those countries in the Treaty of Versailles were forever to be parts of France and Belgium. The British government responded positively to the idea because it would not require them to make a military commitment to France and would reduce tensions that might lead to another war. France believed that since Britain would not sign a military alliance, this agreement was the next best thing and might even persuade Britain to join France in the event that Germany violated the agreement in the future. Germany agreed to the continued demilitarization of the Rhineland as stated in the Treaty of Versailles. France was able to persuade both Britain and Germany to expand the agreement beyond the French and German borders to include those with Belgium.

Briand attempted to extend the agreements to cover Germany's eastern frontiers, but this was rejected by both Germany and Britain. Stresemann did agree to refer disputes with Poland and Czechoslovakia to international arbitration, although he refused to recognize their frontiers with Germany as permanent. The British government was aware that the Polish corridor, Danzig and Upper Silesia, to name a few, were areas where conflict was likely, if not guaranteed. Fully aware that an international agreement could lead to British involvement in a conflict in eastern Europe, the British rejected the idea of extending the agreement to cover Germany's eastern borders.

The Locarno negotiations resulted in seven treaties signed on 1 December in London. The most important of these were agreements confirming the **inviolability** of the Franco-German and Belgian–German frontiers and the demilitarization of the Rhineland which had been set at Versailles (see page 38).

 **KEY TERM**

Inviolability Forbidden to cross.

SOURCE L

Excerpt from *Germany: A Self-Portrait*, edited by Harlan R. Crippen, published by Oxford University Press, London, UK, 1944, p. 214. Crippen was a writer who primarily contributed to the Marxist journal *Science and Society*, published in the USA since 1935.

Thus, under Stresemann's leadership, Germany re-entered world affairs. On 5 March 1925 France and Belgium were offered treaties providing mutual guarantees of frontiers. In July 1925 the Ruhr was evacuated and, a month later, foreign troops moved out of the German districts occupied in 1921. On the basis of the 5 March proposals France, Britain, Belgium, Czechoslovakia, Poland, Italy, and Germany sent representatives to a meeting in Switzerland, where Germany met on equal terms with the other nations for the first time since 1914. The meeting, dominated by Stresemann, Briand and Joseph Austen Chamberlain, resulted in the Locarno Treaties, demilitarizing the Rhineland and providing mutual guarantees of frontiers. In 1926, over Nationalist protests, Stresemann led Germany into the League of Nations.

According to Source L, which nation was the catalyst for international peace negotiations in 1925 and 1926?

Locarno guarantees

The treaties were underwritten by an Anglo-Italian guarantee to assist the victims of aggression. If a relatively minor incident between France and Germany, for example, occurred, the country being disturbed or attacked would first appeal to the Council of the League of Nations (see page 135). If the complaint was upheld, then Britain and Italy would assist the injured state to secure compensation from the country causing the problem. In the event of a serious violation of the treaty, Britain and Italy could act immediately, although they would still eventually refer the issue to the Council.

SOURCE M

According to Source M, how positive were the results of the Locarno treaties?

Excerpt from *Britain and the Problem of International Disarmament, 1919–1934*, by Carolyn J. Kitching, published by Routledge, London, UK, 1999, p. 92. Kitching is a modern history lecturer at the University of Teesside, UK, publishing several books on disarmament and arms control.

In themselves, the Locarno Treaties created neither security nor disarmament. Indeed, the guarantees contained within the treaties were perhaps too vague to be meaningful; how could Britain, for example, draw up concrete military plans if she did not know against whom they would be directed, or with whom joint planning arrangements should be made? The general atmosphere, however, improved markedly. America approved of the treaties, as they seemed to herald a period of stability in Europe; the Italians approved, because their international status was enhanced; Britain and the Dominions approved because stability had been achieved without any precise military commitments having been made. For their part, the Germans were once again legitimate members of the European community and had protected themselves against renewed incursions by the French. The French gained an illusion of security.

Reaction to Locarno

Throughout western Europe and the USA the Locarno treaties were greeted with enormous enthusiasm. It appeared as if real peace had at last come. Had France now achieved the security it had for so long been seeking? Of all the great powers, the French gained least from Locarno. It is true that France's eastern frontier was now secure, but under Locarno it could no longer threaten to occupy the Ruhr in order to bring pressure to bear on Berlin in the event of Germany breaking the Treaty of Versailles.

The British had managed to give France the illusion of security. The provision for referring all but major violations of the Locarno treaties to the League before taking action ensured that the British government would actually be able to determine, through its own representative on the Council, what action, if any, it should take. For Britain there were two main advantages to Locarno. First, it prevented France from repeating the Ruhr occupation which could lead to war. Second, by improving relations between Germany and the western powers and by holding out the prospect of German membership of the League, it discouraged any close co-operation between the Soviet Union and Germany.

Many Europeans felt that the Locarno agreements changed the political atmosphere of the continent and many believed that the threat of war was finally over. This was the **Locarno spirit**. This spirit, however, was mostly felt in western European nations. Eastern European countries were dismayed and felt that they had been betrayed by France, their military ally (see page 112). Some historians believe that separating France from their central and eastern European allies may have been the entire aim of Stresemann as a step towards major revisions of the Treaty of Versailles regarding Germany's eastern borders.

The atmosphere of *détente* created by Locarno quickly led to the evacuation of the Cologne zone in January 1926 and in September 1926, Germany joined the League of Nations and received a permanent seat on the Council (see page 135). Stresemann worked to further revise the Treaty of Versailles and in January 1927 he managed to have the **Allied Disarmament Commission** withdrawn. In August 1928, Britain, France and Belgium withdrew a further 10,000 troops from their garrisons in the Rhineland.

 **KEY TERM**

Locarno spirit The optimistic mood of reconciliation and compromise that swept through western Europe after the signing of the Locarno treaties.

Détente A French term used to describe an easing of tensions between countries.

Allied Disarmament Commission Organization established to monitor the German military to ensure compliance with the Treaty of Versailles.

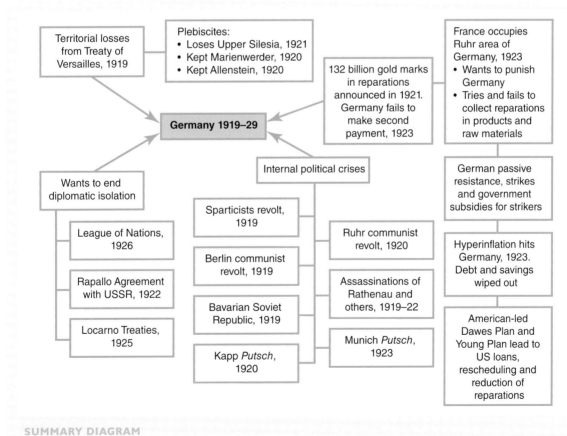

SUMMARY DIAGRAM

Germany 1919–29

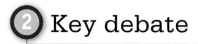

Key debate

▶ **Key question:** *Was Germany strengthened or weakened as a result of the Paris Peace Conference?*

You have learned about the treaties that developed out of the Peace of Paris. The Treaty of Versailles dealt with Germany and is the most famous, but all the treaties are important in understanding the period after the First World War and perhaps even the origins of the Second World War. While it is evident that Germany was punished in the Treaty of Versailles, debate continues on the significance of the treaty. Historians have debated the impact of the treaties since they were issued, with special attention given to that of Versailles. It is important to remember that historians use evidence to make arguments.

Several historians have argued that Versailles was seen as unfair and harsh by Germans. Evidence supporting these points includes those made in Section 1 of this chapter, including political and economic turmoil. Other historians argue that although Germany suffered in the short term, the decisions reached in Versailles actually benefited Germany in the longer term. Evidence for that includes the breaking up of the Austro-Hungarian Empire into small states with hostile neighbours, underdeveloped economic systems and political weakness. The break-up of parts of the Russian Empire allowed Finland, Estonia, Latvia, Lithuania and about half of Poland to further fragment Europe. It must also be remembered that Germany remained relatively intact with its infrastructure and industries undamaged by war since the country was never invaded. By removing the provinces of Alsace-Lorraine and Polish areas, the state was even more ethnically coherent and therefore more united. There is much evidence to support either side of the debate.

Views of some historians who believed that the Treaty of Versailles may not have weakened Germany considerably are presented below.

SOURCE N

Excerpt from *The Origins of the Second World War in Europe*, second edition, by P.M.H. Bell, published by Pearson, London, UK, 1997, p. 27. The book is currently in its third edition, published in 2007. Bell is an honorary senior fellow in the Department of History at the University of Liverpool and has published several books.

Germany remained the centre of Europe, with (even after her losses of territory) a population and industrial resources which were bound, if allowed free play, to give her a predominant position on the Continent. The peace settlement had been harsh enough to infuriate the Germans, but not so crushing as to render them powerless. Machiavelli once advised: 'If you see your enemy in the water up to his neck, you will do well to push him under; but if he is only in it up to his knees, you will do well to help him to the shore.' The peace treaty did neither.

SOURCE O

Excerpt from *The Origins of the Second World War*, by A.J.P. Taylor, published by Penguin Books, UK, 1991, p. 48. First published in 1961 by Hamish Hamilton, this book has been most recently reprinted by Penguin Books in 2001. Taylor was a British historian who wrote many books on European history and was lecturer at many British universities.

However democratic and pacific Germany might become [after the First World War], she remained by far the greatest Power on the continent of Europe; with the disappearance of Russia, more so than before. She was greatest in population – sixty-five million against forty million in France, the only other substantial Power. Her preponderance was greater still in the economic resources of coal and steel which in modern times together made up power. At the moment in 1919, German was down-and-out. The immediate problem was German weakness; but given a few years of 'normal' life, it would again become the problem of German strength. More than this, the old balance of power, which formerly did something to restrain Germany, had broken down. Russia had withdrawn; Austria-Hungary had vanished. Only France and Italy remained, both inferior in man-power and still more in economic resources, both exhausted by the war. If events followed their course in the old 'free' way, nothing could prevent the Germans from overshadowing Europe, even if they did not plan to do so.

SOURCE P

Excerpt from *The Road to War*, second edition, by Richard Overy and Andrew Wheatcroft, 1999, Penguin Books, London, UK, pp. 123–4. Overy is a modern history professor at King's College, University of London, UK. Wheatcroft is a historian at the University of Stirling, UK.

France had not won the war alone, but only with the help of her major allies. Faced by Germany on her own, she would almost certainly have lost the war. The power she enjoyed in the Europe of the 1920s was a result of the weakness of others as much as her own strengths. Revolutionary Russia was isolated, the great powers of Central Europe [sic.] enfeebled beyond recognition …

The war had weakened rather than strengthened France. During the slaughter of the Great War, France lost one-quarter of all her men aged between eighteen and twenty-seven, a higher proportion than any other nation. Four million Frenchmen carried the wounds of that conflict. The war destroyed the enduring value of the French franc, unchanged since Napoleon's time. By 1920 it was worth only a fifth of its pre-war value, while France was saddled with enormous debts from the war and a bill for war pensions, which twenty years later still consumed over half of all government expenditure …

It is against such a background that sense can be made of the almost frantic efforts by French statement to uphold the letter of the Versailles treaty against Germany.

Historians continue to debate the short- and long-term consequences of the Treaty of Versailles for Germany. To what extent are some questions about history unanswerable? (History, Language and Reason.)

③ Russia 1917–32

> ▶ **Key question:** *What factors allowed the Soviet Union success by 1933?*

Russia fell apart in stages in 1917. After agreeing to a harsh peace with Germany in early 1918, a civil war that had already been brewing erupted with full force. By the end of 1921, the Bolsheviks had crushed the vast majority of their opponents and established a communist government which embarked on various economic programmes. The first programme hoped to re-establish a system which could at least feed workers in the cities, the core support group of the Bolsheviks, or communists as they began to be called. Later, after the rise of Stalin, the primary Soviet leader after 1928, a programme of major industrialization was carried out, leading to the death of millions but strengthening the state economically.

Why were there two revolutions in Russia in 1917?

→ Revolutions and Civil War 1917–21

Russia, the largest empire in the world, collapsed in stages in 1917. The first revolution was precipitated by hungry, striking workers in St Petersburg, renamed the less German-sounding Petrograd during the First World War. The so-called February Revolution was essentially a *coup d'état* with the army forcing Emperor Nicholas II aside and replacing him and his administration with a Provisional Government. The army's main concern was to end worker strikes in the major cities, the location of factories, so that war supplies could continue to flow to the troops fighting the Central Powers.

SOURCE Q

What is the importance of Source Q for historians?

Number of strikes 23–6 February 1917 in St Petersburg. From *Years of Russia, the USSR and the Collapse of Soviet Communism* by David Evans and Jane Jenkins, published in 2008.

Date	Strikes	Strikers
23 February	48	99,700
24 February	147	196,632
25 February	296	271,211
26 February	216	314,439

The Provisional Government

The Provisional Government, appointed and supported by the army, set to work on pro-democratic reforms, including freedom of speech and the right to form political parties. Many promises were also made, including **land redistribution** to peasants and supplying cities with affordable food. The Provisional Government was also to organize empire-wide elections for a constituent assembly which would create a constitution and new form of government for Russia. As Russia continued to lose ground to the Central

KEY TERM

Land redistribution In Russia the idea of granting land to peasants.

Powers on the battlefield, the Provisional Government battled various groups of socialists and communists, including Social Revolutionaries, Mensheviks and Bolsheviks, for political control of the country and army.

Social Revolutionaries were a peasant-oriented Marxist Party that advocated massive land redistribution. Mensheviks, an industrial worker-based party, believed that gradual reform of working conditions and the government, in favour of workers, could be achieved by working with other political parties in a parliamentary system. Bolsheviks believed that working with other political parties necessarily meant compromising their beliefs. They believed that the only way to truly achieve a worker-dominated state was through violent revolution, led by a strong central committee.

The Social Revolutionaries were by far the largest party of the three since the peasantry of Russia was over 80 per cent of the population, with Mensheviks a distant second. The Bolsheviks were extremists and their numbers were insignificant in early 1917, perhaps only a few thousand at most. All three groups were opposed to continuing the war which they believed only benefited the wealthy classes that owned industries supplying war goods to the army.

The Petrograd Soviet, a workers' committee dominated by Social Revolutionaries and Mensheviks, established a rival governmental structure to challenge the Provisional Government. The Soviet issued decrees which gave soldiers the right to appoint their own officers and vote on whether to follow orders. Although the Soviet was not the official government, their decrees carried great weight with common soldiers who also wanted an end to the war.

As the army lost cohesion as a result of continued defeat, soldier defections and interference from the Petrograd Soviet, the Provisional Government did not follow through with land redistribution, dragged out preparations for constituent assembly elections, and had difficulty organizing fuel and food distribution to the cities. Eventually the Provisional Government appointed Alexander Kerensky, head of the Petrograd Soviet, as the head of the Provisional Government.

The October Revolution

Kerensky was a Social Revolutionary, but in July 1917 organized a failed military offensive against Germany leading to a loss of support among workers. When faced with more strikes in St Petersburg in August, General Lavr Kornilov decided to move in military units perhaps to seize control of the government. Kerensky feared that he would also be targeted as a Social Revolutionary, so he armed the Bolsheviks who had announced they were willing to fight to defend St Petersburg. Kornilov's attack never materialized, but the Bolsheviks refused to return their weapons and within days overthrew the Provisional Government in the October Revolution, seizing control of St Petersburg and Moscow. Worker councils, soviets, were established throughout Russia with only Bolsheviks allowed to participate. These helped the Bolsheviks control large areas of the country, especially large cities and towns where there were industrial workers.

Before its overthrow, the Provisional Government had finally organized empire-wide elections for the All-Russian Constituent Assembly which went ahead in November 1917. The majority of elected delegates opposed the Bolsheviks as they were Social Revolutionaries, voting down Bolshevik plans during the one day the assembly met in January 1918. The next day, Bolshevik troops locked the delegates out of the Tauride Palace where meetings were being held and dispersed the participants. The Bolsheviks created a new body, the All-Russian Congress of Soviets, where most participants were Bolsheviks, with some representatives of the other socialist

SOURCE R

A Bolshevik propaganda poster from 1919. 'The workers oppressed by Tsar, Pope and Boyar [rich men] – but now the Bolsheviks will put a stop to oppression … '

? What justification do the Bolsheviks present in Source R for stopping the former rulers?

ЦАРЬ, ПОП И БОГАЧ
НА ПЛЕЧАХ У ТРУДОВОГО НАРОДА

parties present. The congress worked to organize the new Russian state on exclusively Bolshevik lines.

By March 1918, the Bolshevik government negotiated the Treaty of Brest-Litovsk with Germany (see page 27), ending Russia's official involvement in the First World War. The terms were exceedingly harsh, but the Bolsheviks needed supportive soldiers released from the front to help them defeat their very well-armed enemies. The Russian Civil War, also known as the Reds versus Whites Civil War, had already begun. Red was the universally recognized colour of communism, while white represented essentially anyone opposed to communism, especially nationalists.

Russian Civil War

The Russian Civil War ended mostly by 1921. The Bolsheviks were successful for several reasons, not the least of which was their control of railroads,

SOURCE S

A Russian Civil War recruitment poster from 1920. 'You, have you signed up as a volunteer?'

What symbolism in Source S informs the viewer which group the poster was recruiting for?

factories and communications. They were an extremely well-organized group who fought the Whites. The Whites represented various Russian factions, including those who wanted Russia to be a democracy, others who wanted a return of the tsarist autocratic system, and so forth. The Whites had difficulty organizing supplies as they did not control many industrial centres. Rival groups often refused to co-operate, communications were difficult, and peasants were usually unsupportive as they felt that Whites would take back land they had been granted by the Bolsheviks. Foreign troops from Japan, Britain, France and the USA that were sent to assist the Whites turned many nationalist Russians against them. During the war, food was unable to reach cities as railroads were damaged or utilized by the military, and peasants often had all their food seized by either the communists or the Whites, leading to mass starvation. Approximately eight million people died in the Russian Civil War.

International isolation

Bolshevism and the events of the Russian Civil War alarmed many in Europe. During the course of the war, newly created Poland invaded the Ukraine, a Russian province controlled primarily by the Bolsheviks. The Bolsheviks counter-attacked, leading an army all the way to Warsaw, the Polish capital, in 1920. The Bolsheviks were defeated and eventually seceded significant territory to Poland partly so that the Bolsheviks could concentrate their armies elsewhere to fight off the Whites. The invasion of Poland, the establishment of the brief communist government in Hungary and Bavaria (see pages 13 and 71), plus the Spartacist uprising in Berlin (see page 13) was evidence for many that the newly named Soviet Union, formerly Russia, was a threat as it supported and encouraged communist revolutions in much of Europe.

During the Civil War, the people of Finland, Estonia, Latvia and Lithuania established independent states, fighting the Bolsheviks and sometimes each other and Poland. Those states, plus Poland, Czechoslovakia, Hungary and an expanded Romania created a geographical barrier of nationalistic republics and a constitutional monarchy between the Soviet Union and the rest of Europe, named the ***cordon sanitaire***. The Soviet Union saw this barrier of small states as a way to prevent them from being part of Europe. Western Europeans saw it as a buffer zone to prevent the spread of communism which would overthrow the existing order (see the maps on pages 37 and 50).

Russia was not invited to participate in the Paris Peace Conference as it was in the middle of civil war. An invitation would have acknowledged the Bolsheviks as the official Russian government, which the Allies were unwilling to do, hopeful that the Bolsheviks would be defeated. When Russia signed the Treaty of Brest-Litovsk in early 1918, it released up to a million

KEY TERM

Cordon sanitaire A French expression that originally meant a barrier to stop disease and that came to mean in international politics the barrier of newly independent and highly nationalistic states that bordered the Soviet Union in Europe between the two world wars.

German soldiers to attack France in the final year of the war, leading to hundreds of thousands of deaths for the Allies. It did not help that the Bolsheviks had repudiated all French loans to Russia and that they were sponsoring, or in the least inspiring, revolts in many areas of Europe.

Russia was also not consulted on any of the treaties established in Paris. The Allies, however, did recognize the independence of some former Russian provinces, officially abolished the Treaty of Brest-Litovsk, but were also unable to help other areas such as Ukraine. Russia, now the Soviet Union, was not invited to join the League of Nations. Diplomatic isolation seemed almost total until 1922 when Germany, also diplomatically isolated, and the Soviet Union achieved an understanding during negotiations at Rapallo to work together against their mutual isolation. This led to economic and military assistance of each other (see page 77).

The Soviet economic system

The Soviet economy 1918–28
The Soviet Union's economic system during the civil war years, referred to as **War Communism**, was one in which there was no currency, no private property and government-directed production. This system was changed to the **New Economic Policy** (NEP) in 1921 in which limited capitalism was allowed, primarily to encourage farmers to grow food which was desperately needed in the cities. Farmers in the new system would not have food confiscated as before, but would instead pay their taxes in grain leaving any remaining grain for the farmers to sell if they wished. In order to get farmers to sell excess grain, the state shifted from producing war supplies to producing consumer goods. Farmers would grow extra grain for cash if they had the opportunity to buy goods they wanted, such as fertilizer, construction materials, cloth, ceramics and furniture.

SOURCE T

Russian economic recovery under the NEP from *Years of Russia, the USSR and the Collapse of Soviet Communism* by David Evans and Jane Jenkins published in 2008.

Year	Industrial production	Agricultural production
1913*	100	100
1921	31	60
1924	45	90
1925	73	112
1926	98	118
1927	111	121
1928	132	124

* Base year = 100.

> **How successful were the various Soviet economic programmes?**

 **KEY TERM**

War Communism
Economic system by the Bolsheviks during the Russian Civil War in which all property and businesses were owned by the state, currency was abolished and strikes were forbidden.

New Economic Policy
Economic system in the Soviet Union between 1921 and 1928 in which farmers paid taxes in grain, surplus grain could be sold on the private market for profit, currency was re-introduced and small businesses were allowed to return to private ownership and operation.

> According to Source T what was the effect of the First World War and the New Economic Policy on the Russian economy? **?**

Within a short period of time, Russia began to recover and by 1928 the economy was mostly restored to 1913 levels. During these years, there were fewer attempts to spread communism as the government sought to stabilize the country and build a base of support.

The Five-Year Plan 1928–32

After a power struggle, Stalin became the primary leader by 1928. He initiated a change in economic policy called the Five-Year Plan starting in 1929, although backdated to 1928. This programme called for mass industrialization of the state, with major targets set to be accomplished by 1932. This was a reflection of Stalin's policy of 'socialism in one country' which intended to strengthen the Soviet Union through industrialization and the expansion of the working class. This had the added benefit of making the country less vulnerable to foreign attack by giving it the ability to produce huge quantities of war goods in case of conflict.

The first Five-Year Plan concentrated on building infrastructure including power plants, railroads, bridges, new cities, mines, steel mills and so forth. In order to accomplish this, the government was massively expanded to control and organize the national effort. Mass industrialization did not go smoothly, with the movement of millions of people in new, poorly constructed cities near factories and mines. Many Soviet officials were former factory workers with limited ability to organize and manage such massive change, sometimes building factories with expensive, imported equipment, but with no access to raw materials to process into products. These difficulties were mostly resolved in time as the Soviet government gained experience through trial and error.

To purchase modern equipment and industrial machinery from the west, primarily Germany, the Soviet Union needed to increase exports of grain which Germany and Britain needed. Instead of producing consumer goods to entice farmers to sell excess grain as had happened in the NEP, **collectivization** was ordered. Collectivization placed agriculture under close control of the government, but also attempted to make it more efficient and industrial. Farmers were to work together on huge farms, dividing up labour, tools and everything else, destroying the traditional family and village systems that might organize against state policies. More efficient agriculture might also allow more peasants to enter the industrial working classes to support the tremendous industrialization taking place.

Collectivization was a disorganized and messy affair. Wealthier peasants were executed or imprisoned as it was assumed they would resist and encourage others to do so. Poorer, less successful peasants moved into communal farms where there was not enough of anything, including tools, farm animals or seeds. This quickly led to a crisis with both collectivized

peasants and industrial workers rationing food as the country faced mass starvation. The government shifted the policy several times in order to produce grain, but it was never particularly successful. Grain quotas were often met by seizing almost all grain grown, even what was needed to feed the peasants, leading to famine in the countryside and rationing in the cities. The death toll in the Soviet Union as a result of collectivization is still debated by historians, but was probably between seven and twelve million people, mostly peasants.

SOURCE U

A table indicating economic goals and results of the Soviet Union's first Five-Year Plan 1928–32.

	1927–8 (millions of tonnes)	1932–3 (planned) (millions of tonnes)	1933 (actual) (millions of tonnes)
Oil	11.7	22.0	21.4
Steel	4.0	10.4	5.9
Coal	35.4	75.0	64.3

To what extent were the Five-Year Plan's goals met according to Source U?

As peasants starved, the first Five-Year Plan produced important results. In 1928, the Soviet Union produced five billion kWh of electricity, but 13.5 billion kWh by 1932. Steel production rose from four million tonnes in 1928 to 5.9 million in 1933. Coal production went from 35.4 million tonnes to 64.3 million. Oil almost doubled from 11.7 million tonnes to 21.4 million. While many targets were not met, there was no doubt that industrial progress had been accomplished. This was done at great cost of lives, but there were major economic successes during these years of the **Great Depression** when Western nations faced severe economic crises. This increased anxiety that Western capitalist nations felt towards the Soviet Union and encouraged communist groups in other countries.

 **KEY TERM**

Great Depression Period starting in 1929 of severe global economic crisis that resulted in millions of people unemployed, thousands of banks closing from lack of funds, and political crises.

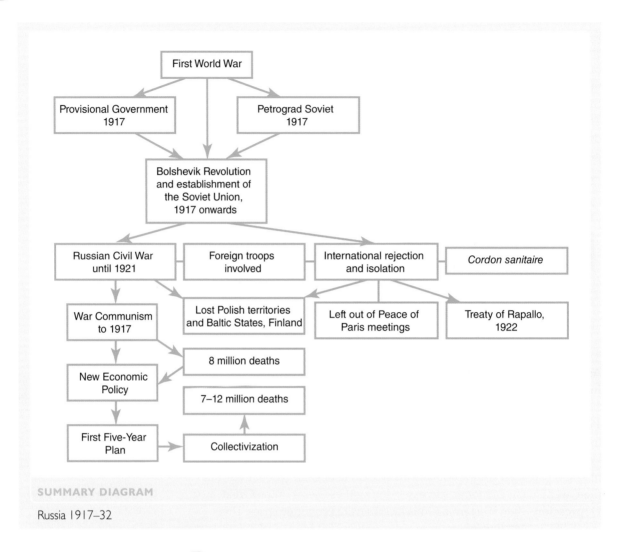

SUMMARY DIAGRAM

Russia 1917–32

Italy 1919–28

> ▶ *Key question: How successful was Italy in overcoming political, economic and foreign policy difficulties after the First World War?*

Italy was severely disappointed as a result of the Paris Peace Conference since lands promised were not all granted to the country. Economic, political and social difficulties that had been suppressed during the war also erupted, producing violence throughout the country. Italy's king was essentially the only stable feature of the **constitutional monarchy** that was the Italian government as prime ministers changed regularly and often. While adventurers caused foreign policy crises, political gangs battled, with the leader of one, Mussolini, becoming prime minister in 1922. This brought an era of oppression, but also unity.

Foreign policy problems

← What were the main goals of Italian foreign policy after the First World War?

The Italian government entered the First World War specifically to gain land which was clearly listed in the Treaty of London in 1915 (see page 24). The Allied Powers meeting in Paris in 1919 decided that Italy would receive only part of the territory promised, with most of the rest going to an expanded Serbia, the new state of Yugoslavia. The city of Fiume, today called Rijeka, was not specifically listed in the treaty, but according to Italy, it contained over 45,000 Italians. Italy demanded the city under Wilson's Fourteen Points, one of which promised self-determination for people. Instead, Fiume was also given to Yugoslavia so that that country would have a deep-water port which would help it develop its economy.

Fiume

Outrage in Italy manifested itself in the seizure of Fiume by Gabriele d'Annunzio in September 1919. A poet and war hero who had led attacks on Austro-Hungarian ships during the war, he led 1000 men into Fiume and set up an independent state: the Italian Regency of Carnaro. This small state was funded by raiding Yugoslav towns and seizing ships in the Adriatic Sea. The Italian government was embarrassed, and although d'Annunzio was hugely popular in Italy, the Italian navy attacked Fiume on 24 December 1920. After three weeks, d'Annunzio surrendered and the town was given to Yugoslavia by the Italian government.

Corfu incident

Italian soldiers were members of a team sent by the **Conference of Ambassadors** to survey the borders of Albania and Greece in 1923 in order to clarify ownership and prevent conflict. Five Italian soldiers in the group were shot by unknown gunmen on a mountain road.

The Italian government publically accused the Greek government of being behind the attack and demanded a large sum of money as compensation. Greece refused to pay, so the Italian navy shelled the Greek island of Corfu. Greece asked for assistance from the League of Nations, but Italy refused to accept any League interference. The new Italian Prime Minister, Mussolini, referred the matter to the Conference of Ambassadors. Greece was ordered to pay Italy 50 million lire as compensation. Mussolini, basking in success, asked Yugoslavia to meet to discuss Fiume. The Yugoslav government believed that they would also be attacked as Greece had been and that the outcome would be much the same. Understanding that they were in no position to fight Italy, Yugoslavia evacuated Fiume and handed over the important port. This was made official in the Treaty of Rome signed in January 1924.

SOURCE V

A postage stamp with a bust of d'Annunzio from the Italian Regency of Carnaro, the temporary state founded by d'Annunzio in Fiume in 1919. The Latin caption says 'The best shall stay here'.

What is the message of Source V?

 **KEY TERM**

Conference of Ambassadors Organization composed of ambassadors from France, Britain, Italy and Japan that formed in 1920 to continue the diplomacy of the Allied Powers after the First World War; it functioned primarily in the early 1920s to settle major disputes involving any of the four represented powers.

Why was the Italian state politically and economically unstable?

🔑 KEY TERM

Papal States Small states in central Italy ruled by the Pope until being annexed to Italy.

Political and economic instability

Italy was politically and economically stressed before the First World War. During Italy's creation between 1858 and 1870, the **Papal States** were annexed. The Papal States were ruled by the Catholic Pope and the loss of these lands and their income created a division between Italian government and the Catholic Church. The Pope refused to accept and acknowledge the new Italian state, leading many in Italy to not participate in elections and politics in the country. In addition, the northern areas of Italy were more developed than the south, which remained over-populated, poor, under-educated and lacked infrastructure for development. Divisions between Catholics who wished to remain faithful to the Pope and those who desired a modern nation-state, between the north and south and even between the old provinces and kingdoms that existed before 1860, kept Italy from being one of Europe's leading nations. The First World War brought a sense of national unity which had been lacking, complete with a goal: expansion to include all Italians and a colonial empire. The war actually brought major losses of life, little battlefield success, and many people to question the *status quo* in Italy in which few owned land or had economic opportunity.

Economic problems

The war also brought economic problems which fed political instability. During the war years, government finances were severely strained and there was a 700 per cent rise in government spending. Higher taxation to pay for the war and major inflation meant a tremendous decrease in real income and a 560 per cent rise in the cost of living. Five lira in 1914 had been worth one US dollar, but by 1920 it took 28 lira to purchase a dollar. Italy was a major importer of coal, wheat and oil, so the devaluation of its currency further undermined the government's finances. There were 2.5 million soldiers who were released by the war's end and returned to a country which could not afford to employ or feed them and did not have the political ability to grant them land, although it had been promised.

Political instability

The inability of the Italian Prime Minister Vittorio Orlando to get France, Britain and the USA to grant all the promises made in the Treaty of London, as well as the demands for Fiume, undermined his coalition government. While Orlando and his delegation fought for more concessions from the other Allied Powers, workers' strikes broke out in Italy demanding better treatment, wages and working hours. Peasants, many of whom had fought for Italy only to return to economic destitution, attacked landlords, demanding lower rents in some cases and land grants in others. Nationalists marched in the cities, demanding everything promised in the Treaty of London and more.

Orlando's coalition government collapsed on June 1919. He was replaced by Francesco Nitti of the Radical Party who formed a new coalition government which concentrated on solving the many internal crises in Italy. Under this new government, Italy agreed that Fiume could be a **free city** under the League of Nations and that Dalmatia could go to Yugoslavia, as other Allied Powers had demanded of Orlando. D'Annunzio seized Fiume as a result of this decision.

The Nitti government was barely able to function with communists, nationalists and others protesting working conditions, demanding land reform or encouraging d'Annunzio's regime in Fiume. Nitti's unstable coalition fell in June 1920, replaced by that of Giovanni Giolitti of the Liberal Party. Fearing a communist revolution in Italy, Giolitti worked to settle the borders with Yugoslavia, gaining for Italy all Istria, a strip of land connecting Italy with Fiume, the city of Zadar on the Yugoslav coast, and various Adriatic islands. Fiume was confirmed as a free city, not under the control of either Italy or Yugoslavia, and Dalmatia was granted to Yugoslavia. D'Annunzio would not accept this and declared war on Italy on 1 December 1920, causing the Italian military to end d'Annunzio's occupation of Fiume in the same month.

Giolitti was beset with a myriad of problems:

- He alienated industrialists, bankers and major landowners by introducing reforms to the taxation system. These included requiring stocks and bonds to be registered and taxed, and introducing **income** and **inheritance taxes**.
- Workers' strikes and unrest continued such as in 1920 when 280 factories were taken over by 600,000 workers.
- Political gangs battled throughout the countryside.

The Fascists

By 1920, two major political parties dominated parliament: the Socialist and Catholic Popular parties. Refusing to co-operate with each other and with major disputes within the Socialist Party, the government was unstable and barely functioned. In this chaos, political gangs battled throughout the countryside. One of the gangs, the Blackshirts, was headed by Benito Mussolini, a former socialist newspaper editor who supported Italy joining the First World War and who became an ultra-nationalist opposed to socialism and communism. Blackshirts usually delivered severe beatings to their opponents and forced their victims to consume large quantities of castor oil.

The Blackshirts were financially supported by industrialists who feared a communist takeover which would certainly deprive them of their businesses and possibly lives. Attacking socialists led to financial support from bank and factory owners and soon major landowners were also supportive when Mussolini's new political party, the Fascists, decided that farmland should belong to investors, not peasant farmers.

The Fascists' beliefs evolved over time, but essentially can be described as ultra-nationalistic. For example, they opposed communists and most

KEY TERM

Free city A city with international supervision, belonging to no particular nation.

Income tax Tax on wages.

Inheritance taxes Tax on money or property granted to someone on the death of another person.

socialists because they called for class warfare, which the Fascists believed weakened Italy and Italians, preventing national unity and therefore greatness. Fascists believed democracy was a failed institution and that the government and industry should be more closely aligned. They also believed in a state where the population was educated and people dedicated time and energy to national goals. The party was open to changing some of its stances, including being anti-Catholic and anti-monarchy – positions they reversed to varying degrees within just two years.

Political crisis 1921–2

In January 1921, the Socialist Party split with the communists who formed a separate party. Giolitti called for new elections, believing that he could create a governing coalition to give him more authority to deal with the political and economic crisis. The election did not greatly reduce the Socialist Party's strength, but communists took fifteen seats and the Fascists 35. Giolitti was unable to create a strong coalition.

Giolitti was forced to resign in July 1921 as a result of industrialist pressure against his law that required the registration of stocks and bonds. He was replaced by Ivanoe Bonomi, a moderate socialist who had supported Giolitti, who immediately suspended the stocks and bonds law. His government was extremely weak and unable to deal with Italy's financial and political crisis.

SOURCE W

An Italian stamp from 1923 advocating a pension fund for the Blackshirts. The Italian caption says 'Pension Fund Blackshirts'.

Compare and contrast Source V (page 99) with Source W.

Luigi Facta took over from Bonomi in February 1922. Mussolini's Fascists continued to act outside the boundaries of law, supported by the army and police, with Facta powerless to deal with the crisis. By October, Mussolini believed he was strong enough to challenge the government itself, calling for a march on Rome. Facta asked the king to declare martial law and the king responded by dismissing Facta and calling on Mussolini, who did not march but stayed in Milan, to become prime minister of Italy. The king and Catholic Church feared socialists and communists and they hoped that the Fascists would operate within the law once they were part of the system and that Fascism would end the communist threat.

Prime Minister Mussolini

Having been lawfully appointed prime minister, Mussolini moved to limit freedom of the press and the Fascists' party leaders were granted more power, as well as government support, in their districts throughout the country. The Acerbo Law of 1923 granted the party with the largest number of votes a two-thirds majority of parliament. This meant that if the Fascist Party received the most votes of any party, then they would rule without a coalition to contain their ambitions. The April 1924 elections occurred with extreme violence, granting the Fascists 64 per cent of the vote and a majority in parliament without help from the Acerbo Law.

In June 1924, a prominent young socialist, Matteotti, was kidnapped by Fascists and murdered. He had been a vocal opponent of Fascist election abuses and called for the recent elections to be annulled. When his body was found in July, a political crisis erupted throughout Italy. Many were upset at the public violence and many non-Fascist members of parliament boycotted it, hoping the king would remove Mussolini from power. This failed when the king refused to dismiss Mussolini and actually allowed the Fascists to pass laws through parliament with little opposition. The king, along with the Catholic Church and industrialists, continued to fear socialism and communism and was willing to accept Fascist methods for the time being. By January 1925, Mussolini fully re-established his authority and soon suppressed political parties and their newspapers, primarily through violence. In 1928, political parties were abolished along with parliamentary elections. Only the king had the authority to remove Mussolini from power. Italy was now stable, but also a dictatorship.

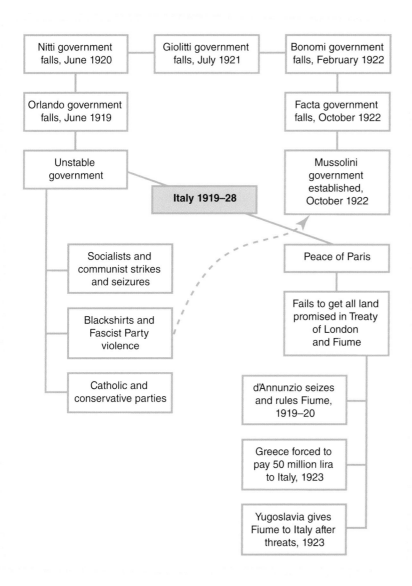

SUMMARY DIAGRAM

Italy 1919–28

Austria, Hungary, Czechoslovakia, Poland and the Balkans

> ▶ *Key question:* How functional were the newly created and expanded states of central, eastern and south-eastern Europe after the Paris Peace Conference?

Central and eastern Europe was full of newly created states after the First World War. Most of these states formed before the Paris conferences, but all were confirmed there. Formerly parts of large empires, the new states all struggled economically and politically, while dealing with border issues through negotiation or war. Ironically, perhaps, it was the most ethnically diverse state in this new group that was the most successful politically and perhaps economically: Czechoslovakia.

What were the main economic and political challenges for Austria after the First World War?

Austria

Austria was essentially a new state by 1920. Formerly the core of the Austro-Hungarian Empire, it was now a land-locked, small country of approximately 6.5 million people. Vienna, the main city, had been the capital of the empire and it alone had 2.5 million residents, giving the country a magnificent capital city that it could not support with food and raw materials. During the final stages of the First World War and through the signing of the Treaty of St Germain-en-Laye in 1920 (see page 47), Austria lacked sufficient food, needing to import it from former provinces that were now hostile, independent nations.

Economic crisis

Vienna was the centre of manufacturing in the new state and had been one of the two main industrial cities of the former empire, the second being Prague. Its factories had formerly been supplied with coal from what was now Czechoslovakia, food for processing from what was now Hungary, and so forth, with the entire empire and beyond having been a market for manufactured goods. Neighbouring states now wanted to develop their own industries, placed taxes on Austrian imports and erected trade barriers. The result was that most Austrian industries shut down for lack of supplies and markets, so unemployed workers were unable to afford food and basic supplies.

The Austrian currency, the crown or krone, lost value in the economic crisis, falling from 16.1 crowns to the US dollar in 1919 to over 70,800 crowns by 1923. Prices increased over 14,000 per cent in the same period.

In October 1922, the League of Nations arranged a 650 million crown loan to Austria, imposing a commissioner to oversee the government's finances. By the end of 1923, the crown was replaced by the more stable schilling, bringing stability to the economy and reassuring potential investors. A year earlier, in 1922, the Treaty of Lana was signed with Czechoslovakia which confirmed the borders between the two countries and arranged for coal to be supplied to Austrian industries, among other points.

SOURCE X

Excerpt from *The World of Yesterday* by Stephan Zweig, published by Viking Press, New York, USA, 1943, p. 333. Zweig was an Austrian journalist, author, and playwright and was one of the world's most famous writers between the First and Second World Wars. *The World of Yesterday* was his autobiography.

Unemployed men took one or two rucksacks and went from peasant to peasant. They even took the train to favorable locations to get foodstuffs illegally which they sold afterwards in the town at three or fourfold the prices they had paid themselves. First the peasants were happy about the great amount of paper money which rained into their houses for their eggs and butter … However, when they came to town with their full briefcases to buy goods, they discovered to their chagrin that, whereas they had only asked for a fivefold price for their produce, the prices for scythe, hammer and cauldron, which they wanted to buy, had risen by a factor of 50.

According to Source X, what was the effect of hyperinflation?

Political crisis

Between 1919 and 1920, a coalition of political groups joined together to help form and protect the new Republic of Austria. The two main political parties, the Christian Social Party and the Social Democrats, dominated Austrian politics. The Christian Social Party was a conservative, Catholic Church-supported group whose bases of power were in smaller cities and in rural areas and included many in the middle class and industrialists. The Social Democrats were socialists and were supported by the working classes of Vienna. By the end of 1920, the coalition had fallen apart.

Throughout the 1920s, the Social Democrats dominated Vienna, reforming the city with worker housing projects, imposing limits on rent, implementing health care reforms while taxing luxuries, transportation and much else to pay for their programmes. The Christian Social Party, the larger party, dominated the national government, supplying the state with all its chancellors. Indicating the political instability of the government, both parties formed paramilitary organizations by the mid-1920s to protect themselves and intimidate their opponents.

Conservative paramilitaries shot and killed several people in January 1927 when they attacked a socialist paramilitary group, but they were acquitted in July of any crime. In July 1927, supporters of the Social Democrats attacked the main court in Vienna and burned it to the ground as a consequence of the acquittal. In street battles and in a general strike, over 80 protestors were dead, approximately 600 wounded and four policemen killed. This created a political rift between the two major groups with no possibility of significant co-operation. Conservative groups called for an end to parliamentary democracy and the establishment of an authoritarian regime. In 1933, in the midst of major economic and political crisis, parliament was suspended and a dictatorship under the Christian Social leader Dolfuss was established which banned other political parties and established an Austrian form of fascism.

SOURCE Y

A 1920 propaganda poster by the Austrian Christian Social Party: 'German Christians Rescue Austria!'

? According to Source Y, who are the opponents of Austria?

Hungary

What were the main features of the Hungarian state after the First World War?

Hungary was severely affected by the First World War. Not only had Hungary been part of the dual kingdom of Austria-Hungary which had been defeated, it also suffered from revolution and invasion, unlike Austria.

Continued war 1919–20

A communist revolt led by Béla Kun in early 1919, inspired by Russian Bolsheviks, temporarily created the Hungarian Soviet Republic in the chaos at the end of the First World War. Fighting broke out within Hungary between Kun's communists and their opponents, some led by Admiral Horthy, a war hero, between Kun's forces and the new state of Czechoslovakia, and between the Hungarian communists and Romania. By August 1919, the Romanian army had defeated the communists, occupied Budapest and much of Hungary, and Kun had fled to Austria. By March 1920, the Romanian army left Hungary, taking factory machinery, 50 per cent of all railroad equipment, 30 per cent of all livestock and agricultural equipment, as well as 35,000 wagon loads of animal feed and grain as compensation for losses in the First World War and the recent conflict. In June, Hungary had to sign the Treaty of Trianon (see page 54) which compounded Hungary's economic and political problems.

SOURCE Z

An Hungarian poster from the 1920s concerning the Treaty of Trianon, with Hungary surrounded by other nations grabbing its territory. 'I believe in God, I believe in the Church, I believe in God's eternal truth, I believe in Hungary …'

How are each of the nations depicted in Source Z and why is Poland absent from the imagery?

Economic crisis

Economically, Hungary, like Austria, was not prepared for independence since its economy had been one of interdependence within a larger empire. Hungary, within the empire, had been a major supplier of agricultural products for the more industrialized areas that became the Republics of Austria and Czechoslovakia. Hungary, for example, produced 500 per cent more farm products than it could consume in the early 1920s. Without a demand for Hungarian agricultural produce, unemployment rose dramatically and grain production declined by 70 per cent.

Hungarian industry suffered from a lack of raw materials as well. The Treaty of Trianon left the new state with only sixteen per cent of its former iron mines and eleven per cent of its former timber resources, for example. Industrial output declined precipitously as exports were curtailed by its hostile neighbours who were also trying to develop their own economies. A major problem was the Hungarian currency, the crown, which suffered from hyperinflation until 1924 when a 250 million gold crown loan was made by the League of Nations and a new currency introduced – the *pengő*. This helped stabilize the Hungarian economy and soon loans from private banks were made available. Although agriculture continued to dominate exports, there was a 75 per cent increase in the number of factories by 1929 and the value of foreign trade increased by more than 100 per cent.

SOURCE AA

?

According to Source AA, how important was the League of Nations' loan?

Excerpt from *Admiral Nicholas Horthy: Memoirs* by Nicholas Horthy, Regent of Hungary, published most recently by Simon Publications, Florida, USA, 2000, p. 158. Horthy was the head of the Hungarian government from 1920 to 1944.

Like many other countries, we also had suffered from inflation in the years after the First World War. The partition of Hungary, the payment of reparations, and the burdens of the aftermath of war made it impossible for us to stabilize our currency unaided, for our most valuable assets were in pawn [held as collateral] to our creditors. Before we could obtain a loan from abroad, it was necessary to reclaim these securities. To this end, we joined the League of Nations on September 18th, 1922, thereby laying ourselves under the supervision of the League of Nations Finance Commission. The loan of two hundred and fifty million gold crowns we used to such good purpose that the [League of Nations imposed] Finance Commissioner, Mr. Jeremiah Smith, on the eve of his departure to Geneva on June 30th, 1926, after a two-year sojourn with us, was able to declare that we had carried out our obligations and had balanced our budget. The following year, our currency was changed from crowns to pengős, the Hungarian word for 'clinking', a pleasing appellation [name] reminiscent of the ringing sound of coins.

Stable government

In March 1920, with the departure of the Romanian army, former Admiral Horthy was named Regent of the newly re-established Kingdom of Hungary. Although technically ruling for an absent king, no one was offered the position of monarch. Instead, Horthy had the powers of a king. The constitution gave him major powers and he appointed prime ministers and worked with various political parties in a parliamentary system that was tightly controlled. István Bethlen, an arch-conservative nationalist, was prime minister from 1921 to 1931, leading the Party of Unity, a coalition of smaller parties.

SOURCE BB

A 1920 Hungarian election poster: 'Horthy!'

Explain the meaning of the imagery in Source BB.

Bethlen kept political opposition tightly controlled and placed wealthy industrialists and landowners in government positions. There was very limited land reform which had been demanded initially by peasants, and minorities, particularly Jews, suffered from varying amounts of discrimination. Hungary desired above all else to revise the Treaty of Trianon and this national goal helped with internal unity. Bethlen, however, was unwilling to challenge Trianon aggressively as this would result in an end to needed foreign loans and could provoke the **Little Entente** powers (see page 112) which were determined to prevent any changes to Trianon.

KEY TERM

Little Entente A coalition of Czechoslovakia, Romania and Yugoslavia who agreed to work together against any Hungarian attempts to reclaim lost lands which they now occupied.

Hungary and Italy signed the Treaty of Friendship in 1927 with hopes that this would lead to political leverage that might see a revision of the treaty; these hopes were in vain and the treaty with Italy ended up meaning little.

What unique issues challenged Czechoslovakia in the 1920s?

Czechoslovakia

Czechoslovakia was created in late 1918 as the Austro-Hungarian Empire collapsed. Unlike Austria and Hungary, which were dominated by Germans and Hungarians, respectively, Czechoslovakia was ethnically diverse. Czechs dominated the government and decided that Slovaks would also be counted as Czechs. This would make Czecho-Slovaks the vast majority nationality; many Slovaks objected to this believing they were a distinct nationality from Czechs. With a population of 13.5 million, Czechoslovakia contained much diversity, including:

- over three million Germans
- about 750,000 Hungarians
- 500,000 Rusyns
- 200,000 Jews.

Czechs managed the government and Czech officials were moved into the regions as government officials and teachers, creating resentment among all other groups. Czechs also did not trust the other groups as Germans wanted to merge with Austria and many Slovaks wanted to return to Hungary, as did Hungarians.

Why, according to Source CC, did Czechs not wish to acknowledge the Slovaks as a separate nationality?

SOURCE CC

Excerpt from 'Czech-Slovak relations in Czechoslovakia, 1918–1939' by Jan Rychlík in *Czechoslovakia in a Nationalist and Fascist Europe 1918–1948*, edited by Mark Cornwall and R.J.W. Evans, published for The British Academy by the Oxford University Press, *Proceedings of the British Academy*, vol. 140, 2007, pp. 22–3. Rychlík is a historian at the Charles University in Prague, Czech Republic and the St Kliment Ochridski University in Sofia, Bulgaria. He has published several books on Czech and Slovak relations and heads the seminar for Modern Czech History.

Recognition of the separate Slovak nation meant also recognition of the right of the Slovak nation to self-determination. If there was no Czechoslovak nation, there could not be any Czechoslovak national programme either. Thus the existence of Czechoslovakia would be only continent and would depend on the goodwill of the Slovak leaders. This was also the reason why Czech leaders were reluctant to agree to Slovak autonomy. Despite the claims of the HSL's [a Slovak political party] that the Slovaks did not wish to leave Czechoslovakia, the Czechs rightly felt that the limits of autonomy would sooner or later be too narrow for the Slovaks and that the next step would be a claim for federation or even confederation. The final result would be the division of Czechoslovakia.

Political stability 1922–38

The parliamentary government was dominated by five major Czech political parties, the Pětka, that formed a coalition that ruled Czechoslovakia for much of the period between 1922 and 1938. This left Czechoslovakia with a stable government that worked to solve the many problems that the new state faced, including tensions between the Germans and Czechs and between Czechs and Slovaks. Most Germans objected to being minorities and desired unification with Austria or Germany. Slovaks pressed for cultural recognition and autonomy which was largely hampered until the late 1930s.

Foreign policy after 1919

One of the first major foreign policy crises that the newly founded state had to resolve was a border dispute with Poland in Silesia, which had recently been removed from Germany. In January 1919, Czechoslovak troops entered Těšín (also known as Teschen in German and Cieszyn in Polish), the coal-rich and industrialized area in dispute, driving out Polish forces. The conflict was resolved by a treaty in 1925, but mistrust remained and affected relations until the Second World War.

A communist Hungarian army attacked Czechoslovak territory in 1919, attempting to restore the former Kingdom of Hungary's borders. Czechoslovak troops were defeated and a Slovak Soviet Republic was founded by the invaders. This was short-lived as the Romanian army crushed

What is indicated regarding nationality and potential nationalism by Source DD?

SOURCE DD

A map of major language groups in Czechoslovakia in 1930.

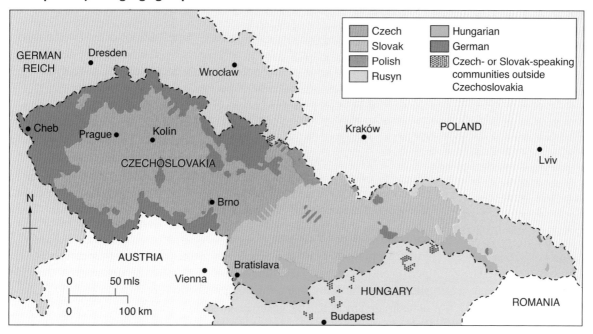

the Hungarian communists a few months later and the Slovak Soviet Republic was abolished. Soon after, in 1921, Czechoslovakia helped form the Little Entente alliance with Yugoslavia and Romania that promised mutual defence and military co-operation against Hungarian aggression.

In 1924, Czechoslovakia was able to form a military alliance with France, although in 1925 France agreed with Germany at Locarno (see page 84) that renegotiation of its eastern borders was possible in the future, which necessarily included Czechoslovakian borders. Germany was unable to disturb Czechoslovakia until the late 1930s when German foreign policy became more aggressive and France vacillated in its treaty obligations.

Stable economy

Czechoslovakia was not as economically stressed as Austria or Hungary at the close of the First World War. In fact, the new country contained up to 80 per cent of all industries that had existed in the Austro-Hungarian Empire. These included glass, porcelain, sugar, shoes and machine-tool factories, as well as chemical, coal-mining and alcohol industries. Czechoslovakia was among the ten most industrialized nations by the mid-1920s, with a relative high standard of living. Industry was heavily concentrated in the province of Bohemia, where most Czechs lived. Slovakia and Ruthenia were both primarily agricultural and therefore poorer, even during the economic boom years of the 1920s. The new state also launched a programme of land reform in 1919, limiting landowners to a maximum of five square kilometres, with excess property seized by the state, with compensation, and distributed to peasants.

What were the main weaknesses of the new Polish state after the First World War?

Poland

Poland was created at the end of the First World War out of lands from three empires: Russia, Austria-Hungary and Germany. The creation of new borders with Germany was complicated and partially dealt with in the Treaty of Versailles (see page 36) and other Paris Peace Conference treaties. The eastern borders of the country, however, were the result of war. Wars broke out between Poland on one hand and Ukraine, Russia and Lithuania on the other, with Poland's enemies also fighting each other. This resulted in Poland expanding its territories beyond those envisioned by the Allied Powers in Paris. The wars ended in 1921, but the borders of Poland left few satisfied; there were many ethnic Poles living in other countries, and many non-Poles living in Poland, especially Germans.

Government 1921–35

In 1921 a parliamentary democracy was formed. Tensions between socialist parties and those that were ultra-nationalist created an unstable political situation in the country and the first president, supported by socialists, was assassinated in 1922. This government system was overthrown in 1926 by Poland's main military leader and former head of government during the

SOURCE EE

A Polish army poster by Kamil Mackiewicz published in 1920: 'Hey, whoever is a Pole, to your bayonets!'

Which three groups does Source EE try to appeal to?

earlier wars, Józef Piłsudski. He refused to be named president, instead simply remaining head of the military. From this position, he appointed the president of Poland, reduced the influence of political parties, limited press freedoms, and enjoyed popular support for working to reduce economic problems that the country faced. His system continued until his death in 1935.

? What does Source FF imply
about the relationship
between the military and the
Catholic Church?

SOURCE FF

Marshal Józef Piłsudski takes his leave of the clergy after a religious ceremony in 1920 affirming the unity of his military government with the Church.

Foreign policy 1919–32

Germany and Poland faced great difficulties throughout the period after the First World War, namely over lands that were absorbed into Poland as the result of the Treaty of Versailles or subsequent plebiscites. Polish uprisings in Silesia led the League of Nations to grant Poland control of key industrial and mining areas in the region, further poisoning the relationship between Germany and Poland (see page 74). France was an early great supporter of Poland, hoping to use it to place diplomatic and military pressure on Germany. An alliance was created between France and Poland in 1921.

The relationship between Poland and its eastern neighbours, Russia and Lithuania, was strained as well. Poland supported **Prometheism** which aimed to encourage nationalities within the Soviet Union, formerly Russia, to work for independence. Essentially, Poland worked to create new states on Soviet territory, with little success. Poland annexed the Vilna region claimed by Lithuania in 1922, in direct violation of a ceasefire (see page 141). Lithuania annexed Memel in 1923, although Poland had demanded some control over this territory as well (see page 142). Lithuania and Poland remained enemies throughout the period.

Problems with Czechoslovakia and their mutual borders were resolved in 1925, but there was not enough trust for a military alliance to be formed. Relations with Romania were positive and led to a series of treaties. The

KEY TERM

Prometheism Polish ideology that worked to create nation states within the Soviet Union which would then be allies with Poland against Soviet, or Russian, aggression.

Convention on Defensive Alliance was signed in 1921 and promised mutual assistance if either was attacked by the Soviet Union. This was expanded in 1926 and 1927, after the Locarno agreements (see page 84), to be an alliance against any attackers on either country. With the rise in popularity of the Nazi Party in Germany, Poland signed a treaty of non-aggression with the Soviet Union in 1932. Later, Poland would also sign a non-aggression pact with Germany in 1935 (see page 211).

Economic crisis 1919–30

SOURCE GG

Excerpt from *Poland, 1918–1945: An Interpretive and Documentary History of the Second Republic* by Peter D. Stachura, published by Routledge, New York, USA, 2004, p. 47. Stachura is a professor of history at the University of Stirling, UK, has written numerous books on European history between the First and Second World Wars, and is Director of the Centre for Research in Polish History.

France, Poland's main ally, was burdened with her own financial and economic problems after the First World War and was not really in a position, therefore, to lend meaningful assistance. Furthermore, the widespread devastation inflicted on the Polish lands by the ferocious battles and rapacious Occupation policies of the First World War were compounded by woefully inadequate transportation, communications, postal and banking systems as well as a chaotic currency situation: in the early 1920s, no fewer than six different currencies were in circulation. Finally, the important pre-war Russian market for Polish goods had now all but collapsed, and was not to revive as the Soviet state began to pursue introspective and largely autarchic policies associated with the doctrine of 'Socialism in One Country', and in response to her defeat by the Poles in the 1919–20 war. In 1918, therefore, Poland faced an overall economic situation akin to [starting from nothing].

According to Source GG, why was Poland's economy in a terrible state after the First World War?

Poland had been the battlefield between Russia and Germany in the First World War. Factories, railroads, mines and other essential economic structures had been destroyed. Poland had been part of three separate countries, so what few railways remained connected parts of Poland with other countries, not with each other. In 1919, industry operated at only 30 per cent of the 1913 level. The acquisition of Upper Silesia in 1921 and the construction of the new Baltic port of Gdynia brought some economic relief, but the vast majority of the population was peasants, approximately 65 per cent of the population throughout the 1920s. Poor relations with neighbouring states limited major trading. Only sixteen per cent of Poles were industrial workers in 1933, indicating limited industrial production. Foreign investors were generally not impressed and Poland therefore received less investment than any other country in central or eastern Europe. Although there was an upturn in the economy in the late 1920s, this was wiped out by the Great Depression (see page 178) by 1930.

What were common
political and economic
features of Romania,
Bulgaria and
Yugoslavia?

→ Balkan states

Romania and Yugoslavia were expanded states after the First World War as a
result of the Paris peace treaties. Romania had gained the vast territory of
Transylvania, complete with about 1.5 million Hungarians who did not want
to leave Hungary, as well as Bukovina and Bessarabia, both ethnically diverse
and rural. Yugoslavia was essentially an expanded Serbia as the government
was dominated by Serbs. Bulgaria had been reduced in size with territory
given to Yugoslavia, Greece and Romania as a result of its defeat. These states
faced similar problems.

Romania

Economic development 1918–30

Romania was primarily an agricultural state that also had vast resources of
raw materials, such as petroleum. Its industry, however, was underdeveloped
leading Romania to depend on other nations for the majority of its
manufactured goods in the mid-1920s. Industry recovered from the war
throughout the 1920s, rising from 86,000 registered businesses in 1918 to
about 273,000 in 1930. It was the oil industry that showed the most growth,
going from less than one million tonnes in 1918 to almost six million by
1930. As impressive as these figures are, Romania remained predominately
agricultural and the population rural.

Government stability and dictatorship

SOURCE HH

?

According to Source HH,
how powerful was Romania's
king?

**Excerpt from *Rumania, 1866–1947* by Keith Hitchins, published by
Clarendon Press, Oxford, UK, 1994, p. 385. Hitchins is a professor of
history at the University of Illinois, USA and has published several books
and articles on Romanian history.**

*In the 1920s political parties retained a key role in the selection of new
governments. As before the war, upon the resignation of the government the king
entered into consultations with the leaders of various parties, after which he
entrusted the formation of a cabinet to one among them. The immediate task of
the new government was to organize elections for the Chamber and Senate. The
process of selecting a new prime minister usually went smoothly, for the king
chose him from only a limited number of parties. Excluded were the leftist
parties, the parties of the national minorities, and, almost always, the small
parties. The leaders of the two largest parties – the Liberals and the National
Peasants   therefore had the greatest influence on the king's decision.*

Politically Romania was fairly stable in the 1920s. In theory it was a
constitutional monarchy with a freely elected parliament which ruled. In
reality, the party that the king chose to form a new government would hold
elections which were carefully controlled and inevitably resulted in that party
receiving the majority of parliament. Peasants had the right to vote, but were
universally disinterested and disengaged in state politics, allowing the small

minority of urban residents to dominate national elections. By the early 1930s, the monarch controlled the government almost totally.

Foreign policy

SOURCE II

Excerpt from *Rumania, 1866–1947* by Keith Hitchins, published by Clarendon Press, Oxford, UK, 1994, p. 426. Hitchins is a professor of history at the University of Illinois, USA and has published several books and articles on Romanian history.

The primary objective of Rumania's foreign policy throughout the inter-war period was to maintain the frontiers drawn at the end of the First World War. All Rumanian political parties, except the Communist, were consistent supporters of the Versailles system, a stance which dictated the choice of allies and provided continuity with the foreign policy pursued in the years immediately before the outbreak of the war. Rumanian politicians regarded France and, to a lesser extent, Britain as the chief guarantors of the peace settlement and relied upon them to counter threats to the territorial status quo in Eastern Europe from the Soviet Union, Germany, and the lesser ... states [of] Hungary and Bulgaria ...

According to Source II, what was Romania's main foreign policy goal?

Romania feared the Soviet Union and to a lesser extent Hungary and Romania. Various alliances (see pages 112 and 114) with Poland, Czechoslovakia and Yugoslavia were arranged in order to prevent any challenges to the treaties signed at the Paris Peace Conference. An understanding was reached with France in 1926 to consult with each other in case one or the other was attacked. Romania was an avid supporter of the League of Nations and the disarmament movement, hoping that both would help preserve its borders and prevent war with its neighbours.

Yugoslavia

Political crisis

Yugoslavia contained many different groups, the two largest and most politically developed being the Serbs and Croats. Many Serbs had lived in the independent Kingdom of Serbia for several decades, while Croats had existed within the Kingdom of Hungary. Serbs, Slovenes and others wanted a centralized government which would protect them from other nations, such as Italy or Hungary. Croats, however, wanted a **federal government** which would allow them autonomy within Yugoslavia. When Croat politicians were unsuccessful, they withdrew from politics as a form of protest, allowing Serbs to dominate the parliament and most government positions. In 1929, after the assassination of a major Croat politician in parliament, King Alexander I abolished the constitution and parliament, assuming all power himself in a desperate move to achieve some national unity. He banned political parties, put restrictions on the press and also removed traditional territorial boundaries, establishing nine new administrative districts in their place. While internal unity was not achieved, enough stability was achieved to create coherent foreign policies.

 **KEY TERM**

Federal government
Governmental system in which individual states have control over local affairs while the national government manages foreign policy, defence and other affairs that affect the nation as a whole.

? According to Source JJ, what were the problems of unification that Yugoslavia faced?

SOURCE JJ

Excerpt from *Yugoslavia in Crisis, 1934–1941* by J.B. Hoptner, published by Columbia University Press, New York, USA, 1963, p. 1. Hoptner was a history professor at Columbia University, USA, and wrote several books on Yugoslavia.

This kingdom, devised in time of war, was a weak amalgam of peoples with contradictory and conflicting ideas of government, particularly in regard to the nature and the form of the new state. Its major internal problem in the years ahead was to make Yugoslavs out of Serbs and Croats, Montenegrins, Slovenes, and Dalmatians, Bosnians, Hercegovinians [sic.], and Macedonians – out of men and women who had lived under seven different political roofs as citizens of the independent states of Serbia and Montenegro, of the Austrian territories which are now Slovenia and Dalmatia, of the Vojvodina and Croatia-Slavonia ruled by Hungary, of Bosnia-Hercegovina [sic.] administered by the Dual Monarchy, and of Macedonia, ruled until 1912 by Turkey and for the next six years by Serbia.

Foreign policy

The new state faced challenges with Italy that we have already reviewed (see page 99). Yugoslavia also joined the Little Entente in 1921 to prevent any Hungarian attempts to seize its former territory. An alliance was signed between France and Yugoslavia in 1927 in which the Yugoslavs hoped for security against Italy, while France was more concerned with encircling Germany. Throughout the late 1920s and early 1930s, King Alexander I attempted diplomacy with Mussolini in Italy to build better relations, but this bore few results. Fears that Bulgaria would attempt to undo the Treaty of Neuilly (see page 52) led to the **Balkan Entente** in 1934 between Greece, Turkey, Romania and Yugoslavia.

Economic difficulties

Economically, Yugoslavia resembled other states in central and eastern Europe. The vast majority of the population was peasants without land or modern machinery. Large estates were seized from primarily Hungarian landowners and land distributed to peasants leading to little economic change. Many of the country's factories had been destroyed in the war, but what few remained were located in Belgrade and a few small cities. Mining was a major industry, but primarily under the control of foreign investors who exported the raw material instead of using it to build local products and factories. The country lacked infrastructure and major ports, especially after Fiume, called Rijeka in Yugoslavia, was given to Italy in January 1924. Trade with its Balkan neighbours was limited since they shared the same type of economy and lack of industry. Instead, Yugoslavia's major trade partners which emerged in the late 1920s and 1930s were Italy, Austria and Germany who needed grain and raw materials, especially timber and mined products. The Danube River and the northern Adriatic Sea became Yugoslavia's economic lifeline.

KEY TERM

Balkan Entente
Agreement between Yugoslavia, Greece, Turkey and Romania to abandon territorial claims against each other and to work together against any aggression, particularly by Bulgaria.

SOURCE KK

'Vox Populi (official)'. A cartoon by David Low, *Evening Standard,* **10 January 1929.** *Vox populi* **is Latin for 'voice of the people'. Low was a cartoonist from New Zealand who worked for many British newspapers from 1919 to 1953. The** *Evening Standard* **is a London newspaper published since 1827.**

The League: 'Good morning, King Alexander. How is your dear mistress?' Chorus of European Dictators : 'It is officially announced that she welcomes the new regime. She remains quiet.'

Bulgaria

Political instability

After the Treaty of Neuilly (see page 52), Bulgaria suffered major political crises. The Bulgarian Communist Party made serious gains in parliament in the March 1920 election, obtaining 51 seats. The Agrarian Party, a pro-peasant group, took 110 seats. The Agrarian Party worked to re-establish Bulgarian's main industry, agriculture, after a disastrous war which left much of the population starving. National service of one year was made mandatory for all men so that the construction of roads, bridges and other projects, especially in the countryside, could be realized to improve the national economy and infrastructure. Land redistribution was initially organized but made few gains before the Agrarians lost power in 1923. The Agrarians were committed to improving peasant education, reducing the size and role of the

What message is David Low conveying in Source KK?

army and improving relations with its former enemies and neighbours. Both the communists and peasants were seen as threats by the old ruling classes which included landowners, industrialists and army officers.

Army officers, known as the Military League, overthrew the Agrarian government in June 1923, killing the prime minister and many others. A communist revolt in September was crushed within a week, but terror attacks, including the 1925 bombing of the capital city Sofia's cathedral that almost killed the king and major members of the government, led to government-sponsored terror. Prominent Agrarians were murdered, even those in exile, thousands were jailed and often disappeared, while others were publically executed. By 1931, the Popular Bloc, a coalition of parties including Agrarians, returned to power briefly before being overthrown in another military-led coup in 1934.

According to Source LL, what was the result of the military coup in Bulgaria?

SOURCE LL

Excerpt from *Bulgaria* by R.J. Crampton, published by Oxford University Press, New York, USA, 2007, p. 235. Crampton is a history professor at St Edmund Hall, University of Oxford, UK and has published several books on Bulgarian and eastern European history.

Bulgaria and its political system paid a terrible price for the coup. Some conspirators had been motivated originally by concern that the Tŭrnovo system [constitutional government] might be overthrown, but the governments which came immediately after that of [assassinated Prime Minster] Stamboliĭski saw constitutional abnormalities and infringements of personal liberties greater than anything yet experienced in modern Bulgarian history. The old sŭbranie [parliamentary] parties which were brought back into the centre of affairs by the coup soon proved little changed from those which had debased the political system before the First World War. The army moved nearer to the centre of political power whilst the Macedonian extremists [who wanted Macedonia to be part of Bulgaria] were given a new lease on life.

Economic difficulties

The Bulgarian economy remained extremely weak throughout the period, primarily because it was almost completely agricultural and competed with countries like Hungary and Yugoslavia which were closer to the consuming nations of Italy, Austria and Germany. Loans from the League of Nations in the late 1920s were able to help the country somewhat before the Great Depression hit in 1930, removing most economic gains.

Foreign policy

In terms of foreign policy, Bulgaria, except for the early Agrarian government, focused on undermining the Treaty of Neuilly. Macedonia was a neighbouring territory that was mostly ruled by Yugoslavia, with some areas under the control of Greece. Both Yugoslavia and Greece were Bulgaria's enemies, so groups that wanted Macedonia to be independent or to join Bulgaria were supported with money, weapons and training by Bulgaria.

Greeks and Yugoslavs were attacked by these groups who often fled into Bulgaria for shelter and rearming. These groups, including the Internal Macedonian Revolutionary Organization, helped the Bulgarian military, even killing the Bulgarian prime minister in the coup of 1923. These cross-border attacks by Bulgarian-supported Macedonian rebels led to a Greek attack on Bulgaria in 1925 which saw the League of Nations intervene (see page 144). Bulgaria remained isolated throughout the period, although a member of the League of Nations, and was seen as a threat to other nations, leading to the Balkan Entente.

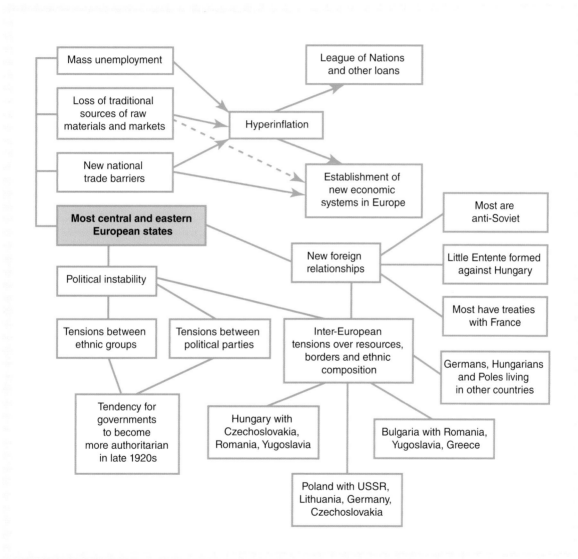

SUMMARY DIAGRAM

Austria, Hungary, Czechoslovakia, Poland and the Balkans

Chapter summary

The geopolitical and economic impact of the Paris Peace Treaties in Europe

Central and eastern Europe was severely affected by the First World War and the subsequent Paris Peace Conference. Germany lost territory, was subjected to large war reparations and suffered multiple political challenges, especially from communist-oriented groups. Continued tensions with France led to a temporary occupation, hyperinflation and finally some reconciliation through diplomacy as represented by the Locarno treaties.

Russia collapsed in 1917 into a civil war that lasted until 1921, affecting much of Europe with Bolshevik-inspired revolutions, after which it entered a period of recovery before mass change as a result of the Five-Year Plans.

An unstable Italy seemed to almost welcome the dictatorship of Mussolini in the early 1920s, with its political and foreign policy success, although economically it continued to struggle.

While old states such as Austria and Hungary, now reduced in size and economic ability, struggled to redefine their existence, other states followed different paths. Poland expanded itself through war, but failed to achieve political or economic stability, ending up with a form of military dictatorship and state-sponsored capitalism.

Czechoslovakia was relatively successful economically, but ignored its disparate ethnic divisions which led to its later demise.

Romania struggled economically although it grew exponentially as a result of the Treaty of Trianon and politically became a dictatorship under its king.

Bulgaria followed in a similar pattern except that it longed to recover territory lost in the war.

Yugoslavia, a nation of diverse ethnic divisions like Czechoslovakia, became a dictatorship under its Serbian king but failed to industrialize, although it enjoyed limited economic success through agriculture and exporting raw materials.

The Paris Peace Conference attempted to solve many of Europe's problems but in the years immediately after the war few saw prosperity, stability or democratic reforms.

 Examination advice

Interpreting visual sources

Visual sources are often included on Paper 1 examinations and can be used in any of the questions. Visual sources include cartoons, maps, graphs, charts, tables, photographs, posters and potentially many other types of graphic art. Some visual sources are easier to understand than others.

Graphs, charts and tables

Graphs, charts and tables usually convey very specific information such as economic data, how many people from a particular political party were in parliament, or how many leaders a country had over a period of time. This type of visual source still needs interpreting, however.

Example: table

Look at Source U (page 97):

SOURCE U

A table indicating economic goals and results of the Five-Year Plan 1928–32

Economic data are shown from the Soviet Union starting with 1927–8 and ending with 1933

	1927–8 (millions of tonnes)	1932–3 (planned) (millions of tonnes)	1933 (actual) (millions of tonnes)
Oil	11.7	22.0	21.4
Steel	4.0	10.4	5.9
Coal	35.4	75.0	64.3

Clearly states oil output in tonnes rose from 11.7 to 21.4, steel from 4.0 to 5.9 and coal from 35.4 to 64.3.

None of the goals were actually met despite the great advances. Oil was short by 600,000 tonnes, steel by 4.5 million tonnes and coal by 10.7 million tonnes.

This table conveys a tremendous amount of information, although it appears quite simple. After reading this chapter, you know that in 1927–8, the Soviet Union used the New Economic Policy which concentrated on rebuilding the Soviet Union from the ravages of the First World and Russian Civil Wars specifically by encouraging farmers to produce more grain. You also know that in 1929 the first Five-Year Plan began and that it concentrated on rapid, massive industrialization, collectivized farming and so forth. The table indicates that oil output almost doubled in that short period of time and coal was close to doubling also; steel rose considerably. It would seem that the Five-Year Plan did achieve great industrial gains for the Soviet Union, yet did not reach any of the targets that were initially set. So, how successful was the first Five-Year Plan? Why was the plan not able to achieve its targets? It is important that you consider this type of question when analysing a table such as Source U.

In Chapter 5 you will discover that all sources must be integrated into an essay on the fourth question of Paper 1 (see page 218) which requires your own knowledge. This means you probably need to consider why the Soviet Union either set targets that they could not achieve or why they failed to meet their goal in the three categories named above. From this chapter it is evident that there was mass starvation in the countryside as a result of collectivization, killing millions, that there was rationing of food in the cities, and that the industrialization process was chaotic for a variety of reasons. Any or all of these and more could be reasons that the Five-Year Plan did not achieve desired results as stated in Source U.

Cartoons, posters, stamps and graphic art

Cartoons and posters can be very similar in terms of symbolism, message and intended effect. Either can be intended to make fun of something, criticize a person or idea, try to get the viewer to agree with their point of view or inform. They can be complex and should be treated very carefully and thoroughly.

Symbolism

First we need to consider symbolism. The chart below gives some of the more common symbols and their potential meanings. However, these are just some of the basics and you should know that the list is almost endless.

Symbol	Represents	Symbol	Represents
Red star, five points	USSR, communism	Hammer and sickle	USSR, communism
Bear	Russia, USSR	Justice	Scales, blind-folded woman
Workers' cap	USSR, communism	Money bags, fat men	Wealth
Swastika	Nazi Germany	Crown of leaves, winged goddess	Victory
Red flag	USSR, communism	Statue of Liberty (one arm holding torch, other holding tablet)	Democracy, USA
The colour red	Communism	Uncle Sam	USA
Outstretched arm salute	Nazi Germany	Olive branch, dove	Peace
Goddess of Freedom (two hands holding torch)	Freedom, democracy	Skull and crossed bones	Death
Star of David, six points	Jews, Judaism, Zionism, Israel after 1948	Hourglass	Time
Turtle	Slow movement	Factory, smokestack	Industry
Chains	Oppression	Bulldog, eagle	War, possibly a nation such as Britain for bulldog or eagle for the USA
Bomb	Disaster, war, major tension	Woman or baby crying	Misery, death, destruction

Representations of people

Additionally, significant people like Lloyd George, Wilson, Clemenceau, Lenin, Stalin, Mussolini and others dealt with in this and other chapters in the book appear in cartoons and other visual sources. Lloyd George always appears with bushy, unkempt hair, Wilson as tall, thin and often with a monocle, Mussolini as short and bald, Stalin with bushy moustache and black hair, and so forth. Cartoons in this and other chapters in the book will help you understand how individuals typically appear in cartoons.

Captions

Captions are the labels that accompany visual sources. These are very important, often informing you of the date of creation, name of artist and perhaps country of origin. All of this information helps determine the message of the source. Often captions include a direct message which is easy to understand such as the message on the Bolshevik poster that clearly states that the 'Bolsheviks will put a stop to oppression …' (see page 92). Read captions carefully.

Example: poster

Look at Source F (see page 78) which is from 1923. 'No – You cannot force me!' is the German message to the invaders, France and Belgium. You are aware after this chapter that France and Belgium occupied part of Germany in an attempt to force Germany to make reparations as well as to seize raw materials and manufactured goods as reparations. The words tell us directly that Germans will not accept French and Belgium pressure to work or co-operate with the occupation. The message, in German, is directed at Germans telling them that they should resist the occupiers and that they should resist any attempt at forcing them to work. In essence, offer passive resistance. The imagery promotes the message as well. The worker has dropped his tool and has his hands in his pockets while the French soldiers point, one at the tool and the other into the distance, presumably motioning the man to go back to work. The worker is a figure for sympathy as there are two armed soldiers against one unarmed worker. We do not see their expressions, but the German worker is sad, angry or disinterested in the soldiers.

Example: cartoon

David Low's 1924 cartoon on the Dawes Plan (Source J, page 82) includes the caption 'FREE AT LAST!' First, the words are in all capitals indicating extreme emotion, screaming or major relief. David Low was from Britain, and Britain was relieved that the Dawes Plan would bring the Ruhr Crisis essentially to an end (see page 81). This meant that Europe was less likely to have war or further strife, at least in the near future. The cartoon also indicates Low's opinion of the crisis as the lady, labelled 'Europe' emerges from the barred gate of the 'International Asylum for the Insane'. His message clearly states that the entire crisis was insane or crazy and that now Europe seems more sensible and reasonable.

Example: stamps

Two stamps appear in this chapter as visual sources. Source V (page 99) is a stamp from the temporary government established by d'Annunzio at Fiume in 1919 and 1920. Stamps often contain political statements and this one is no exception. First notice that d'Annunzio is presented as a stone head or bust, similar to the bust of a Roman emperor for millennia earlier. He wears a crown of leaves which we know from our chart above to represent victory.

The words around his head are Latin, not Italian, again reminding the viewer that d'Annunzio is someone linked to the glory of ancient Rome. The Latin words can be translated in several ways, but essentially mean that 'the best shall stay here'. There were no letter U's in Latin, so Fiume has become a Romanized 'Fivme' to carry the Roman theme further. The stamp reverts back to comprehensible Italian to denote its value and perhaps remind the viewer that Fiume is, or should be, Italian territory.

Photographs

Photographs are another visual source. Photographs can capture a specific moment. Sometimes photographs just record what the photographer saw that particular moment, while many photographs, especially of political events, politicians and conferences are usually ones in which everyone poses in a specific way for an intended effect.

Example: photograph

Source FF (page 114) is a photograph recording the head of the Polish Army, Piłsudski, shaking hands with Catholic Church clergy and officials after attending a ceremony in which he affirms the relationship between the army and the Church. Notice that:

- Piłsudski and the Catholic official he is shaking hands with are essentially in the centre of the photograph.
- While there are soldiers in front of the camera, we do not see their faces.
- There is no one between the soldiers and Piłsudski so that the photographer has a clear view.
- Everyone in the picture is looking at Piłsudski and at no one else.

These observations indicate that the picture was taken for an official reason. While this does not make the source any less valuable, we must realize that this was likely taken for political reasons, perhaps to be distributed to the press. This was perhaps intentional, designed to show that the army and Catholic Church, the two most powerful institutions in Poland, were working together in 1920 to assure Polish independence and victory in war. Poland was in the midst of war with Bolshevik, and therefore atheist, Russia, so another message for Polish Catholics could be that they should support the army which protects their Church and country from the atheist Bolsheviks.

How to answer

It is likely that you will be asked to analyse one of the visual sources that appear on your Paper 1 examination in question 1. The questions are usually very straightforward, asking you to indicate what the message of the source is.

Example 1

This question uses Source BB found on page 109 in this chapter.

What message is conveyed by Source BB? (3 marks)

First, take note of any words. There is only one word on the entire poster: 'Horthy!' The addition of an exclamation mark should be interpreted as a shout or extreme enthusiasm.

Next, notice symbolism:

- Muscular arms = strength.
- Ship's wheel = guiding the state, Horthy was an admiral in the navy.
- Red waves = rough seas or times, red is the colour of communism.
- Shield with cross and other signs = this poster is Hungarian, so likely a symbol of the Kingdom of Hungary recently dismantled by the Treaty of Trianon.
- White = colour of Horthy's name, stands for purity and anti-communism.

Lastly, write your answer to the question.

Source BB is a Hungarian political campaign poster from 1920. The poster enthusiastically supports, as indicated by the capital letters and exclamation point, Admiral Horthy for an important position, likely regent or president of the country. The poster indicates that Horthy, a former admiral in the Austro-Hungarian navy, represented by strong, muscular arms, will be able to steer the ship, Hungary, through difficult times. The red waves are an obvious reference to the threat of communism which already controlled much of Hungary in 1920 under Kun, while Horthy's name is in white, symbolizing his anti-communist stance. Behind Horthy's strong arms is a shield, likely standing for the Kingdom of Hungary which had recently been reduced to a much smaller state with the Treaty of Trianon. This may be a reference to the desire of Horthy or his supporters of re-establishing a unified Kingdom of Hungary. It may be that the cross on the shield is more exposed than the other symbols, perhaps indicating the Catholicism of Horthy in contrast to communist atheism in an attempt to garner support from religious people. The message of this campaign poster is that Horthy should be supported in order to defeat communism and re-establish the Kingdom of Hungary.

The answer indicates which source is being analysed, the type of source and the date.

The caption is thoroughly analysed, including the colour of the words.

All major elements depicted in the poster are discussed and analysed, including the shield, red waves, arms and steering wheel.

Terms and phrases such as 'likely' and 'may be' are used appropriately when presenting a hypothesis based on historical events and probability but where some other interpretation may be possible.

The answer is summarized in the final sentence to make sure all points have been covered.

Answer indicates that question was understood. There are at least three points made about the poster. All points are clear, supported with evidence from the poster, and accurate. Good use of analysis and deduction. Mark: 3/3.

Example 2

This question uses Source KK found on page 119 in this chapter.

What message is conveyed by Source KK? (3 marks)

First, take note of any words. The caption and other words on the cartoon indicate that this is about the voice of the people of Yugoslavia. European dictators answer the League of Nations' question in unison, stating that silence means approval of the Yugoslav king's dictatorship. The king is silent, allowing others to speak for him.

Next, notice symbolism:

- League of Nations is a small woman inferring weakness.
- Yugoslav king sits on another woman who represents Yugoslav people.
- Bag on head of woman may indicate kidnapping or death.
- Each European dictator represents different countries. Mussolini is second from left, Mustafa Kemal is fourth from right. Others are probably Romanian, Bulgarian and Polish dictators or kings.

Lastly, write your answer to the question.

The type and origin of the source are stated in the opening of the answer.	*Source KK is a cartoon by British cartoonist David Low from 10 January 1929. The cartoon clearly indicates that the voice, meaning political expression and power, of the people of Yugoslavia is either dead or unable to be heard. This is clearly represented by the either tied up, or dead, woman with a bag over her head who is labelled 'Jugoslav people'. Second, the League of Nations is represented*
Symbols such as the woman that King Alexander is sitting on, the woman representing the League of Nations and the military uniforms of those standing are interpreted.	*as a woman, usually a sign in this period of weakness, but also perhaps of being peaceful especially when contrasted with the militant individuals depicted together in the cartoon. Finally, five European dictators speak together to affirm that because Yugoslavia is not protesting, the people must agree with King Alexander's*
Some European leaders are identified clearly while others who could be candidates are hypothesized based on historical knowledge.	*expansion of power. Some of the dictators depicted include Mussolini of Italy and Mustafa Kemal of Turkey. Others are probably the kings of Romania and Bulgaria and perhaps Piłsudski of Poland. The*
The concluding sentence clearly states the message of the cartoon.	*message of the cartoon is that the League of Nations is weak while many European nations, including Yugoslavia, limit democracy in their countries.*

Answer indicates that question was understood. There are at least three points made about the cartoon. All points are clear, supported with evidence from the poster, and accurate. Good use of analysis and deduction. Mark: 3/3.

Examination practice

1 What is the message conveyed by each of the following sources:

Cartoons:	Posters:	Photographs:
• Source C (page 76)	• Source S (page 93)	• Source A (page 72)
• Source K (page 84)	• Source Y (page 106)	• Source G (page 79)

2 Using the example of the analysis of the table given on page 123, explain the importance to historians of the following charts and tables:

• Source H (page 80) • Source Q (page 90) • Source T (page 95)

Extended examination practice

Sample question 1s
For guidance on how to answer this type of question see pages 29–30.

Sources can be found on the following pages:

• Source E (page 77) • Source M (page 86) • Source AA (page 108)

1 Why, according to Source E, was the Rapallo Treaty between Germany and the Soviet Union not very important?

2 Why, according to Source M, did the Locarno Treaties have a positive effect on international relations?

3 Why, according to Source AA, did Hungary suffer through an economic crisis?

Sample question 2s
For guidance on how to answer this type of question see pages 65–8.

Sources can be found on the following pages:

• Source D (page 77)	• Source K (page 84)	• Source CC (page 110)
• Source E (page 77)	• Source L (page 85)	• Source JJ (page 118)

1 Compare and contrast the views of Source D and Source E regarding the Treaty of Rapallo.

2 Compare and contrast the views of the Locarno Conference as expressed in Source K and Source L.

3 Compare and contrast Source CC and Source JJ on difficulties faced by some new European states after the First World War with nationalism.

Analysing visual sources from Chapters 1 and 2
1 What is the message conveyed by Source A in Chapter 1 on page 10?
2 What is the message conveyed by Source T in Chapter 2 on page 50?
3 What is the message conveyed by Source Z in Chapter 2 on page 57?
4 What is the message conveyed by Source CC in Chapter 2 on page 60?

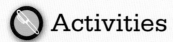 Activities

I Access the David Low cartoon archive that is hosted by the University of Kent at www.cartoons.ac.uk.

* Each student in the class should select a cartoon to analyse with no two students selecting the same one.
* Each student should answer the question 'What message is conveyed by your selected cartoon?' and try and make at least three points.
* Each student should present their analysis to another student for marking, along with the reference number to the cartoon. Students should mark each other out of three possible points.

2 One way to learn cartoon symbolism is to create a bingo-like game where symbols are represented on a grid pattern. Each grid card should have symbols arranged in a different order from any of the others. Someone calls out the meaning of a symbol, keeping track, of course, of which meanings and symbols have been called out. As meanings are matched with symbols, students may cross out or otherwise mark the appropriate symbol. Once a line of symbols is complete, that individual is the winner of that round. Grid patterns can contain any number of symbols with perhaps five across and five down being the easiest to work with.

3 Compare and contrast pro-communist and anti-communist (or anti-socialist) posters from this chapter.

a) What symbolism is used for each group?
b) Who is the intended audience?
c) Are symbols or words more powerful or useful in conveying a message?

4 As a class, debate which form of propaganda presented in this chapter is the most effective. Continue the debate regarding which forms of propaganda and political advertising are the most used and most effective today. Be sure to support your ideas with evidence.

CHAPTER 4

International diplomacy and the League of Nations

The early 1920s saw Allied Powers reverting to their pre-First World War foreign policies. The USA withdrew from international affairs that involved territories outside North and South America. Britain and France could come to few agreements over Germany and disarmament, and argued over Middle Eastern territories, while Japan secured former German territories in Asia and built a large navy. While the League of Nations held great promise for world diplomacy, it was severely weakened at the outset by dominant members such as Britain and France refusing to allow it to deal with major areas of diplomacy, including disarmament. You need to consider the following questions throughout this chapter:

✪ What were the difficulties in international diplomacy that prevented the League of Nations being successful?

✪ What were the main challenges and successes of the League of Nations?

✪ To what extent did the world's major powers successfully disarm after the First World War?

✪ Why was the mandate system established and how successful was it in achieving goals established by the League of Nations?

✪ Why did the British promise a Jewish homeland in Palestine?

 Diplomatic realities after Paris 1919

> ▶ **Key question:** *What were the difficulties in international diplomacy that prevented the League of Nations being successful?*

The Allied Powers were united against the Central Powers in the First World War, but this was an unusual event. The USA had rarely had close relations with Europe before 1917 and Britain and France had come close to war over Africa in 1898. The USA was wary of growing Japanese strength in the Pacific and began to compete for Asian markets. By the end of 1919, much of the unity the war had created had disintegrated, replaced with traditional stances over many issues.

The USA returns to semi-isolationism

The US Senate, the body responsible for the ratification of treaties signed by the US president, rejected the Treaty of Versailles (see page 44). This meant a rejection of the Anglo-American Guarantee that had been promised to

> Why did the USA remove itself from international diplomacy after 1919?

France, as well as US involvement with the League of Nations. France had agreed to abandon the idea of annexing the Saar and creating a separate Rhineland state to weaken Germany and deter future attack; now France felt vulnerable and exposed.

Many people in the USA were pleased with the rejection of the treaties for a variety of reasons. The USA had traditionally not involved itself in European politics and war. The USA preferred to dominate North and South America in line with the Monroe Doctrine, a US policy that rejected European interference in the American continents and therefore guaranteeing US dominance in the region, both political and economic. Many believed that the League of Nations compromised US sovereignty by forcing it to go to war if a member of the League was attacked. The US Senate, and probably the majority of Americans, wanted a return to the traditional stance of the US government in foreign policy: a state of **semi-isolation** where Europe was concerned.

Many also felt that conspiring European nations, including its wartime allies Britain and France, were not to be trusted and that their policies had helped lead the world to war. The nineteenth century had seen a European scramble for territories around the world, leading to war in some cases and certainly to the increase in warships and armies to defend these areas. Imperialism continued after the war as Britain and France rewarded themselves with colonies, masked as League of Nations mandates. Italy, Belgium and Japan also wished to gain colonies under the League. Many in the USA felt that colonial expansion had in part led to the First World War and wanted no part of it.

Why were France and Britain unable to agree on many issues in international affairs?

→ British and French diplomacy after 1920

The withdrawal of the USA from the Treaty of Versailles and the League of Nations removed the world's wealthiest and most industrialized nation from the new network of security that France and Britain attempted to build. The absence of the USA and of the Soviet Union, soon to be the other major world power, weakened the League and allowed Britain and France to dominate international diplomacy. This was not in keeping with their much diminished economic and political importance as a result of the First World War.

Britain

Britain soon reverted to its own traditional stance on European relations in that it did not desire France to completely dominate Europe, nor any other power. Increasingly concerned with the Soviet Union, Britain soon began considering revising sections of the Treaty of Versailles so that Germany could return to the world economy and provide a barrier against communism (see page 19). A return to normal economic relations would mean Germans could purchase British goods, bringing employment and hopefully prosperity to Britain that had been severely eroded by the USA taking over British markets during the early years of the First World War.

France

The French, alarmed at their exposure after the collapse of the Anglo-American military guarantee against German attack, created a system of alliances around Europe that they believed would bring security. France signed treaties with Czechoslovakia and Poland in 1921. Both countries had large militaries and shared borders with Germany. Unfortunately neither of these French allies were inclined to work with the other as they disputed territory (see page 111), the later settlement of which left Poland bitter. The Little Entente (see page 109) was in effect an alliance system under French support as each of the member states, Czechoslovakia, Romania and Yugoslavia, signed separate treaties with France. By 1927, France was formally allied with Poland, Czechoslovakia, Romania and Yugoslavia and potentially able to field millions of soldiers against Germany on its eastern and western borders at a time when the German army was limited by the Treaty of Versailles to 100,000 men with no tanks, artillery or airplanes.

SOURCE A

Excerpt from *Poland, 1918–1945: An Interpretive and Documentary History of the Second Republic* by Peter D. Stachura, published by Routledge, London, UK, 2004, pp. 111–12. Stachura is a professor of history at the University of Stirling, UK and Director of the Centre for Research in Polish History. He has written numerous books on European history between the First and Second World Wars.

The United States had retreated into isolationism, rendering redundant the whole Wilsonian ideology that had been so influential in shaping the peace, while Britain had her imperial interests to oversee and, in any case, where Europe was concerned, she was far more intent on helping to rehabilitate Germany than aiding Poland: Britain's pro-German policies in the dispute over Upper Silesia revealed the orientation her policy on the continent was now taking. France, a haven for Polish exiled revolutionaries in the nineteenth century and generally regarded in Poland and the rest of Europe as being basically sympathetic to the Polish cause, had emerged from the First World War much weakened and rather paranoid about a revival of German militarism. France's policy in Eastern Europe after 1919 was mainly influenced by her desire to construct essentially anti-German alliances with states such as Poland and Czechoslovakia. Even then, France proceeded cautiously, and although she had played a supportive role on Poland's side in the Upper Silesian conflict, it was not until after the Polish-Soviet War that she offered a full alliance.

What, according to Source A, were the foreign policies of the USA, Britain and France after 1919?

Competitors

France and Britain were wartime allies, but it must be remembered that they were colonial and economic competitors as well. During the Paris Peace Conference both countries had serious disagreements over almost all aspects of the various treaties. Competition for areas of the Ottoman Empire was especially tense, with the French accusing the British of breaking various agreements made during the war. While it is tempting to see Britain and France as partners for a peaceful Europe, the reality is that they were fierce competitors who had different objectives and little trust of each other. This lack of trust and diplomatic conflicts with the USA and Italy, severely affected the development of the League of Nations.

Regardless of political realities, people throughout the world were enthusiastic about the League of Nations and hoped that its existence would prevent future conflict and solve many of the world's problems.

? What is the author's opinion of the League of Nations as expressed in Source B?

SOURCE B

Excerpt from 'The League of Nations is alive' by Raymond B. Fosdick, published in _The Atlantic_, June 1920. _The Atlantic_ is a US-oriented political and foreign affairs journal published since 1857. Fosdick was President of the Rockefeller Foundation in the USA, a charitable organization that promotes health and education among other things, started in 1921.

One who examines the minutes of the meetings of the League Council and the proposed programme of the first meeting of the Assembly is impressed by the fact that political questions, such as constituted the bulk of the work of the Paris Conference, are here subordinated to larger considerations of human welfare. It is not boundaries or indemnities, but food and coal and health, which concern the League authorities. Theirs is the task, not of determining the privileges and rights of victorious allies, but of discovering and applying the remedial measures necessary to keep a shattered world alive. Where the Paris Conference sat down with a map and a ruler to make a new heaven and a new earth, the League officials are taking first steps to protect vast populations from starvation and disease, and to reestablish the economic life of the world.

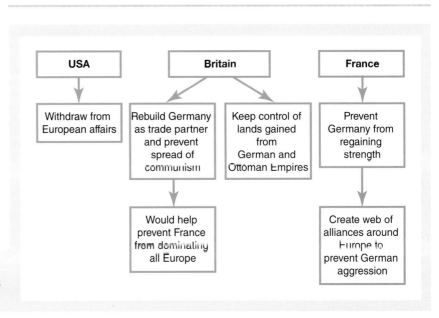

SUMMARY DIAGRAM

Diplomatic realities after Paris 1919

The League of Nations

▶ **Key question:** *What were the main challenges and successes of the League of Nations?*

The League of Nations had been proposed by Wilson in his Fourteen Points, but many diplomats had discussed creating a similar body before 1918. It was a common belief in Europe and the USA that nations often went to war without exhausting diplomatic efforts. The League of Nations, they believed, would provide the forum for conversations between nations, help alleviate disease and slavery, and much more. Although the USA did not join and Germany and the Soviet Union were not invited, people of many nations were extremely supportive of its mission and work.

Organization of the League

The League of Nations consisted of various bodies and commissions, the three most important being the Assembly, the Council and the Secretariat.

← **What were the main divisions of the League and their purposes?**

The Assembly
All members of the League of Nations were allowed representatives in the Assembly. While a nation could have three representatives present, each nation only had one vote. A two-thirds majority vote by the Assembly was required to admit new members, and the Assembly determined the League's budget.

The Council
The Council consisted of important states in the League, including France, Britain, Japan and Italy, with other states selected by the Assembly being allowed to join on a rotating basis. The Council set the Assembly's agenda and issued reports to help the deliberation of the Assembly, theoretically not making any decisions on its own. The fact that the Council was made of the wealthiest and most powerful nations in the League meant that in reality it heavily influenced the decisions of the Assembly.

The Secretariat
The Secretariat was a small body of officials and experts located in Geneva, Switzerland, who functioned primarily behind the scenes researching, issuing reports and documenting the League's work.

The Permanent Court of International Justice
In 1921 a fourth body was added to the League when the Permanent Court of International Justice was set up in The Hague in the Netherlands with the task of both advising the Council on legal matters and judging cases submitted to it by individual states. The Assembly selected the judges for this body.

The mission of the League of Nations

How was the League of Nations supposed to influence international relations?

The heart of the League of Nations Covenant, Articles 8–17 of the Treaty of Versailles (see page 33), was primarily concerned with the prevention of war. The League's long-term strategy for creating a peaceful world was summed up in the first section of Article 8.

SOURCE C

What is required for peace according to Source C?

Article 8 of the *Covenant of the League of Nations*.

The members of the League recognize that the maintenance of peace requires the reduction of national armaments to the lowest point consistent with national safety, and the enforcement by common action of international obligations.

KEY TERM

Arbitration Submitting international disputes to the League and agreeing beforehand to accept whatever decision was reached.

The process for solving disputes between sovereign powers was defined in Articles 12–17. According to Article 12, disputes were to be submitted to **arbitration** by the League. While this was happening, there was to be a cooling off period of three months. Article 13 required members to commit to carrying out the judgments of the Permanent Court of International Justice or the recommendations of the Council. Even if a dispute was not submitted to arbitration, the Council was empowered by Article 15 to set up an investigation into its origins. The assumption in these articles was that states would be only too willing to eliminate war by making use of the League's arbitration systems. If, however, a state ignored the League's recommendations, Article 16 made it clear that a war on one member of the League was a war on all members of the League; this was the principal of collective security (see page 33).

In Article 17, the League's powers were significantly extended by its right to intervene in disputes between non-members of the League, while in Article 11 member states were encouraged to refer to the Assembly or Council any international problem which might threaten the peace.

In theory, the League seemed to have formidable powers, but it was not a world government in the making, with powers to coerce independent nations. Its existence was based, as Article 10 made clear, on the recognition of the political and territorial independence of all member states. Article 15, for instance, recognized that if a dispute arose from an internal issue, the League had no right to intervene. There were several gaps in the League Covenant which allowed a potential aggressor to wage war without a penalty. War, for example, had to be officially declared before the League could act effectively. It had no formula for dealing with guerrilla fighters sponsored by one state against another, in another example, since the instigating state could deny responsibility. Even in the event of a formal declaration of war, if the Permanent Court of International Justice or the Assembly could not agree on a verdict, then League members were free to continue with their war.

The League's diplomatic efforts 1919–25

← **How successful was the League in resolving international crises up to 1925?**

France and Britain agreed to the League of Nations at the insistence of the USA, but once the USA failed to join the League, both nations found themselves the dominant leaders of the organization. Britain, France, Japan and Italy were not interested in referring to the League issues which they felt to be of their national interests since that would imply that the Assembly had the right to comment on or even determine their foreign policies. As the victors in the First World War, they also were determined to expand their own power and spheres of influence.

The Allied Powers had other organizations which they felt were more capable and appropriate for dealing with the aftermath of the First World War. These included the Council of Ambassadors, which represented the Allied Powers exclusively, and the Inter-Allied Reparations Commission that worked to determine the amount of reparations that the Central Powers could pay (see page 34). The League was therefore given a variety of relatively minor tasks, some of which were outlined in the treaties created in Paris. These tasks were simply the ones that the Allied Powers felt were so unimportant that the League of Nations could deal with them.

SOURCE D

'The Gap in the Bridge' a cartoon by Leonard Raven-Hill, *Punch*, 10 December 1919. Raven-Hill was a British artist and cartoonist for many newspapers and magazines. *Punch* was a British humour magazine published from 1841 until 2002.

What, according to Source D, is the main problem of the League of Nations?

THE GAP IN THE BRIDGE.

?

Why, according to Source E, did the League accomplish little in its first years of existence?

SOURCE E

Excerpt from *The League of Nations: Its Life and Times 1920–46* by F.S. Northedge, published by Holmes & Meier, London, UK, 1986, p. 71. Northedge was a professor of international relations at the London School of Economics, UK, writing numerous books on international relations.

The climate in which the League was born being so chilling, the setbacks it suffered needed to be few and far between if confidence in it was to grow; yet confidence was only likely to grow if the new body was seen to be making a real contribution to the welter of problems which oppressed the world when the war ended in 1918. In its first two or three years therefore, the League had to choose between doing little or nothing and risking failures, and the tendency was to lean towards the former. During 1920, 1921 and 1922, the League, which, in the opinion of its supporters, was going to be the saviour of mankind, sat in the sidelines while world politics were filled with tumult. In Eastern Europe was chaos and seemingly endless war, within the Soviet state and between it and its neighbours. In the Near East [Middle East], as it was still called, a revolution raged in Turkey which led to war with Greece, ending disastrously for the latter and almost embroiling Britain, too. In Central Europe, Germany teetered on the brink of revolution and intermittent fighting raged on her eastern borders with the reborn Poland until well into the 1920s. In Western Europe, Britain and France quarrelled over enforcement of the treaty they had made with Germany and seemed at times not far short of resorting to arms to settle the question.

The Saar, Eupen, Malmedy and Danzig

The Treaty of Versailles specifically empowered the newly created League of Nations to establish governments for the Saar (see page 37) and Danzig (see page 39). The Saar was to be governed until 1935 by a commission founded by the League of Nations, while French troops occupied the territory and guaranteed that France would continue to receive the Saar's coal.

Article 34 of the treaty granted Eupen and Malmedy to Belgium as long as the people of these two districts agreed. Belgium was to conduct a plebiscite to determine the wishes of the population and communicate the results to the League in order for the League to confirm and legalize the annexation. Germany protested the results of the plebiscite, but the League ignored Germany and ruled in Belgium's favour.

Article 101 of the treaty established Danzig as a city directly under the protection and administration of the League of Nations, belonging to no particular country. Article 104, however, granted Poland the right to conduct Danzig's foreign policy and Article 107 granted the Allied Powers ownership of former German government property, undermining the League of Nation's authority there.

In all these cases, it was clear that the Allied Powers saw the League of Nations as a tool for their own diplomacy.

Minority rights

The League of Nations was placed in charge of dealing with the rights of ethnic and linguistic minorities in central and eastern Europe, as stated in Article 12 of the League Covenant, where they were to be guaranteed the use of their language in the states where they now found themselves. The League was to investigate complaints by minorities and find solutions. Poland agreed in 1919 to a treaty which allowed the League to monitor the treatment of its ethnic minorities, while the British requested that the League find a way to protect Christian enclaves in the Ottoman Empire which contained about two million people. The League actually refused this request since the Ottoman Empire was collapsing, stating that it could only act with the consent of the Ottoman government. The League, however, agreed to supervise the transfer of Bulgarian and Greek populations that found themselves on the wrong side of their mutual borders in 1919. By 1922, every European country east of Germany and Italy had agreed to allow the League to monitor their minority populations and guarantee that they were allowed various rights.

SOURCE F

Extract from 'Minorities and the League of Nations in interwar Europe', by Mark Mazower, in *Daedalus*, vol. 126, 1996. *Daedalus* is the journal of the American Academy of Arts and Sciences. Mazower is a British historian who is a history professor at Columbia University in New York, USA.

At the Paris Peace Conference, the struggle over the form of an independent Poland eventually brought into being an ambitious new international policy on minority rights. Behind the scenes, the influential New States Committee recognized the need for some such policy if ethnic civil war was not to spread through Eastern Europe and destabilize an area already under the shadow of Bolshevism. Despite bitter protests, the new Polish government was obliged to guarantee certain rights to its minorities as a condition of recognition: they included equality of treatment under the law and religious freedoms as well as rights to certain forms of collective organization in the educational and cultural spheres. The Polish Minorities Treaty was guaranteed by the League of Nations, which apparently meant that complaints could be brought to Geneva (though not directly by the minority concerned). In certain circumstances, the League's Council could take action.

What, according to Source F, was the purpose of the various minorities treaties?

Soviet Union

In 1920, the League worked with some success to **repatriate** between two and three million prisoners of war captured from the Central Powers by Russia, a country now in the midst of civil war (see page 93). This was the first major international relief effort by the League and its success led to further relief efforts. The British government requested in 1920 that the League send investigators to Russia to enquire about its economic condition in hopes that the war would shortly be won and Russia could be returned to

 **KEY TERM**

Repatriate To return someone to their country.

the world economy. The Bolsheviks refused to allow the League to enter Russia claiming that it was clearly a tool of enemy nations. This accusation did not require much evidence since Britain and other League nations supported Poland in its war against Russia at this time.

SOURCE G

'Moral Suasion. The Rabbit: "My offensive equipment being practically nil, it remains for me to fascinate him with the power of my eye" ', a cartoon in *Punch* published in 1920. *Punch* was a British humour magazine published from 1841 until 2002.

? What message does Source G convey?

Persia, today's Iran, was a member of the League and in 1920 it asked for League assistance under Article 11 since the Soviet Union, as Bolshevik Russia was now called, invaded its north. This was the first time that a member nation appealed to the League in the event of armed aggression. The Council investigated and discovered that Persia and the Soviet Union were already negotiating, so the League excused itself from intervening. This was done with much relief since members of the Council would have found attacking the Soviet Union and defending Persia enormously difficult financially, politically and militarily.

Åland Islands

In 1920, Britain requested that the League's Council become involved in a dispute over the Åland Islands located between Sweden and newly-created Finland. Finland initially rejected League involvement as it believed problems in the Åland Islands were an internal issue, not an international one. The Council took up the issue because Sweden demanded a plebiscite be granted to the islands' population so they could determine which country they belonged to. The Council appointed a committee of three experts who recommended in 1921 that the islands be granted to Finland, but with special protection for the Swedish residents. The islands were also to be demilitarized and considered neutral territory. Sweden agreed to the arrangements, but without enthusiasm. This was the League's first international agreement reached solely on the League's authority.

Vilna and the Polish–Lithuanian War

In October 1920, in response to appeals from the Polish foreign minister, the League negotiated an armistice between Poland and Lithuania, whose quarrel over border territories rapidly escalated into war (see page 112). The ceasefire did not, however, hold as a Polish army occupied Vilna, a province of Lithuania, and established a puppet government of Central Lithuania. The League first called for a plebiscite for Vilna to determine if the residents wanted to be part of Lithuania or Poland, but this was rejected by Poland. In March 1922, Poland finally annexed Vilna province which was recognized diplomatically in 1923 by the Conference of Ambassadors. The Conference of Ambassadors, of course, represented the Allied Powers and since the most powerful of the Allied Powers also controlled the League Council, it was recognition that the League could only be as successful as the Allied Powers wanted it to be, regardless of the Covenant or the desires of other nations.

Upper Silesia

Difficulties in determining the fate of Upper Silesia, claimed by both Germany and Poland, were handled by the League of Nations (see page 39). A plebiscite was held which indicated the province should be turned over to Poland, but there were significant numbers of Germans who were determined not to join Poland. The French government referred the issue to the League in 1921. A commission studied the situation and awarded the majority of the territory to Germany, but with most industrial centres and sources of raw materials granted to Poland. The League created new borders between Poland and Germany, allowing the Allied Powers to remove their occupying armies.

Albania

In the second half of 1921, the League focused the attention of the Allied Powers on the plight of Albania which urgently requested help against Greek and Yugoslav aggression. As the Conference of Ambassadors had not yet fixed Albania's borders, the Greeks and Yugoslavs were exploiting the ambiguous situation to occupy as much Albanian territory as they could. The Council responded by dispatching a commission of inquiry, but the Conference of Ambassadors finalized the frontiers and pushed the League Council into threatening economic sanctions against Yugoslavia if it did not recognize them. When this was successful, the League was then entrusted with supervising the Yugoslav withdrawal. The League had played a useful role as a tool of the Conference of Ambassadors where real power resided. The fact that the Conference of Ambassadors then made Italy the protector of Albania's independence indicated further that the Allied Powers were less interested in fulfilling the League's Covenant than in extending their own authority.

Austria

One of the League's greatest successes was its financial assistance to an economically distressed Austria in 1922 (see page 104). The League arranged for short- and long-term loans for Austria to rebuild from the war, but required a League-appointed commissioner-general to reside in Vienna, the Austrian capital, to oversee government financial reform. The League demanded that the Austrian government cut spending and was to have a balanced budget by 1924. By 1924, Austria had recovered from the economic crisis and in 1926 the commissioner-general was withdrawn indicating the success of the League's assistance to Austria. A similar programme was initiated for Hungary in 1924 for much the same reasons and with similar results (see page 108).

Memel

Memel was a small district that the Treaty of Versailles granted to Lithuania. France and Poland, however, wanted this area to be placed under international oversight like Danzig. Lithuania decided to seize the territory by force in January 1923. The Conference of Ambassadors decided that Poland should have some role in Memel's administration, supported by their ally France. Lithuania rejected any Polish involvement, so the Conference referred the issue to the Council as they had done with the Vilna issue. The Council established a three-man commission which decided that Lithuania should control the German port, over-riding Polish protests.

Corfu

In 1923, Italy attacked the Greek island of Corfu (see page 99) prompting Greece to ask the League of Nations to intervene, citing Articles 12 and 15. Italy argued, successfully as it turned out, that this was not an issue for the League of Nations, but one for the Conference of Ambassadors. This was because the mission that was attacked while mapping the borders of Albania and Greece was sent by the Conference of Ambassadors. Four Italians were killed, including a general, and Italy blamed Greece which led to the shelling of the Greek island of Corfu. Since no war had been declared, Greek demands that the League act were essentially ignored since war had to be officially declared to fall under the jurisdiction of the League. The Conference awarded Italy financial compensation from Greece for the death of the Italian officials, but there was great consternation among the League of Nations members. Italy seemed to have gotten away with a criminal act by attacking another League member without any form of punishment. It was another indication that the more powerful nations who sat on the League's Council could and would ignore the League whenever their interests conflicted with the League's Covenant.

SOURCE H

Excerpt from 'The League of Nations' predicament in southeastern Europe' by Laura Garcés in *World Affairs*, vol. 158, 1995. *World Affairs* is a journal concerning US foreign policy and has been published since 1837. Garcés is the author of books on American and Latin American cultural and diplomatic history.

Thus, the Corfu settlement, while representing a peaceful resolution of the Italo-Greek incident, was clearly not the result of pressure from a united international community. To the extent that an understanding had been reached, with 'the League Council and especially the League Assembly act[ing] as catalysts forcing the Conference of Ambassadors to find some sort of reasonable solution to the Italo-Greek dispute,' it was a success. Nevertheless, it was also a precedent that could, if not encourage, at least not frustrate, Italy's ambitions. It therefore instilled concerns on the part of the smaller actors in this area. After the conclusion of the incident, various telegrams of protest from small powers, among others Czechoslovakia, Yugoslavia, and Romania, as well as Sweden and Norway, were sent to … the French representative in Geneva.

What, according to Source H, was the effect of the settlement of the Corfu crisis on the League?

Mosul

In 1924 the League was confronted with another crisis involving a greater power and a lesser one. Turkey claimed the region and city of Mosul, while Britain counted it as part of Iraq, a territory under British control (see page 158). The Treaty of Lausanne (see page 62) provided for direct Anglo-Turkish negotiations over Mosul, but these broke down and the British demanded a withdrawal of all Turkish forces within 48 hours in October 1924. The League intervened and recommended that Turkish forces withdraw to a certain point while a commission of inquiry could be formed to investigate and make recommendations to the League's Assembly. The commission consulted the local Kurdish population who preferred British to Turkish rule. The League recommended that Mosul become part of the mandate of Iraq (see page 157) for 25 years, which was then accepted. As Iraq was a British mandate, this effectively put it under British control.

Bulgaria and Greece

In October 1925, fighting began on the Greek and Bulgarian borders. Bulgaria referred the issue to the Council which demanded a cessation of fighting within three days. A commission was formed to study the conflict and to make recommendations. In December 1925, both countries accepted the League's demand that Greece pay Bulgaria £45,000 and that an officer from a neutral country oversee their mutual border for two years to prevent further fighting.

How successful was the League in addressing international labour, social and health issues?

The League's labour, social and health organizations
International Labour Organization

One of the greatest successes of the League was the International Labour Organization (ILO). This had originally been created as an independent organization by the Treaty of Versailles, but it was financed by the League. In some ways it was a League in miniature. It had its own permanent labour office at Geneva and its work was discussed by a conference of labour delegates that met regularly. Right up to 1939 the ILO turned out an impressive stream of reports, recommendations and statistics which provided important information for a wide range of industries all over the world. The ILO worked to set maximum hours of work, to make factories and mines safer and to encourage nations to compensate those injured while working and to allow sick leave.

SOURCE I

How successful was the ILO of the League according to Source I?

Extract from *The League of Nations: Its Life and Times, 1920–46* by F.S. Northedge, published by Holmes & Meier, London, UK, 1986, p. 180. Northedge was a professor of international relations at the London School of Economics, UK, writing numerous books on international relations.

The first years of the ILO were hectic with activity, symbolised by the holding of its first conference in Washington in October 1919, almost before the ink of the peace treaties was dry: it concerned hours of work in industry. The next meeting, from 15 June until 10 July 1920, concentrated on navigation and workers in the fishing industry, with hours of work again forming a central concern. A third session, held in Geneva from 24 October until 19 November 1921, was mainly occupied with agricultural work. In these three years sixteen conventions and eighteen recommendations were adopted … [In] 1925, three conventions on workmen's compensation were adopted; in May and June of the following year came conventions on labour conditions on ships at sea, then on sickness insurance (1927), the creation and application of minimum-wage-fixing machinery (1928), the conditions of dock workers (1929), compulsory labour (1930), hours of work in coal mines, described as 'the most difficult of all the problems in the field' (1931), and protection against accidents in the loading and unloading of ships (1932). Conventions, recommendations, volumes of statistics, rolled forth. Admittedly the actual impact in the form of legislation passed and put into effect by member-states left much to be desired. But the Organisation formulated norms and standards for those concerned with working standards in the different countries to aim for. Trade unions found in the ILO an ally in their struggle to make life better on the factory floor, in the fields and forests, and at sea.

Health organization and other committees

The League's World Health Organization provided an invaluable forum for drawing up common policies on such matters as the treatment of diseases, the design of hospitals and health education. The League also set up committees to advise on limiting the production of opium and other addictive drugs, on the outlawing of the sale of women and children for prostitution and on the abolition of slavery. The Mandate Commission received reports from those nations that administered mandates around the world.

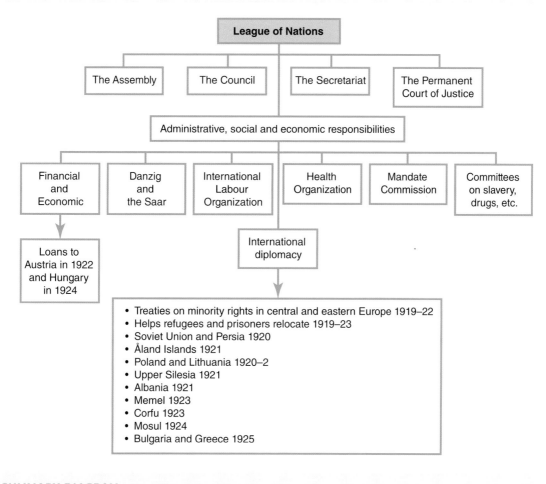

The League of Nations

Disarmament 1922–35

▶ Key question: *To what extent did the world's major powers successfully disarm after the First World War?*

According to Source J, why did the world's nations wish to attempt some level of disarmament?

SOURCE J

Extract from *The League of Nations: Its Life and Times, 1920–46* by F.S. Northedge, published by Holmes & Meier, London, UK, 1986, p. 113. Northedge was a professor of international relations at the London School of Economics, UK, writing numerous books on international relations.

On no enterprise did the League of Nations spend more time and energy than on the attempt, in the words of Article 8 of the Covenant, to reduce armaments 'to the lowest point consistent with national safety and the enforcement by common action of international obligations'. The Article echoed the fourth of President Wilson's Fourteen Points set forth in his speech in January 1918, which called for 'adequate guarantees given and taken that national armaments will be reduced to the lowest point consistent with domestic safety'. Article 8 of the Covenant stated that League Members recognised that peace 'required' disarmament, and this was certainly the belief of many millions of League supporters, at least in the first half of its life. The First World War was widely regarded as having been precipitated by the arms race which preceded it, though it is doubtful whether many governments in the inter-war period ever seriously believed that disarmament by international agreement, on the scale called for by Article 8, was either desirable or feasible. Nevertheless, they had no alternative but to make every effort to achieve it in view of the fervent wishes for a world without arms on the part of their supporters.

Disarmament had been forced on the defeated Central Powers in the various treaties signed in Paris after the First World War. Germany, for example, was limited to an army of 100,000 men, six major warships, no air force, no submarines, no tanks and no heavy artillery (see page 42). This was in keeping with one of Wilson's Fourteen Points which called for the reduction of armaments by all nations. In fact, the Treaty of Versailles stated that German disarmament was the first step towards efforts to lower armaments in all nations. The League of Nations was charged in Article 8 of its Covenant to work towards disarmament. Slowly, the League did set up a commission to study disarmament and make recommendations. As a result, the World Disarmament Conference was finally held in 1932 (see page 151).

Challenges to disarmament

← **Why was disarmament difficult to achieve in Europe after the First World War?**

Disarmament was highly unlikely in the atmosphere of Europe after the First World War, although the idea of limiting the ability to make war was extremely popular with the citizens of most countries in Europe and the USA. France, however, consistently refused to reduce the size of its military for fear of future German attack. France argued that if Britain and the USA would guarantee against German attack, they could then consider disarmament. This guarantee failed to materialize and Britain refused to consider a military alliance with France which could lead it into another European war. Britain was also unable to continue supporting a massive military for an indefinite period of time, having exhausted itself financially during the war and so reduced its military strength rapidly. Britain, as an island nation, did not need to fear an attack except by sea in this period, so a large navy was maintained.

France's European allies all over central and eastern Europe kept their armaments, fearing Hungarian plans to reclaim areas lost in the Treaty of Trianon, invasion by the Soviet Union, rebellions by communists and even seizures of territory from each other. Italy's Mussolini, prime minister after 1922, increased military spending because his governmental system, fascism, glorified war and conquest.

The USA, in contrast to other major nations apart from Britain, reduced its military from approximately three million soldiers to 157,000 by 1921, perhaps to reduce government spending but also as a result of public pressure. This amount was reduced further by 1926 when the USA had approximately 100,000 soldiers.

SOURCE K

Excerpt from *Arms Limitation and Disarmament: Restraints on War, 1899–1939* by B.J.C. McKercher, published by Praeger, Connecticut, USA, 1992, p. 44. McKercher is a professor of war studies at the Royal Military College of Canada and has published numerous books on international relations between the First and Second World Wars.

Lloyd George and Wilson shared other liberal assumptions that affected their approach to the disarmament question at the Paris Peace Conference. They believed that German militarism had been responsible for the outbreak of war in 1914. Confident of the pacific nature of democracies, they thought, too, that democratic public opinion would provide an effective check on the evasion of arms limitation agreements and that the good faith of consenting Powers would therefore be an adequate guarantee of their enforcement. This conviction that democracies do not wage aggressive war had important consequences for the two leaders' positions at the peace conference concerning the enforcement provisions of the treaty and the coercive powers of the League.

Why did Lloyd George and Wilson believe disarmament was possible according to Source K? ❓

Why were the most
successful
disarmaments
achieved outside the
League of Nations?

Disarmament and efforts at reducing tensions 1922–34

Failure of the League of Nations to successfully address disarmament did not deter work towards this end, however. The USA, Japan, Britain, France and Italy, as well as other countries, held a series of conferences and signed several treaties to limit their own strength and to reduce the threat of war.

The Washington Five Power Treaty and Naval Convention 1922

The USA had become alarmed by the rise of Japanese power in the Pacific by 1919. Japan already possessed the third largest navy in the world but now began a major naval construction programme. The Americans responded by forming a Pacific Ocean fleet and embarked on their own formidable building programme, which, when completed, would make the US navy the largest in the world. Britain was a military ally of Japan and therefore in early 1921 it announced its own naval programme in order to support its ally in case of war with the USA. The British government privately told Washington that a negotiated settlement for naval construction was desired as Britain could not afford a naval race.

🔑 **KEY TERM**

Capital ships Large
warships such as battleships
and cruisers that are heavily
armoured and armed.

After three months of negotiations that began in November 1921, the Five Power Treaty, also known as the Washington Naval Convention or Treaty, was signed in February 1922 to last for fourteen years. It halted the building of large battleships for ten years, provided for the scrapping of certain battleships and battle cruisers, and, for those **capital ships** which were allowed, established a ratio of three for Japan and 1.75 each for Italy and France to every five for Britain and the USA. Each nation had limitations placed on the number of aircraft carriers that it could possess as well. There was no agreement on smaller ships and submarines because of a dispute between France and Britain over which destroyers and submarines should be allowed. Japan asked for and received agreements between all nations to not construct fortifications on island possessions throughout the Pacific.

The result of the treaty was that the USA was required to scrap ten old battleships, two new ones and thirteen others that were being built. This left the USA with eighteen warships, Britain with 22, and ten for Japan. Britain was allowed more ships because although many were large, they were not as powerful as more modern vessels. During these negotiations, the Four Power Treaty was signed in December 1921 and was an agreement between the USA, Britain, Japan and France which ended the Anglo-Japanese Alliance and replaced it with an agreement to respect each other's territory. Finally, the Nine Power Treaty was also signed in Washington in February 1922. With this, Japan agreed to remove its military from the Shantung peninsula (see page 41), and all nations agreed to respect China's independence and borders.

SOURCE L

A photograph from the US Navy Historical Center, December 1923. Scrapped guns from the *USS Kansas* and other naval ships are shown with the *USS South Carolina* in the background being dismantled.

What message is conveyed in Source L?

Treaties on submarines, gas and bacteria 1922 and 1925

The USA, Britain, France, Italy and Japan, among others, agreed in 1922 to outlaw **unrestricted submarine warfare**. This meant that crews of merchant ships had to be taken to safety before a submarine was allowed to destroy the ship. Since this was almost impossible, it had the effect of outlawing the use of submarines against merchant ships during war. The use of gas in war was also prohibited. In 1925, the Geneva Protocol for the Prohibition of Poisonous Gases and Bacteriological Methods of Warfare confirmed the outlawing of poison gas and went further, outlawing the use of biological warfare in the form of bacteria. The US Senate failed to ratify this treaty, but Britain finally signed in 1930.

Geneva Naval Conference 1927

The Washington Naval Treaty in 1922 dealt primarily with battleships (see page 148). Britain and Japan decided to increase the strength of their navies instead by building large numbers of cruisers, submarines and destroyers. By 1926, Britain had 54 cruisers in operation and Japan had 25, while the US only had fifteen. The USA requested a conference in 1927 in Geneva, Switzerland, to address this new **arms race**. The USA wished to apply the same ratio to these smaller types of naval vessels as had been applied to

 **KEY TERM**

Unrestricted submarine warfare Policy of allowing submarines to attack any type of ship from an enemy nation without warning.

Arms race Competition between nations to be the most heavily armed.

battleships. Italy and France refused to attend, explaining that they preferred to work through the League of Nations, which the USA conveniently was not a member of, and Britain and Japan sent lower-level diplomats.

Both Britain and Japan claimed that they agreed that something should be done to limit the number of vessels being constructed, but neither would commit to a signed agreement. This diplomatic failure resulted in the US government ordering the construction of fifteen additional cruisers and an aircraft carrier in 1929.

Kellogg–Briand Pact 1928

There was much public pressure on the US government to play a greater role in disarmament as many in the USA had no desire to be drawn into another international conflict. In March 1927 the French Foreign Minister Briand proposed a Franco-American pact that would outlaw war. Kellogg, the US Secretary of State, replied cautiously in December and suggested a general pact between as many states as possible that rejected war as a way for a country to achieve national goals. On 27 August 1928 the Kellogg–Briand Peace Pact, formally known as the General Treaty for the Renunciation of War, was signed by fifteen states, and by 1933 a further 50 had joined it.

Optimists saw the pact as supplementing the Covenant of the League of Nations. It outlawed war, while the League had the necessary machinery for setting up commissions of inquiry and implementing cooling off periods in the event of a dispute. One month later, in September 1928, the General Act for the Pacific Settlement of International Disputes was signed. With this new agreement, countries agreed to allow commissions to study disputes between nations and if those disputes were not resolved to the satisfaction of either nation, then the matter would be referred to the Permanent Court of International Justice. The intention was, along with the Kellogg–Briand Pact, to prevent, even outlaw, war between nations.

Litvinov's Pact 1929

Similar to the Kellogg–Briand Pact, the Litvinov Pact was an agreement arranged by the Soviet Union's Foreign Minister Litvinov and neighbouring countries. The Soviet Union did not have diplomatic relations with the USA and so had not been invited to sign the Kellogg–Briand Pact, yet desired to prevent war between itself and nations sharing its border. In 1929, the Soviet Union, Estonia, Latvia, Poland, Romania, Lithuania, Turkey and Persia, today's Iran, agreed not to go to war to settle disputes but instead to resort to diplomacy to solve problems.

London Naval Conference 1930

The London Naval Conference was called to address concerns with the Five Power Treaty signed in Washington in 1922. In addition, France felt threatened by an increasingly militant Italy in the Mediterranean and wished to increase the number of warships it was allowed. France at the outset absolutely refused to have the same ratio of warships as Italy and wanted

Britain and the USA to agree to a security pact, similar to the failed Anglo-American Guarantee discussed in 1919. A security pact was not achieved and France and Italy refused to agree with the other powers to limit non-battleship construction. Achievements, however, seemed plentiful at the time. The ratio of battleships by the five powers agreed on in Washington was continued. A ratio of seven cruisers, destroyers and other smaller vessels for Japan for every ten held by the USA and Britain was also agreed. All agreed to continue the earlier restrictions on aircraft carrier construction. For the first time in history, there was an agreement on construction of all warships between major nations.

SOURCE M

Excerpt from *British and American Naval Power: Politics and Policy, 1900–1936* by Phillips Payson O'Brien, published by Praeger, Connecticut, USA, 1998, p. 214. O'Brien is a professor at the University of Glasgow, UK, and is the Senior Lecturer in American History. He has published several books on naval history of Britain and the USA.

With the First London Conference the naval arms control process reached its apex. The struggle for naval supremacy between America and Britain that had begun with Woodrow Wilson's 1916 program was finally settled. Parity between the two was agreed to for every type of warship while Japan had accepted a smaller ratio for every category except submarines. The tragedy of the London Conference is that while it marked a considerable success in the arms control process, it was not a lasting achievement. Within six years naval arms control would be at an end.

What, according to Source M, was the importance of the First London Conference?

The results of the conference were several, including an increased naval race in the Mediterranean between France and Italy. In Japan, the treaty was very unpopular with the military who believed it kept Japan weak in comparison to other world powers. This contributed to the assassination of the prime minister in 1932 and the takeover of foreign policy by the military (see page 190). The US and British governments were pleased with the agreement since it meant a reduction in military spending just as the Great Depression began (see page 178). US President Hoover estimated that the London Naval Conference resulted in savings for the USA of $2.5 billion dollars, an enormous sum at the time.

World Disarmament Conference 1932–4

The League of Nations Council called the long-awaited World Disarmament Conference in February 1932 at Geneva after more than six years of preparation. Officially known as the Conference for the Reduction and Limitation of Armaments, it was attended by members of the League of Nations and the USA and Soviet Union. Japan would leave the conference and League early in 1933 as a result of the Lytton Commission of the League (see page 191). France from the start declared that it was unwilling to reduce its armaments unless it was provided with some guarantee against future

German attack by Britain and the USA. The British and the USA refused this guarantee as always, causing the French to simply refuse disarmament. The Conference continued to function until May 1937, although most discussion had been concluded by the end of 1934.

SOURCE N

? What is suggested by Source N about the World Disarmament Conference?

'Mars, the God of War, tied down.' A 1932 poster concerning the World Disarmament Conference.

SOURCE O

? What, according to Source O, is the best way to achieve disarmament?

Excerpt from a speech by US President Franklin D. Roosevelt to the US Congress, 16 May 1933 published in 1983 by the US State Department in *Peace and War: United States Foreign Policy, 1931–1941*.

If all nations will agree wholly to eliminate from possession and use of weapons which make possible a successful attack, defenses automatically will become impregnable, and the frontiers and independence of every nation will become secure.

The ultimate objective of the Disarmament Conference must be the complete elimination of all offensive weapons.

The Germans, disarmed by the Treaty of Versailles, reminded other nations that their forced disarmament was meant to have led to the disarmament of other nations, which had not happened. The Germans continued by declaring that since practically no other country had disarmed, they had the right to expand their military for their own security. In 1933, the government of Germany changed with the appointment of Adolf Hitler as chancellor (see page 186). The Germans declared that since France refused to disarm, Germany would no longer participate in the Conference and withdrew. Soon Germany withdrew from the League altogether. No agreements were reached at the Conference and after 1934 meetings were only called occasionally with equally poor results. The World Disarmament Conference was a complete failure.

SOURCE P

Excerpt from *Arms Limitation and Disarmament: Restraints on War, 1899–1939* by B.J.C. McKercher, published by Praeger, Connecticut, USA, 1992, p. 191. McKercher is a professor of war studies at the Royal Military College of Canada. He has published numerous books on international relations between the First and Second World Wars.

By early 1934, therefore, the World Disarmament Conference existed in name only. The United States was unwilling to make substantive contributions to the deliberations; Germany and Japan had withdrawn; and the other Great Powers, no matter their previous statements and commitment to the process of completing the draft treaty, were not about to limit their armed strength when it remained uncertain what their potential rivals were going to do.

> Why, according to Source P, had the World Disarmament Conference accomplished little by early 1934?

London Naval Conference 1935

The Second London Naval Conference met in 1935 with the purpose of extending earlier naval limitations and clarifying various points such as the size limitations for ships. The agreement reached initially included only the USA, Britain and France. Japan refused to attend and withdrew from earlier naval agreements in January 1935, demanding naval equality with the USA and Britain who refused. Italy also refused to sign the treaty as a result of hostility in Britain and France regarding its invasion of Abyssinia in late 1935 (see page 201). The USA, Britain and France agreed that no battleship could displace more than 35,000 tons or have larger than 14-inch guns. If Japan or Italy refused to sign the agreement by 1937, battleships could be fitted with 16-inch guns. Aircraft carriers could not displace more than 23,000 tons and submarines were limited to 2000 tons or less. The agreement reached in London in 1935 was finally signed by Germany and the Soviet Union in 1937 and Italy in 1938. Japan attempted to achieve parity with the US navy, but only reached a ratio of eight to ten by December 1941.

What does Source Q suggest about naval construction between 1930 and 1935?

SOURCE Q

Surface warships begun by Britain, the USA and Japan 1930–5.

Total ships begun 1930–5	Britain	USA	Japan
Aircraft carriers	2	3	1
Cruisers	17	17	6
Destroyers	45	46	24

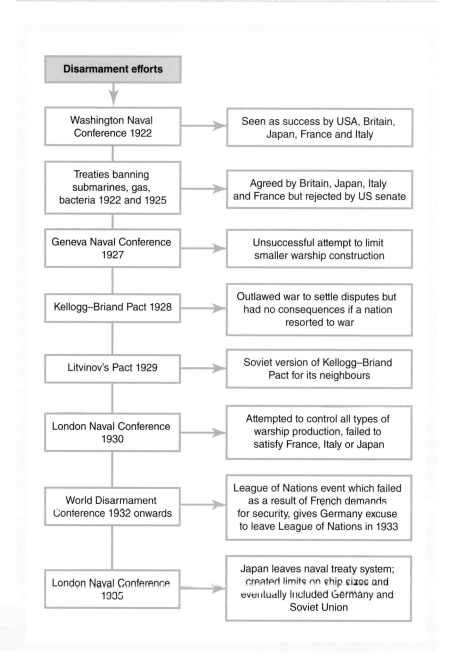

Disarmament efforts

Washington Naval Conference 1922	Seen as success by USA, Britain, Japan, France and Italy
Treaties banning submarines, gas, bacteria 1922 and 1925	Agreed by Britain, Japan, Italy and France but rejected by US senate
Geneva Naval Conference 1927	Unsuccessful attempt to limit smaller warship construction
Kellogg–Briand Pact 1928	Outlawed war to settle disputes but had no consequences if a nation resorted to war
Litvinov's Pact 1929	Soviet version of Kellogg–Briand Pact for its neighbours
London Naval Conference 1930	Attempted to control all types of warship production, failed to satisfy France, Italy or Japan
World Disarmament Conference 1932 onwards	League of Nations event which failed as a result of French demands for security, gives Germany excuse to leave League of Nations in 1933
London Naval Conference 1935	Japan leaves naval treaty system; created limits on ship sizes and eventually included Germany and Soviet Union

SUMMARY DIAGRAM

Disarmament 1922–35

Establishment and impact of the mandate system

> ▶ **Key question:** Why was the mandate system established and how successful was it in achieving goals established by the League of Nations?

During the First World War, armies from the British Empire and Japan, primarily, took control of the German Empire outside Europe. In addition, British armies, along with Arab allies from the Arabian peninsula, took control of large sections of the Ottoman Empire in the Middle East. The British and France, as well as Japan and British Dominions, were able, through the League of Nations, to establish control over these conquered territories with varying degrees of success.

SOURCE R

Excerpt from *Colonialism and Development: Britain and Its Tropical Colonies, 1850–1960* by Michael Havinden and David Meredith, published by Routledge, London, UK, 1993, p. 127. Havinden is a Senior Lecturer with the University of Exeter, UK, for economic and social history. Meredith is Senior Lecturer at University of South Wales, Australia, for economic history.

The exact distribution of ex-German colonial territory amongst the Allies was determined by wartime treaties and agreements between Britain and France, Britain, France and Italy and Britain and Japan. In February 1916 France was offered most of Togoland and the Cameroons by Britain, chiefly as a means of boosting French morale in the face of lack of progress on the western front. This agreement split both German colonies into a British and French sphere (the French share in both cases amounted to about four-fifths), a division which remained in force until the end of the colonial era. In March 1916 the Sykes-Picot Agreement divided Turkish territory in the Middle East between Britain and France. The Treaty of London between Britain, France and Italy signed in April 1915 promised Italy territorial compensation in Africa in the event that France and Britain 'extend their colonial possessions in Africa at the expense of Germany'. Finally, Britain agreed with Japan in February 1917 to support the latter's claim to the German Pacific islands north of the Equator which Japan had conquered, in return for Japan's support of Australia's claim to German New Guinea and its eastern islands and New Zealand's claim to German Samoa.

> What, according to Source R, was agreed upon by the Allies during the First World War? ❓

The creation of the mandate system

← What was the purpose of the mandate system?

Wartime agreements between the Allies promised lands to Italy, France, Britain and Zionists, who wanted to establish a Jewish homeland. These promises, mostly made in secret during the war and clearly seen as prizes by the victors for winning the war, were revealed in Paris in 1919. Awkwardly,

US President Wilson had called for the settlement of colonial claims and for people to have the right to determine their own government (see page 15). Secret agreements were also condemned, further embarrassing the USA's European allies.

Britain and its Dominions, nor France or Japan had no intention of giving up these new acquisitions, especially to each other, but needed to mollify the USA in some way. It was decided, after extremely difficult negotiations, to place the newly conquered lands under the supervision of the League of Nations as mandates. These mandates, organized into three different classes, would then be assigned to the powers that now claimed, and occupied, them. They would be subject to periodic League review.

Classes of mandates

The three classes, A, B and C, indicated each mandate's readiness for independence, with Class A being the most ready. **Mandatory powers** were required to send in annual reports on their territories to the League's Permanent Mandates Commission, which rapidly gained a formidable reputation for its expertise and authority. The Commission had no powers other than to gather data and send reports to other divisions of the League of Nations, so the mandatories managed their mandates in whatever way they determined was best, regardless of the League's regulations. Britain and France were each determined to have their mandates in the Classes B and C, while trying to force the other's possessions into Class A in an obvious attempt to hold on to and exploit their possessions for as long as possible.

SOURCE S

Article 22, *Covenant of the League of Nations, Treaty of Versailles,* 1919.

To those colonies and territories, which as a consequence of the late war have ceased to be under the sovereignty of the states which have formerly governed them, and which are inhabited by peoples not yet able to stand by themselves under the strenuous conditions of the modern world, there should be applied the principle that the well-being and development of such peoples should form a sacred trust of civilisation, and that securities for the performance of this trust should be embodied in this Covenant.

? Why, according to Source S, will some colonies and territories be ruled by other nations?

What challenges faced France and Britain in the Middle East mandates?

→ # Dividing up the Middle East

SOURCE T

Excerpt from *Paris 1919: Six Months that Changed the World* by Margaret MacMillan, published by Random House, New York, USA, 2003, p. 216. MacMillan is a professor of history at University of Toronto, Canada.

One day during the Peace Conference, Arnold Toynbee, an adviser to the British delegation, had to deliver some papers to the prime minister. Lloyd George, to my delight, had forgotten my presence and had begun to think aloud. 'Mesopotamia

… yes … oil … irrigation … we must have Mesopotamia; Palestine … yes … the Holy Land … Zionism … we must have Palestine; Syria … h'm … what is there in Syria? Let the French have that.' Thus the lineaments of the peace settlement in the Middle East were exposed: Britain seizing its chance; the need to throw something to the French; a homeland for the Jews; oil; and the calm assumption that the peacemakers could dispose of the former Ottoman territories to suit themselves. For the Arab Middle East, the peace settlements were the old nineteenth-century imperialism again. Britain and France got away with it – temporarily – because the United States did not choose to involve itself and because Arab nationalism was not yet strong enough to challenge them.

How, according to Source T, was the Middle East divided between France and Britain? **?**

Secret agreements in the Middle East

There were many secret promises that needed to be sorted through concerning the Middle East. McMahon, the British High Commissioner in Egypt, had essentially promised the majority of the Middle East, except for Egypt and parts of today's Syria, to the family of the Sharif of Mecca, Hussein bin Ali in 1915. The intention was to make a large Arab, independent kingdom at the expense of the Ottomans that the British would be happy to supply money and weapons if the revolt would begin; it did in 1916.

Meanwhile, the British and French made the Sykes–Picot Agreement in 1916 dividing up the Middle East into areas of direct and indirect control for each of them, including areas they had recently promised to the Arabs. To complicate the situation further, British Foreign Minister Balfour made the Balfour Declaration in 1917, a statement that the British government would support in some way the establishment of a Jewish state in Palestine, to the delight of Zionists in Europe. This again seemed to contradict promises made to Arab allies who helped the British conquer much of the Middle East.

Middle East divided

Earlier agreements with the Arabs were essentially ignored and the British and French worked to clearly divide the territory between them. It was determined, after many months of haggling, that former parts of the Ottoman Empire, which were highly developed in terms of governance, would need only a short period of time to transition into independent states. Britain and France, supposedly, were to only help develop governing structures and to advise the local government. These mandates were supposed to be able to determine their laws and policies as well. The Class A mandates for Britain were Mesopotamia, today's Iraq, and Palestine, today's Israel, Palestine and Jordan; Trans-Jordan, mostly today's Jordan, was separated from the rest of Palestine in 1922 and treated as a separate mandate thereafter. France's Class A mandate was Syria, which later became the countries of Syria and Lebanon. The only truly independent Arab-led state was the Kingdom of the Hejaz in the western area of today's Saudi Arabia. It was ruled by Hussein bin Ali, and was allowed its independence

principally because no European nation saw any value in it as it had no
known resources in 1920 and its population was less than one million people
with few towns and no development.

SOURCE U

**Excerpt from *The Creation of Iraq, 1914–1921* by Reeva Spector Simon,
published by Columbia University Press, USA, 2004, pp. 117–18. Simon is
a researcher at the Middle East Institute of Columbia University.**

*… they insisted on keeping all territories such as Mosul, which were 'inhabited
by an Ottoman Moslem majority.' The majority of the population of this northern
province were in fact Kurds and there was also a significant Turkoman minority.
Clearly, neither of these groups were Arabs ethnically or linguistically. The
Turkish nationalists insisted, however, that the Kurds did not represent a distinct
non-Turkish national or ethnic group. The Turkish nationals at the time referred
to the Kurds who lived in the mountainous areas along the southern regions of
the Ottoman Empire and northern Iraq as 'Mountain Turks.' The British insisted
that Mosul be part of Iraq to enable modern Iraq to possess the means to pay
for the cost of the British Mandate expenses and also to provide oil for transport
and industry.*

In the mandates of Mesopotamia and Trans-Jordan, the British installed two
sons of the Sharif of Mecca, Faisal and Abdullah, as kings, while in Palestine
a British High Commissioner ruled. Mesopotamia and Trans-Jordan were
relatively stable, if without any real independence from British control. In
1932 Mesopotamia became Iraq and independent, although Britain had
long-term leases which allowed them to continue exploiting and exporting
oil. Iraq was the only mandate to achieve at least nominal independence
before the Second World War.

Palestine

SOURCE V

**Excerpt from 'The Arab–Israeli conflict' by Scott B. Lasensky, published in
The Middle East, eleventh edition, by Congressional Quarterly Press,
Washington, DC, USA, 2007, pp. 45–6. Lasensky is a considered a US
foreign policy expert and has taught at Georgetown University and
Mount Holyoke College, researched for the United States Institute of
Peace, the Brookings Institution, and the Council on Foreign Relations.**

*In Jerusalem in August 1929, a major outbreak of Arab–Jewish violence erupted
around the Western Wall, or Wailing Wall, sparked by increasing Arab fears
about Jewish intentions and newly acquired Zionist confidence and public
displays of political power. The violence then spread to other parts of Palestine
and led the British government to take another look at its policy in the region.
Two investigative reports – the Shaw Report of March 1930 and the Hope
Simpson Report of May 1930 – concluded that insufficient attention was being
paid to the second half of Britain's obligations under its mandate charter,
namely 'ensuring the rights and positions' of the 'non-Jewish communities' of*

According to Source U, why
did the British include the
Mosul area with the rest of
Iraq although it was not
inhabited by many Arabs?

What, according to Source V,
was the main issue that
caused the British problems
in Palestine?

Palestine that remained the majority of the population although waves of Jewish immigration increasingly undermined their demographic strength. Both reports recommended restrictions on Jewish immigration and limitations on future land transfers to 'non-Arabs.' ... This ... provoked a political furor in England ...

What remained of the Palestine mandate after 1922 divided into two camps: primarily urban, prosperous European Jews and agricultural native Arabs, both Christian and Muslim. Violence broke out on many occasions between the two groups, often targeting the British officials as well. The British refused to develop governing institutions, in violation of their mandate agreement, since the Arabs, as a majority, would oppose Zionist immigration legally. Foreign investment poured into Jewish businesses and areas, while investment in Arab businesses and schools paled in comparison, although they too showed great progress compared to the Ottoman era. Jewish immigration would increase dramatically in the years before and during the Second World War leading to increased hostilities. Israel would eventually be proclaimed in 1948 as a Jewish state, leaving Palestinian Arabs essentially stateless.

SOURCE W

Excerpt from The League of Nations' The Mandate of Palestine, 24 July 1922.

Article 2.

The Mandatory shall be responsible for placing the country under such political, administrative and economic conditions as will secure the establishment of the Jewish national home, as laid down in the preamble, and the development of self-governing institutions, and also for safeguarding the civil and religious rights of all the inhabitants of Palestine, irrespective of race and religion.

Article 3.

The Mandatory shall, so far as circumstances permit, encourage local autonomy.

Article 4.

An appropriate Jewish agency shall be recognised as a public body for the purpose of advising and co-operating with the Administration of Palestine in such economic, social and other matters as may affect the establishment of the Jewish national home and the interests of the Jewish population in Palestine, and, subject always to the control of the Administration, to assist and take part in the development of the country.

> What, according to Source W, was the role of a Jewish agency for the administration of Palestine?

Syria

The French ruled Syria through a military officer and soon divided their mandate into six states partly in order to divide opposition to their rule. This did not prevent serious revolts breaking out against the French on several occasions. Instability in Syria continued until its independence after the Second World War. Although politically unstable, Syria developed economically with railroads, roads and harbours constructed.

SOURCE X

? What is the value of Source X for historians?

'**The Syria and The Lebanon. The country of tourism and resorts.**'
A 1920s travel advertisement.

LA SYRIE et LE LIBAN
PAYS DE TOURISME et DE VILLÉGIATURE

To what extent did European powers develop their mandates towards self-rule?

Class B mandates in Africa

Class B mandates were those that would need major assistance from their mandatories and all had been part of the German Empire in Africa. They would be able to achieve independence in the future, but for the moment would be almost completely controlled and administered by the mandatory. The mandatories were to build national institutions and gradually bring local residents into government. Ruanda-Urundi, today's countries of Rwanda and Burundi, was mandated to Belgium in 1922. Tanganyika was a British mandate starting in 1922 and would eventually form the majority of Tanzania. Cameroun, today's Cameroon, was divided between the British and French in 1922, along with Togoland, which would eventually become parts of Ghana and the country of Togo.

A German poster of 1922 concerning French rule of the former German colony of Togoland.

What was the purpose and message of Source Y?

Ruanda-Urundi

The Belgians required that any development of Ruanda-Urundi be paid for by the people of Ruanda-Urundi. The people were heavily taxed, with the majority of funds raised sent back to Belgium to pay for the administration of Ruanda-Urundi. This translated into little development in terms of education, infrastructure or economics. The Belgians did give some authority to the Tutsi ethnic group, a small minority, to rule over the Hutu majority. This division of society would contribute to warfare between the groups throughout much of the twentieth century.

Limited development of African mandates

French and British rule in Africa concentrated on improvements in healthcare and infrastructure, to develop the economies of their mandates. The building of roads and railroads tended to benefit European farmers who settled in the mandates more than the local populations. Both nations treated mandates as they would their other colonies and non-native African populations, again, primarily benefited. In Tanganyika, for example, a Legislative Council was founded to help rule the mandate, yet only resident Arabs, Indians and Europeans were allowed to join. Years later, native Africans were allowed to observe and participate, but not vote. The French tended to rule more directly and require French law and language to be used in schools and administration. Both the French and British improved education, built hospitals and developed agriculture, but even these efforts were limited. The education budget for all Tanganyika in 1935, for example, was only $300,000. In both cases, little effort was made towards the mandates gaining independence or towards developing economies that benefited native Africans.

SOURCE Z

According to Source Z, how did the Belgian mandate of Ruanda-Urundi compare with the British mandate of Tanganyika and the British colony of Kenya?

Excerpt from *Mandates under the League of Nations* by Quincy Wright, published by University of Chicago Press, USA, 1930, pp. 569–71. Wright established the first doctoral programme in the USA for international relations at the University of Chicago and authored over ten books on international politics.

All the African mandates areas showed trade increases from 1921 to 1926, and the exports and imports nearly balanced with the exception of British Togoland whose exports were four times her imports. In per capita foreign trade these territories varied greatly; Southwest Africa ranked near the top of Africa south of the Sahara, $100, compared to $103 for South Africa, $83 for Zanzibar, and $54 for Southern Rhodesia. Ruanda-Urundi, on the other hand, had the lowest, $0.18 … Tanganyika with $7 was considerably below Kenya with $19 and Uganda with $13 but above Mozambique with $6, Nyasaland and Northern Rhodesia with $5 …

Another way to review the development of mandates under Britain, France and Belgium is to review the amount of money invested in various projects such as building infrastructure and the emigration of Europeans. From 1921 until 1930, the total amount of funds invested was approximately $20,000,000, mostly loans. By contrast, the Germans had invested $7,500,000 per year from the mid-1880s until the outbreak of the First World War, equivalent to $75,000,000 every ten years. Historians have noted a remarkable increase of European settlement in mandate territory in the 1920s. While this may have been the result of economic difficulties in Europe, it may also demonstrate a political reality that mandates were truly seen as colonies.

SOURCE AA

Which mandates experienced the largest amounts of European immigration between 1921 and 1927 according to Source AA?

Excerpt from *Mandates under the League of Nations* by Quincy Wright, published by University of Chicago Press, USA, 1930, p. 551. Wright established the first doctoral programme in the US for international relations at the University of Chicago and authored over ten books on international politics.

In most of these territories [in Africa] an increase in the non-native population is noticed from 1921 to 1927: French Cameroons, 200 per cent; French Togoland,

100 per cent; British Cameroons, 300 per cent, Ruanda-Urundi, 350 per cent; Southwest Africa, 24 per cent … Impartial investigators are fairly unanimous that white settlement is disastrous for the native, and it appears that the British proposals for an East African federation including Tanganyika has the object of stimulating white settlement …

Class C mandates in the Pacific and southern Africa

← **How were Class C mandates affected by their mandatories?**

Class C mandates were territories that were not expected to gain independence in the foreseeable future. Class C mandates were to be ruled as if they were colonies, as they had been when they were part of the German Empire. British Dominion Australia was made the mandatory of New Guinea in 1920, while it administered Nauru for Britain. British Dominion New Zealand took control of Western Samoa, while Japan was granted the South Sea mandate, a wide swathe of islands east of the Philippines and north of New Guinea in the Pacific. The only non-Pacific Ocean Class C mandate was German South West Africa, today's Namibia, which was granted to the British Dominion of South Africa.

Economic exploitation

Class C mandates contained vast resources, but few people. Nauru, for example, was a large island with just over 3000 people and New Guinea, one of the largest islands in the world at 240,000 sq km, had a population estimated to be around 500,000. The Japanese mandate consisted of hundreds of islands with few people, giving Japan control of mineral and fishing rights over a vast territory. South West Africa had a population under 300,000, but over 800,000 sq km of territory. There was practically no development of local government, but investments were made in developing export industries, limited education and healthcare, similar to the Class B mandates. Primarily Class C mandates were exploited economically by the country which administered them with little to no regard for native populations.

SOURCE BB

Excerpt from *Mandates under the League of Nations* by Quincy Wright, published by University of Chicago Press, USA, 1930, p. 566. Wright established the first doctoral programme in the US for international relations at the University of Chicago and authored over ten books on international politics.

The phosphate concession in Nauru is virtually the government itself, which may render its influence all the more dangerous, and the same is true of the government-operated ex-enemy estates in New Guinea and Western Samoa. Such concessions, unless carefully regulated, instead of developing the country may milk it, and instead of benefiting the native may enslave him …

According to Source BB, what was the danger that many Class C mandates faced? ?

Nauru, an island rich in phosphates, was strip mined during the mandate era. This led the island, with such a small local population, to have the highest per capita income of any mandate and perhaps of most other territories in the world. This did not translate into political or economic power since most profits went to Australia and Britain, with the mining company essentially running the island's government. New Guinea's development was severely limited by the fact that the Australian government refused investment, determining that any funds used for development had to come from New Guinea itself. This was much the same for Western Samoa.

SOURCE CC

What does Source CC suggest about the mandate of New Guinea under Australian rule?

A photograph of a European or Australian man and woman with New Guinean guide in the 1920s.

All the Pacific mandates increased their exports dramatically as a result of the mandatory powers mining, logging, fishing and generally using their newly acquired territories as sources of raw material. There was little interest in improving the lives of local populations who usually provided manual labour and little else to foreign-owned enterprises.

SOURCE DD

According to Source DD, why were Class C mandates in the Pacific region valuable?

Excerpt from *Mandates under the League of Nations* by Quincy Wright, published by University of Chicago Press, USA, 1930, p. 571. Wright established the first doctoral programme in the USA for international relations at the University of Chicago and authored over ten books on international politics.

The Pacific mandated territories, with the exception of Western Samoa, showed substantial increases of trade between 1920 and 1925. Nauru and New Guinea each increased its exports by 80 per cent though the imports were fairly constant *while the Japanese mandated islands more than tripled their imports, the exports increasing about 50 per cent ... Nauru, with its valuable phosphate deposits and small population, had a per capita trade of $1,100, Western Samoa followed with $74, the Northern Pacific islands with $46, and New Guinea with $19.*

Colonization by mandatories

The Japanese settled large numbers of Japanese, Koreans and Taiwanese people on islands in their mandate. This was partly to ease population pressures in other parts of the Japanese Empire. It had the added benefit of potentially making the islands too Japanese to be easily granted independence in the future. South West Africa, ruled by South Africa, suffered from rebellions by native Africans as European settlers, including Germans who had moved there when it had been part of the German Empire, received special privileges and self-governance. The South African government seized farmlands from native Africans and encouraged South Africans of European descent to settle in the region.

SOURCE EE

Excerpt from *Namibia's Liberation Struggle: The Two-Edged Sword* by Colin Leys and John S. Saul, published by Ohio University Press, USA, 1995, p. 9. Leys has worked for universities in the UK, Uganda, Tanzania, Kenya and Canada. His numerous books include studies of African and British history and politics.

In 1915 South African forces fighting on the British side in the First World War seized control of South West Africa from Germany, and in 1920 South Africa assumed a mandate for the territory under the League of Nations. German settlers were largely replaced by Afrikaner settlers, and the process of evicting Namibians from the highlands was resumed ...

The German policy of violent repression was continued under South African rule: at various times between 1917 and 1932 the Kwanyama-speaking and Kuambi-speaking Ovambo in the north, and the Bondelswart and Rehobothers in the south, were all disciplined through punitive expeditions.

According to Source EE, how did South Africa treat the native people of South West Africa?

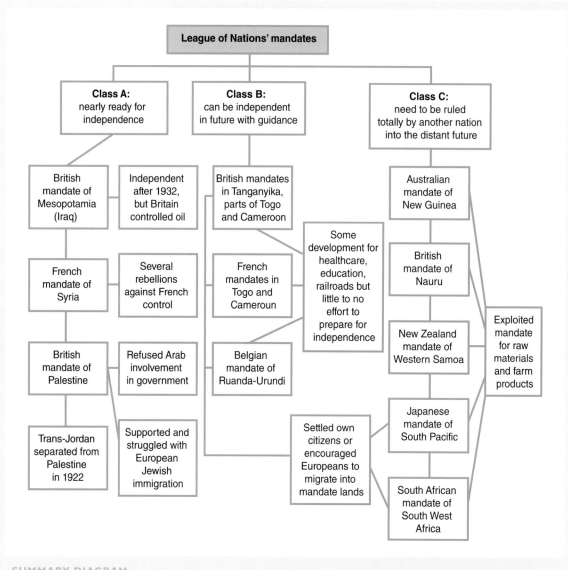

League of Nations' mandates

Class A: nearly ready for independence

Class B: can be independent in future with guidance

Class C: need to be ruled totally by another nation into the distant future

British mandate of Mesopotamia (Iraq)

Independent after 1932, but Britain controlled oil

British mandates in Tanganyika, parts of Togo and Cameroon

Australian mandate of New Guinea

French mandate of Syria

Several rebellions against French control

French mandates in Togo and Cameroun

Some development for healthcare, education, railroads but little to no effort to prepare for independence

British mandate of Nauru

British mandate of Palestine

Refused Arab involvement in government

Belgian mandate of Ruanda-Urundi

New Zealand mandate of Western Samoa

Exploited mandate for raw materials and farm products

Trans-Jordan separated from Palestine in 1922

Supported and struggled with European Jewish immigration

Settled own citizens or encouraged Europeans to migrate into mandate lands

Japanese mandate of South Pacific

South African mandate of South West Africa

⑤ Key Debate

▶ **Key question:** *Why did the British promise a Jewish homeland in Palestine?*

In the midst of the First World War, the British government issued the Balfour Declaration which promised a Jewish homeland in the Ottoman region called Palestine. The consequences of this declaration continue today. Historians continue to debate the actual reasons for the Balfour Declaration.

Some historians see the Balfour Declaration as the result of the romantic views of Arthur Balfour, the British Foreign Secretary. Balfour, according to historian Margaret MacMillan, had stated that he saw Jews as a powerful source of political and religious conservatism in the world. He may have also believed the nineteenth-century idea that spreading the British Empire brought civilization and order to a chaotic and primitive world. Inserting European Jews into what was perceived to be a less politically and economically developed region, at least along European lines, was an extension of this idea. In the Balfour Declaration, Balfour did indicate that there were non-Jews living in Palestine without mentioning anyone specifically or reference to the size of the population. For whatever reason, he was relatively unconcerned or interested in the native population of Palestine. Many British diplomats at the Paris Peace Conference in 1919 assumed that few to no people actually lived in Palestine at all.

SOURCE FF

Excerpt from *Paris 1919: Six Months that Changed the World* by Margaret MacMillan, published by Random House, New York, USA, 2003, p. 420. MacMillan is a professor of history at University of Toronto, Canada.

The Balfour Declaration had promised such protection for what it called 'the existing non-Jewish communities in Palestine,' a curious formulation when Palestinian Arabs, most of them Muslim but including some Christians, made up about four fifths of a population of some 700,000. It also reflected a tendency on the part of both the world's statesmen and Zionist leaders to see Palestine as somehow empty. 'If the Zionists do not go there,' said Sykes firmly, 'someone will; nature abhors a vacuum.' A British Zionist is supposed to have coined the phrase 'The land without people – for the people without land.'

What was ironic, according to Source FF, about Balfour's statement on non-Jewish people in Palestine?

Some historians believe that persecutions against Jews in Europe, primarily in Russia in the late nineteenth and early twentieth centuries, led to western European sympathy. In this line of thought, the creation of a Jewish homeland, wherever that might be, could be a refuge for eastern European Jews escaping from discrimination and violence.

Other historians believe that there was no real deep belief or interest in Zionism by non-Jewish politicians in western Europe. Zionism was instead seen as a useful tool for foreign diplomacy by both Germany and Britain with absolutely no regard for the consequences for the inhabitants of Palestine or even for Zionists who would settle there. The British may have been interested in creating a pro-British European colony in Palestine to protect the Suez Canal from the French who had recently been promised Syria in the Sykes–Picot Agreement (see page 157).

SOURCE GG

Excerpt from *From Sarajevo to Potsdam* by A.J.P. Taylor, published by Thames & Hudson, London, UK, 1966, p. 53. Taylor was a British historian who wrote many books on European history and was lecturer at many British universities.

In November 1917, the British government announced that Palestine was to provide a national home for the Jews. Their immediate aim was to win Jewish support for the Allied cause and, rather more urgently, to devise an excuse for keeping the French at a safe distance from the Suez Canal. The British did not weigh seriously the effects of their promise. In particular, they did not contemplate how Jews could be settled in Palestine without disturbing the existing Arab population. The consequences were, however, remarkable. Though often persecuted, the Jews had been embedded for centuries past in the societies of many European countries and, despite their difference in religion and customs, sometimes as much at home there as any other inhabitants. Now the Jews were being invited to become an ordinary nation like the Irish or the Poles. Most of the Jews who returned to Palestine were Europeans in nearly everything, and their community became a piece of Europe inserted into Asia – a twentieth-century version of the Crusader states.

According to Source GG, what was the main reason the British supported a Jewish homeland in Palestine?

Both Germany and Britain were interested in using Zionism to their own benefit. It was believed by both Germany and Britain that Zionists were politically powerful in the USA and that support for Zionism might, in the case of Germany, lead to less support for Britain from the USA and perhaps ensure US neutrality in the war. The British believed that if they supported Zionism, US Zionists might help bring the USA into the First World War on the side of Britain. The USA entered the war in early 1917 before either Germany or Britain would declare open support for Zionism and a Jewish homeland, ending these arguments.

SOURCE HH

Excerpt from *Reshaping Palestine: From Muhammad Ali to the British Mandate, 1831–1922* by Martin Sicker, published by Praeger, Connecticut, USA, 1999, p. 123. Sicker is a lecturer of Middle East and Jewish history and religion and has taught at the American University and George Washington University in the USA.

On March 11, 1916, Grey [British Foreign Secretary] sent a message to the allied governments that alluded to the significant benefits that might be realized in

According to Source HH, why did Britain support a Jewish homeland in Palestine?

terms of Jewish support for the war effort in the still-neutral United States. These could be realized if only the allied governments would give their stamp of approval to some arrangement that would be supportive of Jewish colonization in Palestine.

A stronger argument along these lines is that the British feared the creation of a Jewish homeland in Palestine allied to Germany. Germany was interested in the possibility of using Zionism to weaken Russia in the midst of the First World War. The creation of a Zionist state in Palestine beholden to Germany would threaten the Suez Canal and therefore the connection between Britain and its all-important possessions in India and east Africa, severing trade links to China and other lands in the process.

SOURCE II

Excerpt from *Reshaping Palestine: From Muhammad Ali to the British Mandate, 1831–1922* by Martin Sicker, published by Praeger, Connecticut, USA, 1999, p. 116. Sicker is a lecturer of Middle East and Jewish history and religion and has taught at the American University and George Washington University in the USA.

… the German government came to believe that the Zionist Organization could be used as an instrument to further German strategic interests. Indeed, some influential officials were convinced that the Zionist movement was sufficiently powerful in Eastern Europe to be able to have significant impact on Russia's ability to prosecute the war. Thus, one report to the German high command predicted that the Zionist Organization, in Germany's hands, 'would be able to provide information on all political and military events in enemy countries and, should we avail ourselves of its useful intelligence and guidance, we might reduce substantially the heavy losses of our forces.' Another report suggested that since 'all supplies of cereal and livestock for the Russian Army are delivered by Jewish middlemen, so we have in the Zionists an effective means to impede the catering and the operation of the Russian Army.' It was also believed by some German officials that the Zionists could be used to influence international Jewish opinion in the West in a way that would tend to reduce the popularity of waging a war against Germany.

According to this source, why did German government want to support Zionism?

There were many reasons for Europeans to support Zionism and its goal of a national homeland in Palestine for European Jews. Whatever the reasons, it is clear that the Balfour Declaration had a major impact on Palestine. The British had made apparently conflicting promises to the Arabs and Zionists, while also making promises to France while also working against the French. Britain hoped to use Zionism, as it also used the Arabs, against the Ottoman Empire and was not alone in its desire to manipulate Zionist desires. Britain raced against Germany to formulate a pro-Zionist stance, winning with the Balfour Declaration. Ironically, the declaration only brought difficulties to the British. According to historian R.J. Overy, Britain had more troops in Palestine in the mid-1930s suppressing violence between European Jews and Arab Palestinians than they had on hand to send to France in case war broke out with Germany over the reoccupation of the Rhineland.

TOK: Historians use evidence to make arguments. What gives evidence value and makes it convincing? (History, Ethics, Language, Emotion and Reason.)

Chapter summary

International diplomacy and the League of Nations

Failure of the USA to end its traditional semi-isolated stance in international diplomacy, especially where European powers were concerned, led to Britain and France reverting to their traditional stances as well. Dominating the League of Nations, they preferred the Conference of Ambassadors to handle major issues of diplomacy, sending to the League minor disputes to resolve. While the League had notable successes, it failed to achieve any significant disarmament partly as a result of France's determination to prevent any future attack by maintaining a large army and building military alliances throughout Europe. What disarmament did take place, and other efforts to prevent war, mostly occurred outside the League. The USA, Britain, Japan and others made major progress for a decade in limiting the construction of ships of war, including battleships and aircraft carriers, with limited success regarding smaller vessels.

Among the League's many tasks was the supervision of mandates, as the new colonies of the British Empire, France and Japan were now named. Supervision consisted of annual reports submitted by the rulers of the mandates who treated most of the mandates as they would their other colonies. The mandatories were to build their mandates so that one day they could be independent nations, but this League requirement was simply ignored in all but two or three mandates. The only mandate to achieve independence more or less was Iraq. Perhaps the most problematic mandate was Palestine which, as the result of promises made during the First World War, saw major European Jewish immigration which caused friction with those already living there. Palestine was not alone in terms of violence uprisings, as they also occurred in Syria and South West Africa as well. Yet, the problems created by British administration of Palestine are ones that continue in that area today.

Examination advice

Paper 1 question 3: origin, purpose, value and limitations (OPVL)

Question 3 on the IB History Diploma examination requires to you to discuss the origin and purpose of two sources and then to use that information to determine each source's potential value and limitations. The question always asks you to refer to the origin and purpose of two named sources to assess their value and limitations for historians. Unlike questions 1 and 2, some knowledge of the topic, value of types of sources, or authors can be useful, although this is not required.

Question 3 is worth 6 marks out of the 25 total for Paper 1. This means it is worth 24 per cent of your overall mark. Answering question 3 should take approximately ten minutes of your examination time.

How to answer

Read question 3 carefully. You will notice that it is asking you to discuss the origins and purpose of two different sources and then to determine the value and limitations for these two sources for historians. This question is not like question 2; you must treat each source separately. The first source mentioned in the question should be the one you start with and it should be in its own paragraph, with the second source treated in the second paragraph. At no point should you compare or contrast the sources or discuss them in the same paragraph.

Structure will help you in answering the question. Incorporate the words origin, purpose, value and limitation into your answer. 'The origin of Source B is ...', 'the purpose of Source B is ...', 'the value of this source is ...' and 'a limitation of this source may be ...'. This keeps you focused on the task, making sure you covered all the required elements, but also helps the examiner understand your answers by providing a framework that they can follow.

It is important to remember that you are to use the origins and purpose to determine the value and limitations. The actual text of the source is not to be used as it is just an excerpt from a much larger work.

Origin

The origin of a source is the author, the type of publication, the year it was published, and sometimes the country it originates from. If there is biographical information included as part of the source's introduction, this may also be used in addressing the source's origin.

Purpose

The purpose of a source is usually indicated by the source's title, the type of source, the writer or speaker, if it is a speech, or the location of the source, such as in a newspaper, an academic book or a journal. Purposes can range from speeches that try to convince certain groups or nations that what the speaker is saying is the truth or should be heeded, to explaining the history of a certain time period. If a book's title is 'The League of Nations and the Mandate of Palestine' the purpose of this particular source is likely to explain the League of Nation's work in the mandate of Palestine. If the author of this source is British, it may be that the purpose is to explain British policy in Palestine, to convince the reader that the British government's policies in Palestine were the best it could manage in a tough situation, and so forth. If the source's author is an Israeli academic, then the purpose could very well be to convince the reader that Zionism improved Palestine or perhaps something else. Since this is a hypothesis on your part, be sure to include the words 'perhaps' or 'possibly'. In order to determine the purpose or purposes of a source, be sure to read the title, the date of publication, the name of the author and any biographical information given.

Value

The value of a source flows naturally from the origins and purpose. Perhaps a book exists that is titled 'The League of Nations and the Mandate of Palestine' and was written by a Palestinian leader during the 1920s. The value will be that this leader probably witnessed or participated in certain events, perhaps experienced the effects of European immigration into the region, and may have even met prominent British or Zionist officials. This would give the author first-hand knowledge of the mandate of Palestine. If the author lived 50 years after the mandate of Palestine ended, a value could be that the writer has access to Israeli, Arab and British sources, may be less connected and therefore less emotional about the subject and therefore more objective, or perhaps is able to better determine the long-term impact of the mandate of Palestine on international relations. Your answer will have to be determined by the origin and purpose of the source you are asked to discuss. Do not state primary sources have more value than secondary sources; this is not necessarily true.

Limitation

The limitation of a source is determined in much the same way that you determined the source's value. If the writer of 'The League of Nations and the Mandate of Palestine' is an Israeli, the writer is likely to have more access to Israeli sources than Arab ones. This would be a limitation in that the author is *possibly* unable to present a truly balanced view of some aspects of Palestine when it was a mandate. Other than the author's nationality, there may be other ways to determine possible limitations:

- the title of the source may be of a limited nature or too broad for the topic
- the date of publication may be limiting if it is too close or far from the historical events
- a source that is political in nature may be trying to advocate a certain view or policy instead of being objective.

Do not state that sources are limited because they are secondary sources; this may not be true and often is not.

Visual images

Visual sources will have information explaining to you their origin. Remember that photographs can capture a single moment in time so that they can show exactly what happened, but they can also be staged to send a particular message. A photograph of smiling Africans in mandate Ruanda-Urundi captures a moment when they were either genuinely happy or told to smile, perhaps not knowing even what they were smiling about. Cartoons, posters and even photographs often have a political message. The purpose of any of these could potentially be to convince the viewer of a certain point of view. Another purpose could be to make fun of a particular idea or person for some other reason. Apply analytical skills from Chapter 3 if appropriate.

Example

This question uses Sources B and E found in this chapter on pages 134 and 138.

> With reference to their origins and purpose, discuss the value and limitations of Sources B and E for historians studying the early work of the League of Nations.

You will immediately turn to Source B and read that it is an article in a journal written in 1920. There is no need to brainstorm or outline for this question, so go to your examination paper and start writing. Below is a sample answer to this question.

The origin of Source B is a journal article titled 'The League of Nations is alive' by Raymond Fosdick published in 1920 in the **Atlantic**, *a political and foreign affairs journal in the USA.*

> The terms origin, purpose, value and limitation are used throughout both paragraphs.

The purpose of the article is to explain the important work of the League of Nations in 1920. Another purpose of the article may be to advocate the League's work in the USA since the article was written in June 1920, after the US government refused to join the organization or sign the Treaty of Versailles which contained the League's Covenant.

A value of this source may be that it was written during the first year of the League of Nation's existence, so the author may have witnessed the League's work or was able to actually see positive results of its efforts. Another value may be that since Fosdick was considered an important American leader, as he was President of the prestigious Rockefeller Foundation after 1921, it may show that there was substantial support in the USA in 1920 for the League of Nations and its work.

> Each source is discussed in its own paragraph and nowhere is there comparison or contrasting of the two sources.

A limitation of Source B may be that Fosdick is using the article to encourage the USA to join the League of Nations since the article's title, 'The League of Nations is alive', shows that he supports the League's work. He may be ignoring the fact that the League in 1920 made very little impact on international diplomacy and was certainly not achieving all the US President Wilson had hoped in 1919. Another limitation may be that since the article was written in 1920, the League had only begun to operate, so any major successes that Fosdick may have indicated would probably have lacked much impact or evidence of their success at this time.

> More than one value or limitation was found for each of the sources based on the origin and purpose.

The origin of Source E is an excerpt from **The League of Nations: Its Life and Times 1920–46**, *written by F.S. Northedge, a professor of international relations in Britain, in 1986.*

> The title of each source and its author are clearly stated, as is the year of publication.

The purpose of Northedge's book is to discuss the League of Nations from its beginning until its end in 1946.

A value of Source E is that Northedge is an established professor at the London School of Economics and has written many other books on

Use of the words 'may be' and 'perhaps' are appropriately used since the value and limitations are based on hypotheses.

international relations, indicating that he is an expert in his field. Another value of Source E may be that since it was written 40 years after the end of the League of Nations, Northedge has access to the League's archives, the work of other researchers, and can assess the long-term impact of the League on international diplomacy.

*A limitation of Source E **may be** that since the author is British, he may be primarily interested in the League's effect on British policy or rely more heavily on British sources to evaluate the League's success.*

Answer indicates that the demands of the question were understood. Both sources assessed. There is clear discussion of the origins, purpose, value and limitations of both sources, often with multiple examples. Mark: 6/6.

 Examination practice

The following are exam-style questions for you to practise, using sources from this chapter. Sources can be found on the following pages:

- Source A (page 133)
- Source D (page 137)
- Source M (page 151)
- Source O (page 152)
- Source P (page 153)
- Source Q (page 154)
- Source R (page 155)
- Source T (page 156)
- Source AA (page 162)
- Source EE (page 165)

1 With reference to their origin and purpose, assess the value and limitations of Sources A and D for historians studying problems of the League of Nations in its first years.

2 With reference to their origin and purpose, assess the value and limitations of Sources M and O for historians studying disarmament efforts after the First World War.

3 With reference to their origin and purpose, assess the value and limitations of Sources P and Q for historians studying disarmament before the Second World War.

4 With reference to their origin and purpose, assess the value and limitations of Sources R and T for historians studying the creation of the mandate system of the League of Nations.

5 With reference to their origin and purpose, assess the value and limitations of Sources AA and EE for historians studying the mandate system of the League of Nations.

Extended examination practice

Sample question 1s

For guidance on how to answer this type of question see pages 29–30 and 122–8.

Sources can be found on the following pages:

- Source A (page 133)
- Source B (page 134)
- Source E (page 138)
- Source H (page 143)
- Source I (page 144)

1 What, according to Source A, was the importance of France for Poland after the First World War?

2 Why, according to Source B, is the League of Nations important for the world?

3 Why, according to Source E, was the League of Nations weak?

4 What was the importance of the Corfu settlement on international diplomacy according to Source H?

5 How effective was the League of Nations' International Labour Organization according to Source I?

Visual sources

For guidance on how to answer this type of question see page 29.

Sources can be found on the following pages:

1 What is the message conveyed by Source D on page 137?

2 What is the message conveyed by Source G on page 140?

3 What is the message conveyed by Source N on page 152?

4 What is the message conveyed by Source X on page 160?

5 What is the message conveyed by Source Y on page 161?

Sample question 2s

For guidance on how to answer this type of question see pages 65–8.

Sources can be found on the following pages:

- Source B (page 134)
- Source E (page 138)
- Source G (page 140)
- Source H (page 143)
- Source R (page 155)
- Source T (page 156)
- Source Y (page 161)
- Source AA (page 162)
- Source CC (page 164)
- Source DD (page 164)

1 Compare and contrast the views expressed in Sources B and E regarding the importance of the League of Nations.

2 Compare and contrast the views of Sources G and H regarding the success of the League of Nations in resolving international crises between 1920 and 1923.

3 Compare and contrast the views of Sources R and T regarding the creation of mandates in the Middle East.

4 Compare and contrast the views expressed by Sources Y and AA regarding the development of Class B mandates in Africa.

5 Compare and contrast the views expressed in Sources CC and DD regarding Class C mandates.

Sample question 3s

These questions use sources from earlier chapters to practise your skills at determining the value and limitations of sources based on their origin and purpose.

Chapter 1

Sources can be found on the following pages:

- Source A (page 10)
- Source B (page 11)
- Source F (page 20)
- Source H (page 22)

1 With reference to their origins and purpose, discuss the value and limitations of Sources F and H for historians studying French aims for the Paris Peace Conference in 1919.

2 With reference to their origins and purpose, discuss the value and limitations of Sources A and B for historians studying the context of the Paris Peace Conference in 1919.

Chapter 2

Sources can be found on the following pages:

- Source A (page 33)
- Source B (page 33)
- Source K (page 42)
- Source L (page 43)
- Source Q (page 48)
- Source R (page 48)

1 With reference to their origins and purpose, discuss the value and limitations of Sources A and B for historians studying the importance of the League of Nations for US President Woodrow Wilson.

2 With reference to their origins and purpose, discuss the value and limitations of Sources K and L for historians studying the disarmament of Germany after the First World War.

3 With reference to their origins and purpose, discuss the value and limitations of Sources Q and R for historians studying the impact of the Treaty of St Germain-en-Laye on Austria.

Chapter 3

Sources can be found on the following pages:

- Source D (page 77)
- Source E (page 77)
- Source AA (page 108)
- Source BB (page 109)

1 With reference to their origins and purpose, discuss the value and limitations of Sources D and E for historians studying the importance of the Treaty of Rapallo signed in 1922 by Germany and the Soviet Union.

2 With reference to their origins and purpose, discuss the value and limitations of Sources AA and BB for historians studying the importance of Admiral Horthy in Hungary after the First World War.

Activities

1 It helps to know some of the more familiar historians who have written extensively on the period 1918–36. Create a flashcard game with the name of a historian on one side and biographical information about the historian on the other side. You will find these historians throughout this book. Some of those historians might be Margaret MacMillan, P.M.H. Bell, Payson O'Brien, Quincy Wright, A.J.P. Taylor, as well as many others. Once you are familiar with their names and areas of expertise, you may wish to create another set of cards regarding their values and limitations based on their works, dates of publication and other factors to help you review further.

2 Create five Paper 1 question 3-type questions per chapter in this book:
   - each chapter's questions should be on a separate sheet of paper
   - exchange a single chapter's question 3s with your classmates
   - complete as homework
   - exchange answers with classmates and correct each other's work.

3 With the help of your teacher or school librarian, research the works of the authors you made flashcards for in activity 1. Create a list of some of the works of the authors you have chosen and then look online and on information databases your school may have for either the works themselves, or for reviews of them. Use this information to make a presentation to your classmates to add more information about the origins and purpose of the authors presented in this book.

CHAPTER 5

The Great Depression and threats to international peace and collective security

This chapter investigates international diplomacy from 1930 to 1936 in the context of the Great Depression. It examines the following key questions which you need to consider:

✪ What were the economic and political effects of the Great Depression?

✪ How significant was the Manchurian Crisis in world affairs?

✪ What role did the Abyssinian Crisis have in destroying the League of Nations' credibility?

✪ What were the main international agreements and diplomatic actions during the Great Depression?

The economic and political effects of the Great Depression

▶ **Key question:** *What were the economic and political effects of the Great Depression?*

🔑 KEY TERM

Wall Street Crash A rapid decline of the US stockmarket, located on Wall Street in New York, in October 1929 which led to an economic crisis.

The Great Depression, triggered by the **Wall Street Crash** in late 1929 in the USA, marked a turning point in interwar history. Not only did it weaken the economic and social stability of the world's major powers, but it also dealt a devastating blow to the progress made towards creating a new framework for peaceful international co-operation. It has been called by historian Robert Boyce 'the third global catastrophe of the century'along with the two world wars.

How did the Great Depression affect the economic policies of different countries?

Economic effects

Between 1929 and 1932 the volume of world trade fell by 70 per cent, leading to mass unemployment in most industrialized nations. By 1932, for example, Germany suffered from 26 per cent unemployment, with the USA, the world's largest economy, close behind with 25 per cent unemployment. The banking industry was in crisis and loans were recalled as stocks lost value and industry shrank. American banks called in the short-term loans they had granted to Germany in the 1920s on which much of its industrial recovery and expansion depended. Eventually banks started collapsing including 9000 in the USA alone during the 1930s.

Trade barriers

In order to keep money and investment within their own borders, most nations erected **trade barriers** by taxing imports, further hindering world trade and an economic recovery. US-erected trade barriers especially affected Japan and Germany, exporting nations that relied on the US market, causing a 50 per cent decline in Japanese heavy industry and mining and a 61 per cent decline in German industrial production overall. British international trade declined by 60 per cent and the United States, the largest importer of raw material and manufactured goods, saw its international trade retract by 70 per cent.

SOURCE A

The effect on unemployment and loss of trade of the Great Depression between 1929 and 1933. Statistics taken from *The Inter-War Crisis: 1919–1939*, second edition by R.J. Overy, published by Pearson Education, UK, 2007, p. 52, and *The European World: A History*, second edition, by Jerome Blum *et al.*, published by Little Brown & Co., USA, 1970, p. 885. Overy is a modern history professor at King's College, University of London, UK. Blum was chairman of the history department of Princeton University, USA.

According to Source A, which nation was affected the most between 1929 and 1933 by the Great Depression?

Great Depression 1929–33

Country	USA	Britain	France	Germany
Estimated percentage of unemployed workers by 1933	25	23	5	26
Percentage decline in wholesale prices	−32	−33	−34	−29
Percentage change in exports	−69	−49	−63	−53
Percentage change in industrial production	−36	−4	−19	−34

Countries did not just erect trade barriers to protect their own industries, but also turned to their colonies, if they had any. Britain turned to its empire, establishing a system of **imperial preference**. This placed large taxes on imports from outside the empire, stimulating industry in the more industrial areas of the empire, such as Britain, and allowing Australia and Canada, producers of agricultural products, to sell their products to Britain and India. By the mid-1930s over half of all British exports were to other parts of the British Empire which covered 23.9 per cent of the earth's land area. The French imperial preference system was even more successful. The French Empire covered just over nine per cent of the globe and was a market for one-third of France's industrial production.

 **KEY TERM**

Trade barrier
A government policy to restrict trade with other countries usually by placing high taxes on foreign imports so that domestic goods can be sold more cheaply.

Imperial preference
A system of commerce created by lowering import taxes between areas of an empire, while increasing taxes on imports from countries outside the empire.

According to Source B, how did the French government respond to the Great Depression?

KEY TERM

Import quota A maximum amount of imports of specific products allowed into a country.

SOURCE B

Excerpt from *The Origins of the Second World War in Europe*, second edition, by P.M.H. Bell, published by Pearson Education, UK, 1997, p. 149. The book is currently in its third edition, published in 2007. Bell is an honorary senior fellow in the Department of History at the University of Liverpool, UK and has published several books.

The problem of imports was met by the second element in French policy: the imposition of quotas on imports, and a system of imperial preference more far-reaching and effective than the British equivalent. In July and August 1931 **import quotas** *were introduced arbitrarily on nearly all agricultural products, followed later by quotas on industrial products which were usually negotiated with the countries concerned. French colonies were exempt from these quotas, and also had considerable tariff [tax] advantages over foreign countries.*

Both Britain and France had exported their surplus population to North America in former centuries, as well as to southern Asia and to Oceania in more recent times. In this era of economic hardship, many left their European homelands and settled in the League of Nations mandates that they had been granted after the First World War (see page 155).

The USA and the Soviet Union were physically massive, containing many of the resources needed for most types of industry and manufacturing. It appeared to smaller, industrialized countries that larger states, as empires or otherwise, had cheap raw materials, food and markets that they were lacking and wanted.

How did the Great Depression affect the formation and policies of national governments differently?

Political effects

The Great Depression brought political crises to several countries, often leading to coalition governments that were relatively unstable. Other countries saw long-established governments voted out in preference for an alternative. Political parties and governments throughout the world feared violence and the spread of communist ideology, which seemed to go hand in hand to many observers.

The USA

The Republican Party fell from political power when they lost control of the presidency and both divisions of Congress, the US parliament, in elections at the end of 1932. Franklin D. Roosevelt, commonly known by his initials as FDR, won the presidency, leading the Democrats to victory. Democrats took control of both the House of Representatives and the Senate with huge majorities. Roosevelt was seemingly a man of action and inspiring speeches, who passed a barrage of laws in the first 100 days of his presidency in 1933 with support from Congress. Banks were temporarily closed to give the government the opportunity to investigate their financial soundness, taxes were raised and government spending was increased while government salaries were reduced and trade barriers were erected.

SOURCE C

Comparison of US national election results of 1930 and 1932.

Election Year	President	House	Senate
1930	Republican with 58.2 per cent of vote	Republicans 218 Democrats 216	Republicans 48 Democrats 47
1932	Democrat with 57.4 per cent of vote	Democrats 313 Republicans 117	Democrats 59 Republicans 36

According to Source C, how did the US federal government change between 1930 and 1932 elections?

 **KEY TERM**

Deficit spending When a government spends more money than it brings in through taxation, usually to stimulate a country's economy.

Gold standard A system by which the value of a currency is linked to gold. When the British pound came off the gold standard in September 1931 its value fell from $4.86 to $3.49.

Roosevelt advocated a policy of **deficit spending**, where the government borrowed and spent more money than brought in by taxes as a way to stimulate the economy into recovery. Republicans opposed this policy and continued to advocate a reduction in government and in spending, and for the depression to run its natural course. Republican ideas had not alleviated the effects of the Great Depression from 1930 to 1932, so they were unpopular and Roosevelt and his Democratic Party were able to dominate politics throughout the 1930s.

Roosevelt continued to support the American public's view that foreign wars and conflicts were not the concern of the USA and he put this succinctly in economic terms in a memo to his advisor Adolf Berle: 'Don't forget that I discovered that over 90 per cent of all national deficits from 1921 to 1939 were caused by payments for past, present and future wars.' The USA was a country isolated from most European foreign affairs in the 1930s, primarily allowing Britain and France to take the lead in international diplomacy as the so-called Great Powers.

Britain

The British Labour government under Prime Minister Ramsay MacDonald continued until August 1931 with a heavy economic burden of mass unemployment. The government spent money to help the unemployed, but, as more and more people lost jobs, government tax revenue also decreased, leading the government to attempt to borrow money from US banks. These banks were also stressed and therefore placed many conditions and guarantees on the British that the government was unwilling to accept.

The Labour government fell that August to be replaced by a coalition government, known as the National Government, which was primarily Conservative but also had Liberal and Labour ministers, including a Labour prime minister: MacDonald. Many in the Labour Party disagreed with the formation of the coalition government, so the party split into two unequal groups with the minority supporting the coalition. This National Government continued throughout the 1930s and adopted several strong economic measures. For example, Britain:

- ended its use of the **gold standard** in September 1931, making its products cheaper to importing countries

- established the system of imperial preference (see page 179)
- made lending rates cheaper to stimulate the construction of homes.

These measures enjoyed some success and by 1934 Britain had surpassed its 1929 industrial production numbers.

International impact of British policies

Historian P.M.H. Bell has argued that British trade barriers to countries outside the empire, specifically those in central and eastern Europe, caused many countries to economically gravitate towards Germany. This helped the German economy and caused countries to form closer relationships with Germany as well. Germany soon became as important as France and Britain in these economies, if not more so in some cases.

? According to Source D, what were two results of the imperial preference system?

SOURCE D

Excerpt from *The Origins of the Second World War in Europe*, second edition, by P.M.H. Bell, published by Pearson Education, UK, 1998, pp. 148–9. The book is currently in its third edition, published in 2007. Bell is an honorary senior fellow in the Department of History at the University of Liverpool, UK and has published several books.

A Foreign Office memorandum put to the Cabinet in December 1931 warned that a high protective tariff along with imperial preference would separate Britain from European affairs and diminish British influence on the Continent … In 1933 and 1934 the Foreign Office urged the importance of Britain providing a market for bacon, eggs, butter and timber for the Baltic states and Poland, which might otherwise come into the economic orbit of Berlin or Moscow. Similarly, it was argued that Britain should buy cereals and other farm produce from Hungary and Yugoslavia, to prevent them from becoming over-dependent on the German market. In both cases the government refused …

Effect on military programmes

All political parties had to compromise in various ways to make sure the National Government remained in power. The Labour Party would not compromise on the issue of military spending. They believed that large numbers of weapons made war more likely and argued that the stockpiling of huge amounts of weaponry, ships and other tools of war, was one of the key causes of the First World War.

Economic stress also meant that Britain did not have the funds to invest in rearmament and it instead worked to limit armaments, specifically warships, through treaties signed in 1930 and 1935 (see pages 150 and 153). Rearmament programmes in the early 1930s were politically impossible, at a time when it was obvious that Italy and afterwards Germany were starting to rebuild their militaries.

It is important to keep the coalition government, a product of the Great Depression, in mind when we turn our attention to the Manchurian and

Abyssinian Crises (see pages 189 and 201), as well as the remilitarization of the Rhineland (see page 205).

France

France was in a different economic position from Britain. Whereas Britain had to import many raw materials and was almost completely dependent on imported food, France was essentially self-sufficient in food production. The French government established a very strict quota on imports of all kinds, including food. A very thorough system of imperial preference (see page 179) was created whereby France and its colonies formed an exclusive trade zone. Government wages were reduced by about twelve per cent and government spending was slashed. France did not suffer from mass unemployment as experienced in Britain, partly because vast numbers of people were employed in agriculture and the huge French army used conscription to keep young men occupied. Foreign workers were sent back to their own countries and 1935, the worst year of the depression for France, saw only 500,000 unemployed. Although France seemed much more successful than the British and the USA in fighting the effects of the Great Depression, its government was extremely unstable during this period.

The effect of coalition governments on foreign policy

Coalition government was the rule in France, where a myriad of parties gathered together to form majorities in the parliament to pass a few pieces of agreed-upon legislation, before collapsing. This collapse would lead to new elections being called or new coalitions being formed to create some unity for another list of agreed items. In 1932 there were three different governments, four in 1933, two more in 1934 and then two in 1935; that is eleven governments in four years. Governmental instability meant that foreign policy was often inconsistent in order to appease various political factions in France.

Conservatives and national extremists, fascists in fact, were politically successful in the 1930s and supported Mussolini during his invasion of Abyssinia (see page 202). They were, however, opposed to the Soviet Union whom they saw as the ultimate threat to world peace, and desired a large, active military in order to counteract the perceived threat. A large military would also protect them from Germany.

Socialist parties also grew dramatically in France and by 1935 the Communist Party was active on the political scene. These groups opposed the French fascists and conservatives as well as military build-up, believing funds for the military would be better spent on social welfare programmes. They supported the League of Nations and collective security.

The most difficult year of the Great Depression for France was 1935 with rising unemployment and growing political unrest. The French were unwilling to end their system of imperial preference, although it limited their economic ability to influence their allies in central and eastern Europe while

German economic strength began to be felt. In 1935 Germany announced its rearmament programme and Italy attacked Abyssinia, neither of which France was able to effectively address partly as a result of divided government and economic stress.

Germany

In the early years of the Great Depression, some governments decided to reduce government expenditure. Tax revenues were in decline and leaders believed the economic downturn would be temporary at best. Reducing spending would be better than saddling their people with debt which they believed would make matters worse over the long term. Germany was one such country, at the time led by Chancellor Brüning. Germany kept its currency at a high exchange rate while other countries were devaluing theirs so that their products were cheaper than those of competitors. Brüning also tried to reduce prices on consumer goods and keep the government's budget balanced. These policies failed to stimulate or protect the German economy, contributing to the unemployment of six million people by 1932. Economic conditions were so poor that Britain and France suspended indefinitely reparation payments from Germany at the Lausanne Conference in 1932.

National Socialism versus Communism

As the traditional coalition parties were linked with economic failure, other parties such as the National Socialist and Communist Parties grew in popularity as they seemed to offer legitimate alternatives to an obviously broken system. The Communist Party also benefited from the apparent success of the first Five-Year Plan in the Soviet Union (see page 96).

The **National Socialists**, the Nazis, were more popular than the Communist Party, and most other parties, by 1932. Hitler, their leader, ran for president in 1932, losing to General Paul von Hindenburg, president since 1925, in both the first and second rounds. Hitler did, however, poll far ahead of the leader of the Communist Party, Ernst Thälmann, and became better known to the German people through speeches, propaganda posters, radio addresses and visits to their towns and villages; he took thirteen million votes out of about 36 million cast.

Hitler was a nationalist and preached that a powerful Germany could prosper, take its place on the world stage and end the humiliation of Versailles. Hitler argued that the German economy was too dependent on other countries for raw materials and markets, which meant that when these nations had economic problems, Germany had them also. He preached a need for *lebensraum*, or living space, in lands ruled or won by Germany in the First World War against Russia but taken away in the Treaty of Versailles (see page 32), roughly Poland and parts of Ukraine. He claimed that *lebensraum* would provide raw materials for industry, food and land for Germans to settle. Non-economic beliefs of the Nazis were many, but included a hatred of Jews, homosexuals and others, that women should stay

 **KEY TERM**

National Socialists Abbreviated name for the National Socialist German Workers' Party or Nazi Party, an ultra-nationalist group.

Lebensraum German for living space, loosely defined as parts of eastern Europe.

home and rear children, and that Germans were a master race that was meant to rule over other nationalities.

National Socialism appealed to more people than strict communist ideology. This was partly because communism opposed the concept of nationalism, preaching that working-class people around the world were the same. Communism also believed in the ending of all social classes, the confiscation of private property, and that religion was just a creation of people in power to control people not in power. The violence of the Bolshevik takeover of Russia and the Russian Civil War, as well as various revolts in the first years of the German Republic, made many nervous about communist government.

SOURCE E

Excerpt from *Hitler: A Study in Tyranny* by Alan Bullock, published by Harper & Row, New York, USA, 1962, p. 199. Bullock was a British historian who served as vice-chancellor of Oxford University, UK.

When Hitler sat down [from the speech,] the audience, whose reserve had long since thawed, rose and cheered him wildly. 'The effect upon the industrialists,' wrote Otto Dietrich [Nazi Party Press Chief], who was present, 'was great, and very evident during the next hard months of struggle.' … as a result of the impression Hitler made, large contributions from the resources of heavy industry flowed into the Nazi treasury. With an astuteness which matched that of his appeal to the Army, Hitler had won an important victory. As the Army officers saw in Hitler the man who promised to restore Germany's military power, so the industrialists came to see in him the man who would defend their interests against the threat of Communism and the claims of the trade unions, giving a free hand to private enterprise and economic exploitation …

According to Source E, which two groups supported Hitler's stance against communism?

Industrialists and large landowners naturally opposed communism and poured money into the Nazi Party coffers. This allowed more Nazi propaganda, paid staff workers, offices and the employment of tens of thousands of young men in armed gangs who often violently opposed the opponents of the Nazis.

SOURCE F

Excerpt from 'Why the German Republic fell' by Bruno Heilig published in *Why the German Republic Fell and Other Lessons of War and Peace Upholding True Democracy through Economic Freedom*, edited by Arthur Madsen, published by The Hogarth Press, London, UK, 1941. Heilig was a journalist for newspapers in Vienna, Budapest, Prague and Berlin who was arrested in Austria in 1938 for being Jewish. He was released from a concentration camp in 1939, immigrated to Britain, and served in the Royal Air Force during the Second World War.

Was there a link between the economic and the political collapse? Emphatically, yes. For as unemployment grew, and with it poverty and the fear of poverty, so grew the influence of the Nazi Party, which was making its lavish promises to the frustrated and its violent appeal to the revenges of a populace aware of its

According to Source F, how did Hitler and the Nazi Party come to power in Germany?

wrongs but condemned to hear only a malignant and distorted explanation of them.

In the first year of the crisis the number of Nazi deputies to the Reichstag rose from 8 to 107. A year later this figure was doubled. In the same time the Communists captured half of the votes of the German Social Democratic Party and the representation of the middle class practically speaking disappeared. In January 1933 Hitler was appointed Reichskanzler [chancellor]; he attained power, as I said before, quite legally. All the forms of democracy were observed. It sounds paradoxical but it was in fact absolutely logical.

Hitler comes to power

While Hitler himself was not elected as president, the Nazi Party went from 2.6 per cent of the representatives in the *Reichstag*, the German parliament, in 1928, to 37.3 per cent in July 1932. There was another election in late 1932 as a stable government coalition could not be formed between the various political parties, none of which had a majority. In this election the National Socialists lost seats, yet still had more than any other individual party. In January 1933, in an attempt to stabilize the country politically, President von Hindenburg appointed Hitler as chancellor. An election was called afterwards to see if the election returns would confirm the appointment.

SOURCE G

A photograph of Adolf Hitler shaking hands with German President Paul von Hindenburg, 21 March 1933.

? What message is conveyed by Source G about the relationship between von Hindenburg and Hitler?

The Nazi Party returned in March 1933 with its largest percentage ever at almost 44 per cent of the *Reichstag* seats. The election, it must be noted, was held with Hitler as chancellor. He had outlawed the Communist Party which had been accused of burning down the *Reichstag*. Other parties had many of their candidates attacked and harassed by Nazis during their campaigns since Hitler intentionally withdrew their police protection for this purpose. Within a few days after the election, the Nazis combined with other nationalists and the Catholic Centre Party (they joined the coalition after Hitler promised to protect the rights of the Catholic Church) to form a parliamentary majority. The Enabling Act was immediately passed which gave Hitler the power to pass laws and sign treaties for the next five years without consulting the *Reichstag*. The economic desperation in Germany was so great that a large number of its citizens, or at least their political representatives, were willing to forfeit their republican government in order to solve their economic problems.

German economic response to the Great Depression

With the new Nazi government came new policies to deal with the depression. From October 1933, Germany worked to do business only with countries that would purchase Germans goods of equal value to those Germany imported from that country. If Romania, for example, wanted Germany to purchase oil or wheat, then Romania had to purchase an equivalent amount of German industrial goods such as cameras or automobiles. While this programme had limited success, it did have political consequences in making central and eastern European countries less dependent on British or French markets, bringing them closer to Germany economically.

The 'New Plan'

In 1934 this policy, now called the 'New Plan', was expanded by the German Economics Minister Hjalmar Schacht, and the German government came to have much more control over the economy, dictating what could and would be imported.

SOURCE H

Excerpt from *The Origins of the Second World War in Europe*, second edition, by P.M.H. Bell, published by Pearson Education, London, UK, 1998, p. 158. The book is currently in its third edition, published in 2007. Bell is an honorary senior fellow in the Department of History at the University of Liverpool, UK and has published several books.

… he [Schacht] introduced his 'New Plan' for German foreign trade, based on the principles of buying nothing that could not be paid for by foreign exchange earned by German exports, and of making imports conform to national needs as decided by the government. All imports were subject to licenses, which were used to differentiate between essential and non-essential items, with raw materials and food classified as essential. Whenever possible, imports were to be bought

What is the message conveyed by Source H? ?

only from the countries which were willing to accept German goods in return; and any foreign exchange involved was to be paid into a clearing account, and not used freely by the exporting country.

Schacht's plan meant that Germany:

- imported 284 million German marks' worth of materials and products more than it exported in 1934
- exported 111 million marks' more than it imported in 1935
- exported 550 million marks' more than it imported in 1936.

The success of the 'New Plan' meant cheaper food prices in Germany and surplus funds to purchase raw materials that could be used for **rearmament**.

KEY TERM

Rearmament The rebuilding or re-equipping of an army.

Germany's economic recovery also benefited from Germany being the largest, most industrialized nation east of France, except for an introverted Soviet Union. At the end of the First World War many new central and eastern European countries, such as Czechoslovakia, Yugoslavia, Poland, Romania and Hungary, had been created from the former Russian, Austrian and German empires. They were mainly producers of raw materials and agricultural products rather than industrial goods, although Czechoslovakia was quite industrialized. This meant they needed imports of industrial goods which Germany could supply, and once bilateral and highly-controlled trade mechanisms were established between Germany and each of these states, Germany was able to recover economically faster than the USA, Britain or France and began to have political influence with these nations.

German rearmament

The German military was severely limited by the Treaty of Versailles (see page 32). The pre-Nazi governments of Germany had early on violated this aspect of Versailles, experimenting with planes and poison gas in the Soviet Union after the Treaty of Rapallo (see page 77). At the Paris Peace Conference it had been made clear that German disarmament was only a step towards general world disarmament, which had not occurred. If the world had not followed through with their promise to disarm, Germany believed it had the right to rearm to defend itself against attack (see page 153).

In 1935, rearmament began in earnest:

- With the introduction of conscription, Germany had a standing army of over 700,000 men and three million in reserve within four years.
- In 1935 there were 2500 military planes of various types in operation and in 1936 Germany had the ability to produce over 5000 planes per year.
- A naval agreement was signed with Britain permitting the German navy to greatly expand without fear of attack and Germany immediately began a massive shipbuilding programme.

While many historians question the quality and equipment of this army, rearmament was accomplished in the midst of the Great Depression when most countries worked to control spending and reduce imports and certainly not build up massive, expensive armies. German rearmament appeared as some miracle to most observers, not least because much of it was built with imported materials and because it led to practically no unemployment. It was the fear of this army, the fear of war in general and the fear of the costs of rearmament in the midst of a crushing Great Depression that need to be considered when studying international relations post-1933.

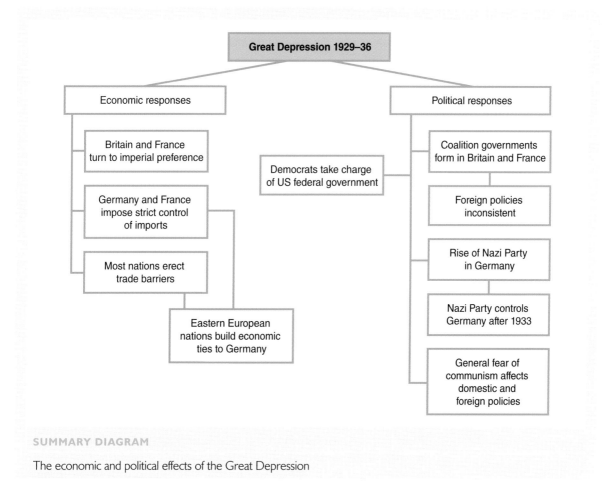

SUMMARY DIAGRAM

The economic and political effects of the Great Depression

2 The Manchurian Crisis

▶ *Key question: How significant was the Manchurian Crisis in world affairs?*

Japan suffered more than many countries in the Great Depression. It imported most of its raw materials, including oil and metals, and exported manufactured goods throughout Asia and to the USA. With the closure of markets with the erection of trade barriers throughout the world, Japanese trade collapsed. The problem was compounded by the fact that Japan had to pay for imports in gold or in other currencies, neither of which Japan had much of since it was unable to sell its products to gain gold or foreign currency.

Japan had a growing population in a land of few resources. Japan had heavily settled the South Seas Mandate it had been granted at the end of the First World War (see page 165). Colonization had also taken place in Taiwan, added to the Japanese Empire in 1895, and in Korea, annexed in 1905. The USA, however, was the greatest recipient of Japanese immigration. Economic hardship in the USA during the Great Depression, coupled with racism, led to severe limitations placed on Japanese immigration. Many in Japan believed an expanded empire would help alleviate population pressures.

The Japanese military had grown more powerful than the civilian government by the early 1930s, perhaps partly as a result of support from the Emperor of Japan, Hirohito. In addition, the constitution of Japan itself made the military powerful as the army and navy ministers had to come from the military and therefore were part of all cabinets. If the military withdrew its ministers, by law the government collapsed. This meant that the military had to be appeased by the civilian government in order to function. As a result, by 1931 the civilian government was no longer able to command the military or control its spending. From 1932 to 1936 the prime minister's position was held by admirals from the navy.

SOURCE I

Excerpt from _The Global Impact of the Great Depression, 1929–1939_ by Dietmar Rothermund, published by Routledge, London, UK, 1996, p. 116. Rothermund is professor emeritus of south Asian history at the Ruprecht-Karls Univeresity in Heidelberg, Germany.

These events were paralleled by deep social tensions in Japan. The army had emerged as a decisive political force, defending the interests of the peasants against the big corporations. It also followed an aggressive policy of expansion abroad and had invaded Manchuria in September 1931 without the approval of the Japanese government. The army was also behind the murders of Inouye [prime minister] and of Baron Dan, the head of the Mitsui corporation, in the spring of 1932. They were, so to speak, 'executed' for betraying the interests of the Japanese people. Finance minister Takahashi, Inouye's successor, who piloted Japan through the years of the depression, was also murdered by army officers in 1936. It was clearly very dangerous to be in charge of Japan's financial affairs in this crucial period.

The economic crisis, coupled with extreme nationalism and a weak civilian government dominated by the military, led directly to the idea that Japan should expand its empire. This expanded empire would provide Japan with raw materials and food, and perhaps serve as a place to move many of its citizens from the overcrowded Japanese home islands. Japan did not have to

? According to Source I, who did the army claim to represent?

look far to find Manchuria. Manchuria was a massive province in northern China with a low population, ostensibly full of natural resources like iron and coal and relatively close to Japan itself. Japan already ruled Korea, just to the east of Manchuria, and Korea could be used as a staging area for any invasion of China. Japan already had a foothold in Manchuria as well, having leased the South Manchurian Railway in 1905 with the right to protect it with 15,000 troops.

China was a massive country in terms of land area and population, but had a very unstable government and civil war. The Republic of China was formed in 1911, but had been unable to bring political stability to the country. Instead, military rulers, commonly known as warlords, fought each other and carved out essentially independent states within China starting in 1916. There was also fighting between communists and republican forces and even an attempt to re-establish the monarchy. A disorganized and unstable China would not be able to resist the Japanese army, a highly trained and professional force. The only possible difficulty was that China was a member of the League of Nations, as was Japan.

The Mukden Incident and the Lytton Commission

> **What was the main result of the Mukden Incident?**

On 18 September 1931, a bomb exploded on the railway line just outside Mukden, the leading city of Manchuria. This very minor explosion, known as the Mukden Incident, did not even prevent trains from using the railway, but it had conveniently taken place near a garrison of Japanese soldiers guarding the South Manchurian Railway operated by Japan. Although many historians believe that the bomb was placed by Japanese troops, Japan blamed the explosion on Chinese soldiers. The Japanese army used this as an excuse to occupy the entirety of southern Manchuria. Once this task was complete, the Japanese army defeated Chinese troops in the north, occupying all Manchuria.

SOURCE J

Excerpt from *The Manchurian Crisis and Japanese Society, 1931–33* by Sandra Wilson, published by Routledge, London, UK, 2002, p. 1. Wilson is a professor of Asian history at Murdoch University, Australia.

On the night of 18 September 1931, a minor explosion occurred on a section of the Japanese-owned South Manchurian Railway near Mukden (now Shenyang) in the north-east of China. Japanese troops, stationed in Manchuria since 1905 to protect the railway and its associated operations, moved swiftly and decisively to defend Japan's interests. Meanwhile their leaders loudly asserted to the world that Chinese soldiers were responsible for the explosion, which was branded as only the latest in a series of anti-Japanese 'outrages'. Actually, damage to the railway had been slight, and the 'incident' had in any case been perpetrated not by Chinese soldiers but by Japanese troops, as part of a wider plan to extend Japanese power in Manchuria.

> According to Source J, what was the purpose of the explosion on 18 September 1931?

While Japan completed the occupation of all Manchuria, China appealed to the League of Nations. The League responded with great caution; this was the first major military conflict between members of the League. The League requested that Japan pull its armies back to the area along the South Manchurian Railway where Japan had the right to have troops; this request was ignored. The Lytton Commission was established and began a leisurely fact-finding operation in the spring of 1932.

While the Lytton Commission investigated the issue of Japanese aggression in Manchuria, Japan consolidated its grip on Manchuria, creating Manchukuo. This new state was dominated by the Japanese, but the last Emperor of China, an ethnic Manchu who had been overthrown in 1911 as a child, was installed as Emperor of Manchukuo. Emperor Kang-de, more commonly known as Pu-Yi, is considered by modern historians to have been little more than a puppet for the Japanese military. His installation as ruler, however, helped Japan justify its invasion as a way to free the Manchurian people from Chinese domination. Japan also argued that by separating Manchuria from the chaos of China's politics and internal wars, it was bringing peace and stability to the people who lived there.

SOURCE K

? What is the origin and purpose of Source K?

Excerpt from 'Manchuria: what is it all about?' by Uthai Vincent Wilcox, *Popular Mechanics*, February 1932, vol. 57, number 2. Wilcox was a research economist who wrote many journal articles and contributed to several books on economics. *Popular Mechanics* has been published since 1902 in the USA and has focused primarily on technology and science.

First, there is the Fushun colliery. This great coal mine, or rather series of mines, is but twenty-two miles southeast of Mukden. The mines are remarkable for the thickness of their seams. The daily output at present is 20,000 tons, with a conservatively estimated potential output of 1,200,000,000 tons… The Japanese themselves claim that the future source of steel in the Far East is located at Anshan [in Manchuria]. The [South Manchurian Railway] acts as the godfather to these factories and to the extensive mines of iron ore. There are several blast furnaces in operation with an ultimate annual production of 1,000,000 tons in sight.

It would be tiresome, perhaps, to note in detail the long list of industries operated in that ancient land. Such a list includes coke ovens, sulphate-of-ammonia factories, gasworks, libraries, technical schools, playgrounds, and bean mills. There is a medical college (Nanman Igakudo) which should be included. The school work of the railway is another evidence of the vision of the owners [the Japanese Empire].

In order to encourage education among the children, the railway grants free passage to those who attend schools along its right of way.

SOURCE L

Empire of Japan and areas under its control by 1940.

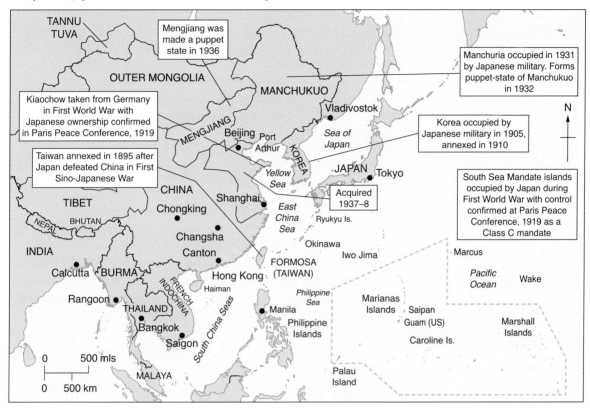

The Lytton Commission was released in September 1932, a full year after the Mukden Incident. It essentially agreed that Japan had special interests in China and in Manchuria in particular. It also stated that there had been a bombing in Mukden, although it did not actually investigate who had carried this out, and noted that there had been no Manchurian uprising for independence despite Japanese claims. The report continued that the Japanese army had gone beyond defending its railway interests by occupying the entire province of Manchuria. It suggested Japan should not have used such aggression. The report failed to outright condemn Japan for the invasion although Japan had clearly violated many of the articles in the Covenant of the League of Nations (see page 33). Britain, France and Italy half-heartedly protested about Japanese actions against China, but did little else.

What information is conveyed by Source L? You should be able to state at least three facts.

?

According to Source M, what were members of the League of Nations to do if a member state went to war with another member state?

SOURCE M

Treaty of Versailles, Part I [1], Article 17, 1919.

Should any Member of the League resort to war in disregard of its covenants under Articles 12, 13, or 15, it shall ipso facto *[by the fact itself] be deemed to have committed an act of war against all other Members of the League, which hereby undertake immediately to subject it to the severance of all trade or financial relations, the prohibition of all intercourse between their nationals and the nationals of the covenant-breaking State, and the prevention of all financial, commercial, or personal intercourse between the nationals of the covenant-breaking State and the nationals of any other State, whether a Member of the League or not.*

The Japanese response

Japan left the League of Nations in 1933 in protest over criticism of its actions in Manchuria. This had the added benefit of conveniently removing Japan from possible penalties from the League as only League members could be punished with economic sanctions. Japan consolidated its hold on Manchuria, developing mines and industries and extending its control into northern China, outside Manchuria. China offered little military resistance, but did boycott Japanese goods. By mid-1935, Japan had taken control of Hebei Province south of Manchuria, placing Beijing, one of China's main cities, within striking distance. In 1936 Japan signed the Anti-Comintern Pact with Germany, ending its diplomatic isolation.

Why did the Great Powers fail to protect China from Japan?

→ # The failure of collective security and consequences of the Manchurian Crisis

Collective security through the League failed for many reasons, including:

- reluctance to use force
- opposition to communism
- a better off Manchuria.

Nevertheless, the invasion of Manchuria affected the relationship between Japan and the USA while China continued to protest.

Reluctance to use force

At this time the League was dominated by the French and British, as the USA and Soviet Union were withdrawn from most international affairs. Japan and China were far from Europe and the British and French public would not tolerate their governments sending off their men to die far from home over a conflict they knew little and cared less about. People were more concerned with their immediate economic situation as banks collapsed and unemployment increased, and with how to maintain national governments that were made of many different political parties attempting national unity to get through the worst effects of the Great Depression.

To send an army to defend China would have required a massive military build-up, including a navy of transport ships and vessels to protect them, an air force to fight a modern war, and a fully equipped army with tanks and artillery. No member of the League of Nations could do that alone and no country had the political will or the financial ability to even contribute in part to such an undertaking. Japan, on the other hand, was geographically near Manchuria, had a large standing army that was very recently battle tested, and had its industries and newly sequestered raw materials for those industries nearby. It was also a government opposed to communism. Japan also had a substantial navy as seen in naval treaties in 1922 and 1930 (see pages 148 and 150) which would be difficult to oppose.

Opposition to communism

The Soviet Union was the only communist country in the world at the time and was opposed to the capitalist countries of the west ideologically and often politically. Many in Europe feared a Bolshevik-style revolution in their own countries (see page 10) and were nervous about the first Five-Year Plan of the Soviet Union (see page 96), which was in operation during the Manchurian Crisis. Communists in China were supported by the Soviet Union and if a capitalist, imperialistic Japan could fight and destroy the communism there, western nations would not object. A stronger Japan could also put military pressure on the eastern Soviet Union. This might cause the Soviets to be more cautious in any military plans they might have against eastern European states for fear of attack in the east. The Soviet Union would necessarily have to expend major resources to build an army and navy to defend itself from an attack by Japan as well, hindering the Soviet economy.

A better off Manchuria

The other realities were that Japan, having set up a Manchurian ruler over Manchukuo, could easily say that Manchuria was better off, that Manchurians had the right to rule themselves as did various eastern European nationalities at the end of the First World War, and this view was shared by many. If China could not even govern itself, then why not let the Japanese establish law and order?

Impact of Manchurian Crisis on Asia

← **How did the Manchurian Crisis lead to further conflict in Asia?**

Japanese government

The Japanese military, which already had substantial power in the government, now acted on its own initiative, dictating Japanese foreign policy and expecting the civilian government to simply follow. On 15 May 1932 members of the Japanese military assassinated the head of the civilian government, Prime Minister Inukai Tsuyoshi. According to the eleven assassins, they acted to protest against limitations placed on the Japanese navy at the London Naval Conference of 1930 (see page 150). All participants received very light sentences, proving to many that the military was not to be opposed and that killing civilian ministers had little consequence if carried out by members of the armed forces. The military's command over the Japanese government increased as a result of the 15 May Incident so the Japanese army's actions in Manchuria became state policy. In February 1936 there was another attempt by members of the military to take over the government, but by this time the government was already all but completely subservient to the military.

US reaction to the Manchurian Crisis

With Britain, France and Italy being primarily concerned with economic issues and with their foreign policies focused on European affairs, Japan was essentially free to act in Asia as it desired. The only possible threat to the country was the USA which had a small military, a relatively limited navy as the result of treaties signed in 1922 and 1930 (see pages 148 and 150), and little desire to confront Japan. In 1932, the USA protested against Japanese actions by formulating the **Stimson Doctrine**, named after the US Secretary of State Henry Stimson. This doctrine simply stated that the USA would not recognize any territorial changes made to China by Japan and that the USA would continue to insist on the **open-door policy** which stated that all countries had equal access to Chinese markets. This produced no result other than to alienate the Japanese government, preventing any possible negotiations.

The Sino-Japanese and Second World Wars 1937–45

A direct result of the Manchurian Crisis was the Second Sino-Japanese War that began in 1937. Controlling Manchuria allowed the Japanese army, which now essentially operated the Japanese government, to build up its strength on the Chinese border in preparation for invasion. In July 1937, Japanese and Chinese troops exchanged fire at the Marco Polo Bridge which connected Beijing with the south of China. Both sides mobilized for war and Japan soon moved to seize Shanghai, the largest city in China's south. At the end of November 1937, Shanghai finally fell after three months of fighting and within a month Nanjing, the capital of the Republic of China, was also captured by Japan. Although Japan suffered some defeats, it had mostly taken control of all eastern China by 1940. China appealed to the League of Nations in 1937 and barely received a response; Britain and France were preoccupied by events in Europe and could not afford to worry about Asia, even though their colonies were threatened by Japanese expansion. Japan was now the unrivalled power of Asia, with only the USA to contend with in the Pacific Ocean region.

 **KEY TERM**

Stimson Doctrine
US policy to not recognize border changes to China, specifically China's separation from Manchuria.

Open-door policy
US policy that expected all nations to allow all nations to freely trade with China.

SOURCE N

Excerpt from *The Origins of the Second World War*, second edition, by R.J. Overy, published by Pearson Education, London, UK, 1998, pp. 12–14. Overy is a modern history professor at King's College, University of London, UK.

In 1933 Japan left the League and effectively removed the Far East from the system of collective security. In 1934, in violation of international agreements to preserve an 'Open Door' policy in China (to allow open and equal access to Chinese markets), the Japanese government announced the **Amau Doctrine***, a warning to other powers to regard China as Japan's sphere of influence and to abandon trade with the Chinese and the provision of technical aid to them. There is no doubt that Japanese leaders, spurred on at home by the military, were encouraged to go further after 1932 than they might otherwise have done because of the weak response from the major powers. Even the United States, architect of the 'Open Door' policy and naval limitations in the Pacific, hesitated to do anything that would alienate the Japanese. Neither Britain nor America was willing, in the difficult political climate of the early 1930s, to confront Japan militarily, and each suspected the other of trying to pass on the responsibility and cost of doing so.*

According to Source N, what caused the Japanese to become aggressive in their policies after 1932?

 **KEY TERM**

Amau Doctrine Japanese government's declaration that China and Asia were Japan's area of interest and that other nations were not to interfere in the region.

Neutrality Acts US laws in the 1930s that required the US government to remain isolated from world affairs so as not to be drawn into war.

Embargo A ban on trade in order to isolate a nation.

Petroleum products Products based on oil, including gasoline, rubber and diesel fuel.

Japanese troops committed great atrocities in China during the war. In Shanghai and many other cities, civilians were bombed by Japanese planes. In Nanjing perhaps 300,000 mostly civilian Chinese were intentionally killed, as well as captured Chinese troops; tens of thousands of women were raped, regardless of age and then also killed. These actions by Japanese troops, in addition to concern about the growing military and economic strength of Japan, alarmed many countries, the USA in particular.

US President Franklin D. Roosevelt was limited by several laws called **Neutrality Acts** which prevented US involvement in conflicts that did not specifically involve the USA. This meant that the USA could only respond to the Japanese invasion of China with verbal condemnations. An **embargo** on raw materials or products to Japan would have brought the Japanese military to a halt since it relied almost entirely on US **petroleum products**, but this would have violated the Neutrality Acts.

War in Europe broke out in September 1939 and by 1940, the USA had changed its laws to allow the export of materials to Britain and other countries fighting Germany. As the Neutrality Acts expired in July 1941, Japan moved against French Indochina, today's Vietnam, Cambodia and Laos. The USA responded by freezing all Japanese assets in the USA and placing an oil embargo on Japan. With only two years of oil stockpiles for military operations, Japan decided it had to expand to take control of oilfields in Dutch Indonesia, something the USA was likely to resist. To either shock the USA into not fighting Japan or to delay a US attack on Japan long enough for Dutch Indonesia to be absorbed into the Japanese Empire, the Japanese navy attacked the US Pacific naval fleet in December 1941 at Pearl Harbor, Hawaii. This brought the USA into the Second World War against Japan. The economic power of the USA and its military might that resulted from a massive rearmament programme eventually led to the defeat of a heavily destroyed Japan in 1945, allowing Manchuria to rejoin a liberated, independent China.

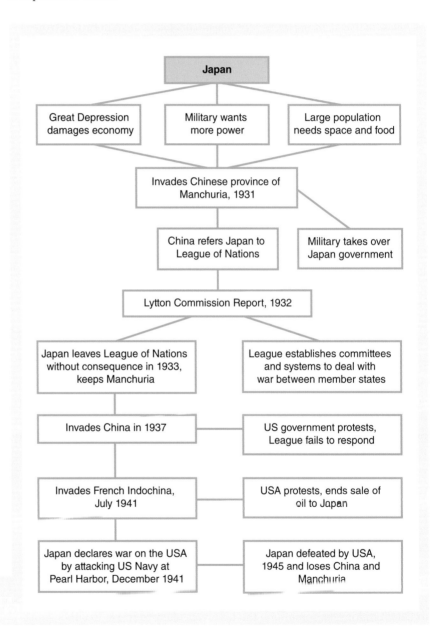

The Manchurian Crisis

Key Debate

▶ *Key question: What was the significance of the Manchurian Crisis for the League of Nations?*

The institution of collective security, where each member of the League of Nations would defend the other members in case of war, failed and many historians have claimed that the road to the Second World War began in 1931 at Mukden and that profound weaknesses of the League were revealed.

SOURCE O

Excerpt from 'Great powers paid price for "peace": history shows that the pacifist movement of the 1930s ultimately helped to usher in the horror of World War II by allowing rogue nations to rise to power unabated' by Stephen Goode, in *Insight on the News*, Vol. 19, 2003. Goode was senior writer for this conservative US news magazine that stopped publication in 2008.

The League of Nations declined to recognize Manchukuo, but it also refused to place any sanctions on Japan's behavior, in part because neither Great Britain nor any other member nation was strong enough to enforce them. The United States had not joined the League of Nations, nor did it support sanctions. The result: Japan continued to occupy Manchukuo and to make war in China. And it removed itself from membership in the League.

The failure to put an end to Japanese aggression had ramifications beyond the Far East. Benito Mussolini, dictator in Italy since 1922, noted the failure of the League of Nations to say 'no' to Japan. In October 1935, Italy invaded Abyssinia …

According to Source O, what was the main result of the Manchurian Crisis?

While weaknesses were revealed, some historians state that the failure of the League of Nations to confront Japan actually demonstrated a new reality. This reality was that the Great Powers within the League of Nations, such as Britain, France, Italy and Japan, would not oppose each other's dealings with smaller states. These historians go further and state that smaller, less powerful states realized that they were now more vulnerable and would be expected to give in to the demands of more powerful nations.

SOURCE P

Excerpt from *The League of Nations: Its Life and Times 1920–46* by F.S. Northedge, published by Holmes & Meier, London, 1986, p. 164. Northedge was a professor of international relations at the London School of Economics, UK, writing numerous books on the subject as well.

Britain and the other great Powers did not worry overmuch about the implications of the Manchurian affair for collective security. As always, they had more immediate questions to think about. In the result, collective security was dealt a blow from which it never fully recovered. The smaller countries were left

According to Source P, what did the Manchurian Crisis acknowledge in international diplomacy?

to conclude that, if the League was to protect them, it would have to be when the great Powers were united against a common enemy, which happened to be victimising a small country. But it was as likely as not that the great Powers, so far from joining together to defend the small country, would join together to attack it, or to shut their eyes if one of them attacked it. Something like that had happened in the Corfu crisis in 1923, when Italy was sheltered by [being a member of the Conference of Ambassadors]. Japan profited in the same way in the Manchurian affair. Later in the 1930s the European dictators were shielded by sympathisers in the form of states which were supposed to be the very pillars of the League system. And what were the smaller states to do in such a situation? They could make their peace with one or other of the great Powers in good time, perhaps losing part of their territory in the process of accommodation. Or they could relax their links with the collective system in the hope of diverting from themselves the predatory attentions of great Powers. In either case, the solidity of the League system was bound to be affected as it prepared for the next great challenge. That challenge was not long in coming.

Other historians claim that the Manchurian Crisis actually strengthened the League by forcing it to set up committees and internal structures to deal with conflict between states, machinery that had never been set up before because it had never been needed. A.J.P. Taylor makes this argument in *The Origins of the Second World War* and claims that historians only later gave significance, wrongly, to the Manchurian Crisis.

SOURCE Q

Excerpt from *The Origins of the Second World War* by A.J.P. Taylor, published by Penguin Books, UK, 1991, p. 92. First published in 1961 by Hamish Hamilton, this book has been most recently reprinted by Penguin Books in 2001. Taylor was a British historian who wrote many books on European history and was lecturer at many British universities.

The Commission did not reach a simple verdict. It found that most of the Japanese grievances were justified. Japan was not condemned as an aggressor, though she was condemned for resorting to force before all peaceful means of redress were exhausted. The Japanese withdrew in protest from the League of Nations. But in fact British policy succeeded. The Chinese reconciled themselves to the loss of a province which they had not controlled for some years; and in 1933 peace was restored between China and Japan. In later years the Manchurian affair assumed a mythical importance. It was treated as a milestone on the road to war, the first decisive betrayal of the League, especially by the British government. In reality, the League, under British leadership, had done what the British thought it was designed to do: it had limited a conflict and brought it, however unsatisfactorily, to an end. Moreover, the Manchurian affair, far from weakening the coercive powers of the League, actually brought them into existence. It was thanks to this affair that the League again on British prompting set up machinery, hitherto lacking, to organize economic sanctions. This machinery, to everyone's misfortune, made possible the League action over Abyssinia in 1935.

? According to Source Q, what was the main result of the Manchuria Crisis?

Debate about the significance of the Manchurian Crisis continues today. Did the failure of collective security in the Manchurian Crisis lead to the fall of the League? Did this crisis contribute to the origins of the Second World War? Was the League really prepared for another crisis between its member states? While these questions continue to be debated, it is important to understand that whatever the overall significance of the Manchurian Crisis may have been, the League clearly failed to protect China from Japan. This moved Asia closer to war since Japan invaded the rest of China in 1937, but it is still unclear if this also moved Europe closer to the Second World War. Establishing internal structures within the League to deal with any future aggression by member states was important, but addressing the lack of political will power and financial ability of the Great Powers to intervene in conflicts was more complicated.

TOK

We know much about the Manchurian Crisis, but continue to debate its importance. What is it about history that makes it important? (History, Language and Reason.)

4 The Abyssinian Crisis

▶ *Key question: What role did the Abyssinian Crisis have in destroying the League of Nations' credibility?*

SOURCE R

A speech by Benito Mussolini, 2 October 1933 regarding the invasion of Abyssinia, from *Lend Me Your Ears: Great Speeches in History*, edited by William Safire, published by W.W. Norton, New York, USA, 1997. Safire wrote speeches for several US presidents and was a political columnist for *The New York Times* in the USA, a newspaper with one of the largest circulations of any newspaper in the world.

It is not only an army marching towards its goal, but it is forty-four million Italians marching in unity behind this army. Because the blackest of injustices is being attempted against them, that of taking from them their place in the sun. When in 1915 Italy threw in her fate with that of the Allies, how many cries of admiration, how many promises were heard? But after the common victory, which cost Italy six hundred thousand dead, four hundred thousand lost, one million wounded, when peace was being discussed around the table only the crumbs of a rich colonial booty were left for us to pick up. For thirteen years we have been patient while the circle tightened around us at the hands of those who wish to suffocate us.

With reference to Source R's origin and purpose, what are some values and limitations of this source?

The Italian Empire

The leader of Italy, Benito Mussolini, wanted to create an empire in order to make Italy a Great Power, like France and Britain were perceived to be. While Italy held Libya, Eritrea and part of Somalia, there were not particularly important or developed and Libya's oil remained undiscovered at this time. The Italian Empire was not impressive to the Italians or anyone else.

What were the main reasons that Italy sought an empire?

When casting about for suitable territory to conquer in nearby Africa, there remained only Abyssinia, more commonly known as Ethiopia today, and Liberia, a state formed by freed American slaves in the nineteenth century and under the indirect supervision and sponsorship of the USA. Abyssinia was conveniently located beside the Italian colonies Somaliland and Eritrea and its borders were loosely defined, if at all. Mussolini was completely uninterested in its economic potential and also disregarded the state of the Italian economy which was totally unprepared to finance a war for any purpose.

? What is the message conveyed in Source S?

SOURCE S

'The Jap in the Vase' a cartoon by Sidney George Strube, *Daily Express*, 29 November 1935. Strube was a British cartoonist who worked at this British daily newspaper from 1912 to 1948.

The Wal-Wal Incident and war

What was the significance of the Wal-Wal Incident for Italian foreign policy?

In December 1934 a clash occurred between Italian and Abyssinian troops at the small oasis of Wal-Wal, some 80 km on the Abyssinian side of the border with Italian Somaliland, leaving at least two Italian soldiers and over 100 Ethiopian troops dead. Italy demanded compensation and an official apology from the Abyssinian government. Abyssinia responded by appealing to the League of Nations of which both Italy and Abyssinia were members. An arbitration committee was established that announced in September 1935 that the Wal-Wal Incident, as it became known, was minor and that no country was at fault. Mussolini, however, had already directed the Italian army in December 1934 to prepare for the invasion of Abyssinia and armies prepared to invade from neighbouring Italian colonies. Britain and France were very aware of Italy's plans, but were unwilling to jeopardize their relationship with Italy which they believed was important in opposing German foreign policies.

SOURCE T

Abyssinian troops marching near the northern frontier during the occupation of their country by Mussolini's Italy, 18 November 1935.

What information does Source T indicate about the Abyssinian army?

October 1935 saw the long-expected invasion of Abyssinia. The relatively modern Italian forces annihilated Abyssinian armies sent against them that used a variety of antique weapons. Aerial bombing by the Italians and the liberal use of poison gas over large areas of Abyssinia led to the deaths of hundreds of thousands of men, women, children and livestock, poisoning water and destroying crops. The Emperor of Abyssinia, Haile Selassie, escaped to Britain while practically all organized opposition to the Italian occupation collapsed in the midst of the destruction in early 1936. **Guerrilla attacks**, however, continued, leading to Mussolini himself ordering that prisoners be shot, that various villages be gassed where resistance had been discovered, and that priests and others suspected of complicity in armed resistance be executed without hesitation.

 **KEY TERM**

Guerrilla attacks Military attacks by small groups usually on a larger military force.

SOURCE U

What is the value of Source U for historians studying the Abyssinian Crisis?

Telegrams from Mussolini to army commanders in Ethiopia, 1936 from *Mussolini Unleashed 1939–1941: Politics and Strategy in Fascist Italy's Last War* by MacGregor Knox, published by Cambridge University Press, UK, 1982, p. 4. Knox is an American professor of modern European history at the London School of Economics, UK.

Secret – 8 June 1936. To finish off rebels as in case at Ancober use gas. Mussolini

Secret – 8 July 1936. I repeat my authorization to initiate and systematically conduct policy of terror and extermination against rebels and populations in complicity with them. Without the law of ten eyes for one we cannot heal this wound in good time. Mussolini

21 February 1937. Agree that male population of Goggetti over 18 years of age is to be shot and village destroyed. Mussolini

What were the main
concerns of Britain
and France in the
Abyssinian Crisis?

The dilemma of Britain and France

Mussolini was convinced that neither Britain nor France would raise serious objections to the invasion and therefore the League of Nations would not interfere. In fact, in January 1935, Laval, the French foreign minister, had verbally promised him a free hand in Abyssinia. The British Foreign Office was desperate to avert the crisis either by offering Mussolini territorial compensation elsewhere or by helping to negotiate an arrangement which would give Italy effective control of Abyssinia without formally annexing it.

SOURCE V

?
What are the origins,
purpose, value and
limitations of Source V?

Excerpt of a memo from Sir Robert Vansittart, Permanent Under-Secretary of the British Foreign Office, to Sir Samuel Hoare, British Foreign Secretary, and Anthony Eden, Minister for League of Nations Affairs, 8 June 1935. Quoted in *The Making of the Second World War* by Anthony Adamthwaite, published by Routledge, London, UK, 1992, p. 138. Adamthwaite is a history professor at the University of California, Berkeley, USA.

The position is as plain as a pikestaff. Italy will have to be bought off – let us use and face ugly words – in some form or other, or Abyssinia will eventually perish. That might in itself matter less, if it did not mean that the League would also perish (and that Italy would simultaneously perform another volte-face *[change of policy] into the arms of Germany).*

Why then could such a compromise not be negotiated? The scale and brutality of the Italian invasion confronted both the British and French governments with a considerable dilemma. The British government faced an election in November 1935 and was under intense pressure from the electorate to support the League. In an unofficial ballot in June 1935, organized by the League of Nations Union formed in 1918 to win public support for the League, ten million out of eleven million votes backed the use of economic sanctions by the League in a case of aggression, as opposed to military intervention. In France, public opinion was more divided, with socialists supporting the League and conservatives supporting Italy.

France believed it needed Italy to help guarantee the borders of its central and eastern European allies in the Little Entente against Germany which Britain refused to do. Britain and France both believed Italy could be a valuable and potent ally against Germany, at least diplomatically, perhaps militarily if needed, since Mussolini had seemingly been ready to resist a German annexation of Austria in 1934.

Germany announced rearmament in early 1935 and a plebiscite held in the Saar, an industrial area bordering France and Germany but ruled by the League of Nations since 1920 (see page 37), showed that 90 per cent of the population there wanted to rejoin Germany, and they did. This boosted Hitler's confidence. The German economy, as noted above, was beginning to move forward rapidly, unlike the economies of most nations. Resurgent Germany needed more attention than whatever was happening in eastern Africa, many believed. To further prove that a war of intervention against Italy, if even possible, would have been beneficial to Germany, Germany proved the point in March 1936 by remilitarizing the Rhineland, the land bordering France where the Treaty of Versailles had expressly forbidden Germany to have any troops.

SOURCE W

'A picture remarkable for its composition, made on the bridge leading over the Rhine River and into the city of Mainz, shows a company of German infantrymen marching into the demilitarized area, to the accompaniment of cheers and "hails" of enthusiastic townsmen who can be seen giving the Nazi salute. Before the night fall, of March 7th, it was estimated that 20,000 troops had again occupied the regions forbidden to them by the Locarno Pact. It was the first time the armed soldiers had occupied these cities since 1918.'

What is the importance of Source W for historians studying the remilitarization of the Rhineland?

Britain and France, in addition to all other pressures, did not want to militarily threaten Italy as this could lead to a war which they could not afford to fight. Again, in the midst of the Great Depression, no country wanted to have to rearm, much less rearm to defend a land far from home. Italy was virulently, at least in speeches, anti-communist, so there were many, especially in France, who believed Italy should be given free rein in Ethiopia if not outright support so that a united front could be presented against a potentially aggressive Soviet Union.

Why were the League's actions against Italy ineffective?

The League's reaction

KEY TERM

Sanctions A ban on trade.

Suez Canal An important shipping route linking the Mediterranean and Red Seas and therefore the Atlantic and Indian Oceans.

In October 1935 the League condemned the Italian invasion of Ethiopia, voting for a gradually escalating program of **sanctions**. In the meantime, both Britain and France continued to search for a compromise settlement. In December, Laval and the British Foreign Minister Samuel Hoare, produced a plan which involved placing some two-thirds of Ethiopia under Italian control and giving what was left to Ethiopia including a land corridor to the sea to build trade and a better economy for its people. There was a strong possibility that it would have been acceptable to Mussolini, but it was leaked to the French press and an explosion of rage among the British public forced Hoare's resignation and the dropping of the plan. *The Times*, a major British newspaper, ridiculed the idea of the corridor as a 'corridor of camels'. The sheer violence and aggression of Italy against Ethiopia, not to mention war being built on the flimsy excuse of the Wal-Wal Incident, meant that a compromise sought by various governments was destroyed by public opinion bent on not rewarding war and not wanting to be drawn into one.

The failure of diplomacy did not translate into vigorous action against Mussolini. The League put no embargo on oil exports to Italy which would have brought the Italian economy to its knees quickly. Backed by public opinion, Britain did not threaten Italy with war or even consider it an option, so a divided French government did not either. Britain refused to close the **Suez Canal** to Italian shipping on the grounds that this might lead to war in the Mediterranean, for example. British admirals believed that Italy could win a naval conflict in the Mediterranean, perhaps then depriving Britain of control of Egypt, Cyprus, Malta and Gibraltar and severing a vital trade route to the Indian Ocean region and Asia. The lack of an oil embargo and use of the Suez Canal condemned Ethiopia to a brutal defeat which was accomplished by May 1936.

SOURCE X

The Hoare–Laval Plan for the partition of Abyssinia.

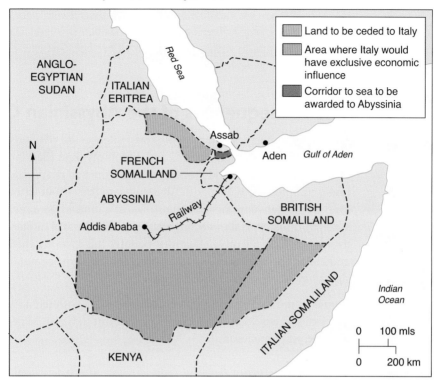

SOURCE Y

**Excerpt from a speech by Emperor Haile Selassie of Ethiopia to the
League of Nations, 30 June 1936.** *Haile Selassie I: Ethiopia's Lion of Judah*
**by Peter Schwab, published by Nelson-Hall Publishers, USA, 1979,
pp. 168–70. Schwab is a professor of political science at the State
University of New York, USA.**

*In December 1935, the council made it quite clear that its feelings were in
harmony with those of hundreds of millions of people who, in all parts of the
world, had protested against the proposal to dismember Ethiopia. It was
constantly repeated that there was not merely a conflict between the Italian
government and Ethiopia but also a conflict between the Italian government and
the League of Nations, and that is why I personally refused all proposals to my
personal advantage made to me by the Italian government if only I would betray
my people and the Covenant of the League of Nations. I was defending the cause
of all small peoples who are threatened with aggression.*

*… The Ethiopian government never expected other governments to shed their
soldiers' blood to defend the Covenant when their own immediate personal
interests were not at stake. Ethiopian warriors asked only for means to defend
themselves. On many occasions I have asked for financial assistance for the*

According to Source X, what
were the most significant
territorial changes proposed
and who benefited?

What is the message
conveyed in Source Y?

purchase of arms. That assistance has been constantly refused me. What, then, in practice, is the meaning of Article 16 and of collective security?

… Should it happen that a strong government finds it may, with impunity, destroy a weak people, then the hour strikes for that weak people to appeal to the League of Nations to give its judgment in all freedom. God and history will remember your judgment …

Why was the Abyssinian Crisis much more important than the Manchurian Crisis?

The consequences of the Abyssinian Crisis

The Abyssinian Crisis had multiple consequences, all of which had a greater impact on international relations and diplomacy than the Manchurian Crisis of 1931–2. The British and French governments had desperately worked to find a compromise which both Abyssinia and Italy could agree in order to avert a split between the European allies at a time when a revival of German strength threatened them economically, politically and militarily. Only together could they most effectively counter this growing threat, but British and French citizens were unwilling to grant their governments the right to sign away Abyssinia or reward aggression.

People feared that warring states, once rewarded with territory or concessions, would only seek more reward through war. Mussolini himself glorified war repeatedly.

SOURCE Z

According to Source Z, what is the benefit of war?

Benito Mussolini quoted in *Social Darwinism in European and American Thought, 1860–1945: Nature as Model and Nature as Threat* by Mike Hawkins, published by Cambridge University Press, UK, 1997, p. 285. Hawkins is a sociology professor at Kingston University, UK.

… societies are formed, gain strength, and move forwards through conflict; the healthiest and most vital of them assert themselves against the weakest and less well adapted through conflict; the natural evolution of nations and races takes place through conflict …

SOURCE AA

Why, according to Source AA, does Mussolini not believe in peace?

Benito Mussolini quoted in *You Might Like Socialism: A Way of Life for Modern Man* by Corliss Lamont, published by Modern Age Books, New York, USA, 1939, p. 173. Lamont was a socialist, professor of philosophy at Columbia, Harvard and other universities, and Chairman of the National Council of America–Soviet Friendship.

War is to man what maternity [giving birth] is to a woman. From a philosophical and doctrinal viewpoint, I do not believe in perpetual peace.

The League of Nations did respond with economic sanctions, although, as noted, oil was not among them, the one item that would have likely brought an abrupt end to the war since Italy produced none of its own. However,

Italy was a nation poor in most resources and thus needed imports, so sanctions did inflict massive economic damage to the country. This quickly led to a breakdown in relations between Britain and France on one side and Italy on the other which had serious consequences for European diplomacy.

Germany was not a member of the League since dropping out in 1933, so did not participate in the international embargo, instead increasing trade with Italy. A treaty of friendship and co-operation was signed in October 1936 between Italy and Germany, known as the **Rome–Berlin Axis**. This agreement helped delineate each other's foreign policy objectives which included recognizing Germany's interest in Austria.

Collective security failed in an effort by the governments of Britain and France to keep Italy as an ally while satisfying the demands of its citizens. Italy was actually driven closer to Germany by League actions. After the blatant failure of the League to address the destruction of a member state, it ceased to be considered as an influential body. It was shown that the League's major sponsors and leaders were only willing to use it as a tool of their own foreign policy, jettisoning key sections of the League's Covenant at will. The Convenant was the very thing which gave the League any meaning and a reason to exist.

KEY TERM

Rome–Berlin Axis Treaty of friendship between Germany and Italy in 1936, signalling an end to Italy's diplomatic co-operation with Britain and France.

SOURCE BB

The Origins of the Second World War by A.J.P. Taylor, Penguin Books, London, UK, 1961, pp. 127–8. First published in 1961 by Hamish Hamilton, this book has been most recently reprinted by Penguin Books in 2001. Taylor was a British historian who wrote many books on European history and was lecturer at many British universities.

What is the message conveyed in Source BB about the League of Nations?

On 1 May the Emperor Haile Selassie left Abyssinia. A week later, Mussolini proclaimed the foundation of a new Roman empire.

This was the deathblow to the League as well as to Abyssinia. Fifty-two nations had combined to resist aggression; all they accomplished was that Haile Selassie lost all his country instead of only half. Incorrigible in impracticality, the League further offended Italy by allowing Haile Selassie a hearing at the Assembly; and then expelled him for the crime of taking the Covenant seriously. Japan and Germany had already left the League; Italy followed in December 1937. The League continued in existence only by averting its eyes from what was happening around it. When foreign Powers intervened in the Spanish civil war, the Spanish government appealed to the League. The Council first studied the question, then expressed its regrets, and agreed to house the pictures from the Prado [Spanish art museum] at Geneva. In September 1938 the Assembly actually met at the height of the Czech crisis; it managed to get through the session without noting that a crisis was taking place. In September 1939 no one bothered to inform the League that war had broken out. In December 1939 the League expelled Soviet Russia for invading Finland. The Assembly loyally observed Swiss neutrality by not mentioning the war between Germany and the Western Powers.

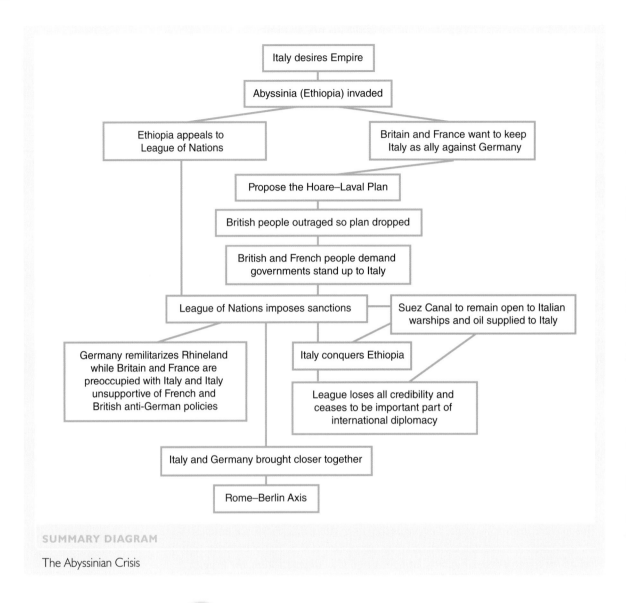

The Abyssinian Crisis

⑤ International agreements and diplomatic actions 1934–6

▶ *Key question: What were the main international agreements and diplomatic actions during the Great Depression?*

The years 1934–6 saw a number of pacts, treaties, conferences and military actions. Germany claimed it sought peace by making an agreement with Poland and then announcing major rearmament. While Britain, France and Italy appeared to want to work together to keep Germany isolated, each nation's diplomacy led to tensions with the others, allowing Germany to rearm and reoccupy the Rhineland. British and French reaction to the invasion of Abyssinia by Italy led to greater co-operation between Italy and Germany, ending Germany's diplomatic isolation.

The Polish–German Non-Aggression Pact, January 1934

Hitler's first major initiative in foreign policy was the conclusion of a ten-year pact of non-aggression with Poland. While many historians have argued that the purpose of the pact was to weaken an earlier alliance of mutual military assistance between France and Poland, obviously aimed at Germany, it must be remembered that German mass rearmament had not been accomplished and was only in the planning stages at this time. Poland's military was far larger, and even more modern in 1934, than that of Germany. Poland also wanted a non-aggression pact because it meant that it was less likely to be required to go to war to protect France.

Poland's primary enemy was the Soviet Union with which it had fought a successful war that ended in 1920, effectively doubling the size of Poland (see page 94). The second Five-Year Plan of the Soviet Union was already in progress and the future industrial, and therefore military, might of the Soviet Union needed to be observed and potentially opposed if Polish independence was threatened.

France believed that the pact with Germany weakened its own security since Poland could no longer be counted on to put military pressure on Germany's eastern borders. The French believed that this would mean that the Germans could now make a single, large army bent on the invasion of France instead of being divided between attacking Poland and France. Hitler was warned in August 1934 by a senior German diplomat, B.W. von Bülow, that France remained very powerful and capable of action during any rearmament programme.

Why did the Polish–German Non-Aggression Pact have major support in both Poland and Germany?

SOURCE CC

Excerpt of a memo from State Secretary B.W. von Bülow to Hitler, German Chancellor, August 1934. Quoted in *Documents on Nazism 1919–1945* by Jeremy Noakes and Geoffrey Pridham, published by University of Exeter Press, UK, 1995, p. 662. Noakes is a professor of history at the University of Exeter, UK. Pridham is a senior research fellow in politics at University of Bristol, UK.

In judging the situation we should never overlook the fact that no kind of rearmament in the next few years could give us military security. Even apart from our isolation, we shall for a long time yet be hopelessly inferior to France in the military sphere. A particularly dangerous period will be 1934–5 on account of the reorganization of the Reichswehr [German army].

What is the message conveyed in Source CC?

What factors prevented Germany successfully supporting a coup in Austria in 1934?

🔑 **KEY TERM**

Satellite state A state that is technically independent, but under some control by another state.

Coup Overthrow of a government.

The attempted Nazi coup in Austria, July 1934

Hitler was certainly aware of Germany's lack of security with its small military, but over Austria he adopted an aggressive policy. Hitler was himself Austrian and believed, as did most Germans, that all Germans should have the right to live in Germany, even an expanded one that included all lands where Germans lived, including Austria. In June 1934, he met Mussolini and tried to convince him that Austria should become a German **satellite state**. When Mussolini rejected this, Hitler gave the Austrian Nazis strong, unofficial encouragement to stage a **coup** a month later that was disastrously unsuccessful.

Mussolini was determined to keep Austria as a buffer state between Italy and Germany and to perhaps demonstrate to Britain and France that he was a powerful and important ally. He immediately mobilized troops on the Italian–Austrian frontier and forced Hitler to disown the coup which immediately failed. Hitler was unable and unwilling to take a military risk at this early stage of his political career, not least because he did not have complete control of the army. The army was led by officers from the old nobility who had little respect for Hitler, a former corporal who was not only non-noble, but to them not even a real German.

The incident brought about a sharp deterioration in German–Italian relations and appeared to rule out any prospect of an alliance. Within a few years, however, the Rome–Berlin Axis would be signed and Hitler would assume complete control of the army in 1938. In 1938 Austria was annexed to Germany with Mussolini's apparent consent.

What was the most significant result of the Stresa Conference and why was the so-called Stresa Front doomed to fail?

The Stresa Conference, April 1935

In April 1935 the British, French and Italian heads of government met in Stresa, Italy, to discuss forming a common diplomatic front against Germany. In March, Germany had announced that rearmament would begin in earnest since France and Britain, among others, failed to abide by the Treaty of Versailles which stated that those countries would work towards their own disarmament. Britain and France had not disarmed but had forced Germany to do so, so Germany now must rearm to protect itself. At the conference all three countries condemned German plans to rebuild its military and agreed to work together.

Hitler quickly launched a diplomatic offensive to reassure the powers of his peaceful intentions. In a speech that repeated many aspects of German foreign policy of the 1920s, he proposed a series of non-aggression pacts with Germany's neighbours, promised to observe the Locarno Pact (see page 84) which guaranteed borders in western Europe and agreed to resort to diplomacy to redraw any borders in central or eastern Europe. He also stated that he would accept an overall limitation on armaments if the other countries also agreed to do so.

France responded by contacting the Soviet Union, a state that few countries had normalized relations with, establishing the Franco-Soviet Treaty of Mutual Assistance in May 1935. This pact stated that through the League, France and the Soviet Union would definitely come to each other's assistance in case of attack by another European power. Britain, Italy and Belgium, signatories to the Locarno Pact, were dismayed at this development as they believed this treaty could lead them into a war with Germany over eastern European borders that they were not willing to fight for.

While Mussolini continued to build up forces to invade Ethiopia, Germany and Britain had been as busy as France in breaking up the unity of Stresa by concluding the Anglo-German Naval Treaty in June 1935, completely in contradiction to the declarations at Stresa made just two months before. The British believed that they had scored a diplomatic victory because the treaty would limit the German navy to only 35 per cent of the size of the British navy. Germany would then have a small fleet that could never challenge them for control of the seas militarily or threaten their merchant fleet. This had the added advantage of tying down the Germans by allowing them to use up precious national resources and expensive raw material imports on ships that would be unable to challenge British control of the sea.

SOURCE DD

A cartoon by David Low, *Evening Standard*, 24 June 1935. Low was a cartoonist from New Zealand who worked for many British newspapers from 1919 to 1953. The *Evening Standard* is a London newspaper published since 1827.

What is the message of Source DD regarding the League of Nations and the Abyssinian Crisis?

According to Source EE, what was the value of Britain making agreements with Germany?

SOURCE EE

Excerpt of a letter from Sir John Simon, British Foreign Secretary, to King George V, February 1935. Quoted in *Sir Gerald Fitzmaurice and the World Crisis: A Legal Adviser in the Foreign Office 1930–1945* by Anthony Carty, published by Springer, USA, 2000, p. 179. Carty is a law professor at the University of Aberdeen, UK.

The practical choice is between a Germany which continues to rearm without any regulation or agreement and a Germany which, through getting a recognition of its rights and some modification of the Peace Treaties, enters into the comity [community] of nations and contributes, in this and other ways, to European stability.

The Anglo-German Naval Treaty must be seen in the context of British diplomacy which worked to treat Germany as a state with legitimate concerns. Treating Germany otherwise might lead to war which Britain was not prepared, and perhaps unwilling, to fight.

Italy and France, however, believed that German rearmament had been encouraged and the Treaty of Versailles had been violated with British consent. This brought France and Italy temporarily closer together and in mid-1935 there were talks about mutual military co-operation in case of war with Germany. The Stresa Front was severely damaged as a result of the diplomacy of France and Britain, but collapsed completely with the Italian invasion of Abyssinia and economic sanctions placed on Italy.

Why, despite the Locarno Agreements, was there no effective opposition when Germany remilitarized the Rhineland?

→ # The remilitarization of the Rhineland, March 1936

The remilitarization of the Rhineland marked an important stage in Hitler's plans for rebuilding German power. The construction of strong fortifications there would enable him to stop any French attempts to invade Germany. Hitler had originally planned to reoccupy the Rhineland in 1937, but the favourable diplomatic situation created by the Abyssinian Crisis persuaded him to act in March 1936. In December 1935 the German army was ordered to start planning the reoccupation. Meanwhile, German diplomats began to make a legal justification for such action by arguing that the Franco-Soviet Pact was contrary to the Locarno Agreement (see page 84).

According to Source FF, what made the reoccupation of the Rhineland by Germany possible?

SOURCE FF

Excerpt from *The Origins of the Second World War* by A.J.P. Taylor, Penguin Books, London, UK, 1961, pp. 129–30. First published in 1961 by Hamish Hamilton, this book has been most recently reprinted by Penguin Books in 2001. Taylor was a British historian who wrote many books on European history and was lecturer at many British universities.

Hitler's excuse was the French ratification of the Franco-Soviet pact on 27 February 1936. This, he claimed, had destroyed the assumptions of Locarno;

not much of an argument, but a useful appeal no doubt to anti-Bolshevik feeling in Great Britain and France. The actual move on 7 March was a staggering example of Hitler's strong nerve. Germany had literally no forces available for war. The trained men of the old Reichswehr [German army] were now dispersed as instructors among the new mass army; and this new army was not yet ready. Hitler assured his protesting generals that he would withdraw his token force at the first sign of French action; but he was unshakably confident that no action would follow.

The reoccupation of the Rhineland did not take the French by surprise. They had been brooding on it apprehensively ever since the beginning of the Abyssinian affair.

Crucial to the success of his plan was the attitude of Italy. Mussolini, isolated from the other Stresa Powers because of his Abyssinian policy, assured Hitler that he would not co-operate with the British and French in opposing the remilitarization of the Rhineland.

German troops entered the Rhineland on 7 March 1936. In order to reassure France that they did not intend to violate the Franco-German frontier, they were initially few in number and lightly equipped.

France did not move to intervene. This was partly because the French border had not been violated and there was little support in both France and Britain for preventing Germany from controlling its own territory. The French army had planned only for a defensive war with the assumption that Germany would attack along its shared border, not through the demilitarized Rhineland. The French government refused to fight Germany alone and Britain made it clear that it was unwilling to go to war over the Rhineland.

The British government did reassure France that in the event of an unprovoked German attack on French territory, it would send two divisions of troops to France. British public opinion was convinced that Hitler was merely walking into 'his own back garden'. In fact, the British government was pleased at the reoccupation of the Rhineland because it removed a major German grievance against Britain and France and meant that France could no longer threaten Germany with invasion.

The remilitarization of the Rhineland was a triumph for Hitler, and, as an internal French Foreign Office memorandum of 12 March 1936 stressed, there was a feeling in Europe that Germany was now the centre of European power.

What is the origin and purpose of Source GG?

Excerpt from a memorandum for the foreign minister from René Massigli, deputy political director of the French Foreign Ministry, 12 March 1936. *The Foreign Policy of France* by J. Néré, published by Routledge, London, UK, 2002, p. 337. Massigli was a senior French diplomat who was secretary-general of the Conference of Ambassadors from 1920 to 1931 and by 1937 political director in the Foreign Ministry. Néré is a historian of modern French history.

A German success would likewise not fail to encourage elements which, in Yugoslavia, look towards Berlin … In Rumania this will be a victory of the elements of the Right which have been stirred up by Hitlerite propaganda. All that will remain for Czechoslovakia is to come to terms with Germany. Austria does not conceal her anxiety. 'Next time it will be our turn' … Turkey, who has increasingly close economic relations with Germany, but who politically remains in the Franco-British axis, can be induced to modify her line. The Scandinavian countries … are alarmed.

While Germany's brazen reoccupation of the demilitarized zone was a victory for Hitler and a diplomatic victory of sorts for the British, the reality was that the Treaty of Versailles no longer functioned. The Stresa Front, if it ever existed, was now dead and Germany was again an emerging economic and military power.

The Rome–Berlin Axis and the Anti-Comintern Pact, October and November 1936

What was the main advantage for Germany of creating a relationship, even if just on paper, with Italy and Japan in 1936?

The Rome–Berlin Axis

The summer of 1936 saw increasingly cordial relations between Berlin and Rome. While Britain refused to recognize the King of Italy as the 'Emperor of Abyssinia', Germany did so. Italy's growing hostility towards Britain, France and especially the Soviet Union, a country that Italy had positive relations with until the start of the Spanish Civil War in 1936, meant closer relations with Germany and its goals. One German goal was to influence or even annex Austria, something that had been prevented by Italy in 1934. In January 1936 Mussolini assured the German Ambassador in Rome that 'If Austria, as a formerly independent state, were … in practice to become a German satellite, he would have no objection'.

The understanding between Italy and Germany over Austria prepared the way for a German–Italian agreement which was signed in Berlin in October 1936. This formed a new diplomatic relationship commonly known as the Rome–Berlin Axis. Mussolini announced this new alignment to the world at a mass meeting in Milan on 1 November.

SOURCE HH

Speech by Benito Mussolini in Milan, Italy, 1 November 1936, quoted in *The Causes of the Second World War* by Anthony Crozier, published by Blackwell, UK, 1997, p. 121. Crozier was a history lecturer at Queen Mary College, University of London.

The Berlin conversations have resulted in an understanding between our two countries over certain problems which have been particularly acute. By these understandings … this Berlin–Rome line is … an axis around which can revolve all those European states with a will to collaboration and peace.

What, according to Source HH, was the purpose of the Rome–Berlin Axis?

The Anti-Comintern Pact

Three weeks later Hitler overrode advice from his professional diplomats and signed the Anti-Comintern Pact with Japan. This was more of symbolic than practical importance as it was aimed against the Comintern, the Soviet institution established to sponsor and spread communism to other countries, rather than the Soviet Union itself. For Hitler, coming so soon after the Rome–Berlin Axis, the pact trumpeted to the world that Germany was no longer isolated, as it had appeared just a year earlier.

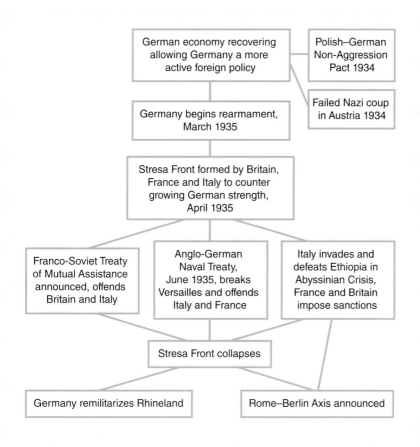

SUMMARY DIAGRAM

International Diplomacy 1934–6

The Great Depression and threats to international peace and collective security

International Relations and diplomacy between 1930 and 1936 must be seen in the context of the Great Depression. Economic hardship led many countries to erect trade barriers and turn to their empires to stimulate their economies. Other countries, such as Japan, sought economic relief by expanding their territory at the expense of others. Economic stress led to the formation of coalition governments in Britain and France, while in Germany it was directly connected to the formation of a National Socialist (Nazi) government in 1933. The Nazi government, through strict controls on imports and a series of trade agreements, resurrected the German economy which allowed major rearmament to begin in 1935, violating the Treaty of Versailles and causing diplomatic problems for Britain and France.

Collective security arrangements through the League of Nations were ineffective against Japan and Italy in the Manchurian and Abyssinian Crises for several reasons. Britain and France were the main world powers involved in the League of Nations and their populations did not want war. Military intervention was financially impossible due to the effects of the Great Depression and politically member parties of British and French coalition governments would not support war except in self-defence. Diplomatically, Britain and France were reluctant to interfere with the Abyssinian Crisis because they wished to retain Italy as an ally against Germany. Italy, however, moved closer to Germany in 1936 as League of Nations economic sanctions affected its economy.

A flurry of diplomatic activity from 1934 to 1936 saw Germany not only strengthening its position through pacts with Poland and Italy, but also remilitarizing the Rhineland. British and French diplomatic efforts to build an anti-German coalition failed and these two powers disagreed on such things as whether Germany should be allowed to rearm, remilitarize the Rhineland or be allowed to rebuild its navy. These were all violations of the Treaty of Versailles.

 # Examination advice

Paper 1 question 4: how to integrate sources and write a good essay

Question 4 is always an essay question. It requires you to write what you know while integrating the sources provided. The sources are there to support your own knowledge. Therefore, it is important that you prepare yourself for this type of question by knowing and understanding the history of international diplomacy between 1919 and 1936 that we have presented in this book.

Question 4 is always worth 8 marks. This means it is worth about one-third of the overall mark possible. We suggest that you spend 30–35 minutes answering this question, using the first five to eight minutes of this time to summarize the sources and outline your response.

How to answer
Summarize the sources and outline your essay
It is best to first list and summarize your sources to focus your thoughts. This should be done in about five minutes and should be in the form of short bullet points. Once you have summarized the sources, briefly outline your essay's structure. This outline should include some sort of introduction to your essay and a concluding answer to the question. Write your outline down on your examination paper, but put a single line through everything that you do not want the examiner to mark.

Writing the essay
When you write your essay make sure you follow your outline and use all the sources. This should take the remainder of your time, which should be at least 25 minutes.

You need to start with a good introduction to focus your essay and which defines anything that might be open to interpretation. Your introduction should conclude a definite answer to the question. This should further serve to focus your essay. Usually you can introduce one or more of your sources into the introduction to support what you are going to cover.

All sources must be used at least once, but use them multiple times if they will help your essay. Remember the sources should support your essay.

If you write something you want the examiner to ignore, draw a single line through this and move on. Finally, under no circumstances are you to actually just list the five sources and a couple of bullet points beneath each in a sort of preamble to a real essay. Sources should be integrated and quoted to support your essay.

Your concluding paragraph should clearly answer the essay question, summarizing your main arguments. For example, if the question asks you 'to what extent', answer the question:

- 'to a great extent'
- 'to some extent' or
- 'to no extent'.

Your conclusion will then include a summary of your main points.

Source I: see page 190
Source J: see page 191
Source K: see page 192
Source L: see page 193
Source M: see page 194

Example

This question uses Sources I–M found in this chapter:

> Using these sources and your own knowledge, explain the importance of the Manchurian Crisis for Japan.

First, very briefly summarize the sources just for your own information in five minutes or less.

Source I: Japan army has political power, acted in Manchuria on its own, killed PM.

Source J: Japan army in Manchuria since 1905, staged railway bomb at Mukden 1931, blamed Chinese, planned to take all Manchuria.

Source K: Japan had major investment in mines, factories, schools, etc. in Manchuria because of S. Manchu. Railway.

Source L: map of Japanese Empire.

Source M: TOV Art. 17. If League member makes war on another same as war on all League members.

Second, briefly outline in bullet points the main parts of your essay in five minutes or less.

Introduction
- Was important
  - Made army stronger
  - Gave Japan economic help
  - League reaction = expansion/defeat

Paragraph 2: Military in constitution
- Part of cabinet
  - Could collapse gov. at will
- Civilian gov. must agree with military demands
  - Military acting in Manchu. on its own
- Military kills PM, proves strength
    PM from military

Paragraph 3: Great Depression
- Industry problems

- Trade barriers in USA, Britain, France
- Empire small
  - Taiwan
  - Korea
- European Empires
  - Large
  - Economic benefits
- Manchuria
  - Coal
  - Iron
  - Helps Japan in GD

Paragraph 4: League weakness = Japan expansion
- China asks for help
- League criticizes Japan
- Japan leaves 1933
- League shows no punishment for war
  - Japan expands empire into China
  - Into French Indochina
  - Attacks USA
  - Leads to defeat in WW2

Conclusion: MC had great impact, great importance:
- Made military stronger
- Helped in GD
- League weakness encouraged Empire

Third, write an answer to the question.

The Manchurian Crisis of 1931 was important for Japan in many ways. The Crisis allowed the military to consolidate and expand its authority over the Japanese government. Bringing Manchuria into the empire gave Japan raw materials in the midst of the Great Depression as well as land for settling its growing population. Finally, the actions of the League of Nations caused Japan to end its membership and expand into the rest of China within a few years, sowing the seeds of destruction for the Empire.

   The constitution of the Japanese Empire gave great power to the military. Ministers for the navy and army both sat in the cabinet and if the navy or army objected to any government policy, they could

The introduction clearly indicates that the Manchurian Crisis was important and then presents three reasons that it was so.

simply refuse to join the cabinet causing the government to collapse. This created a situation where the military could dictate the policies of the state to their liking and meant that the civilian government had little control over military policy, as indicated in <u>Source I</u>, if the civilian ministers wished to accomplish anything and stay in office. When the Japanese army invaded Manchuria, after staging a bombing on the South Manchurian Railway to provide an excuse, according to <u>Source J</u>, the civilian government had to agree. Perhaps to prove their power over the civilian government, the Japanese Prime Minister Inouye was killed by members of the military in 1932, as stated in <u>Source I</u>. The assassins received light sentences and military officers took over the prime minister's office for several years. The Manchurian Crisis consolidated and expanded the military's control over the government of Japan.

The Great Depression created a major economic crisis in Japan. Major industries, like that of silk production, collapsed as the USA, France and Britain created trade barriers to protect their own industries. France and Britain turned to their empires to alleviate the effect of the depression on their economies. According to <u>Source L</u>, a map of the Japanese Empire, Japan had expanded since 1895 when it took control of Taiwan and in 1905 when Korea was annexed, but these areas were small especially when compared to the British and French Empires which occupied about 35 per cent of the earth's surface. Japan also wanted sources of raw material, markets for its manufactured goods, and areas to settle its growing population. Manchuria was already providing some of this along the South Manchurian Railway which Japan operated. Uthai Wilcox in <u>Source K</u> indicates that just in the area controlled by Japan before the invasion, Manchuria provided coal in huge quantities, specifically 20,000 tons of coal per day but with 'an estimated potential of 1,200,000,000 tons'. <u>Source K</u> states also that it was believed that 1,000,000 tons of iron per year could be produced from Manchuria. The addition of Manchuria would be of great benefit to Japanese industry to help recover from the Great Depression and into the future.

Manchuria was part of China and both China and Japan were part of the League of Nations and China asked the League to

All five sources are used in the essay and explicitly mentioned. Some sources are quoted which demonstrates the importance of particular sources in making a historical argument.

The essay makes three strong arguments in three tightly focused paragraphs. Each paragraph focuses on a different topic relating to the importance of the Manchurian Crisis for Japan.

intervene. The League only helped China by criticizing Japanese actions, something intolerable to Japan, so it left the League in 1933. Although an attack on China should have caused war between Japan and the other League members, as required by Article 17 in the Treaty of Versailles, <u>Source M</u>, which stated: 'Should any Member of the League resort to war … it shall be deemed to have committed an act of war against all other Members … '. The League did not declare war since no member of the League wanted to fight Japan far from their homes in the midst of the Great Depression. Japan, and its ruling military officers, understood by this that China was vulnerable and no European power would challenge the Japanese in Asia, leading to a much greater conflict in 1937 that would see Japan conquer large areas of China. Perhaps encouraged by this success, the Japanese went on to attack French Indochina in 1941, provoking the USA to end oil exports to Japan. This was a real threat to Japan and had the potential to end its military dominance in Asia. Japan responded by attacking the USA which led to a four-year war in which the USA slowly inflicted a crushing defeat on Japan, ending its dominance over Asia.

The Manchurian Crisis had a great impact on Japan. It confirmed the power of the military and saw that power expand greatly as they took over the government. Japan was able to expand its empire to include mineral-rich Manchuria which helped it during the Great Depression when most other avenues of trade and raw materials had closed. Finally, the lack of interest in Asia by the League of Nations, or the inability of League powers to act, encouraged Japan to expand its empire at the expense of China. This would bring the USA into conflict with Japan in time and finally Japan's defeat at the end of the Second World War in 1945. The Manchurian Crisis was of the greatest importance to Japan.

> The conclusion clearly indicates that the Manchurian Crisis was of the greatest importance to Japan and summarizes the argument.

> This essay uses all the sources in an explicit and appropriate manner. The essay also goes beyond the sources to indicate that the student also used their own knowledge and that this knowledge was correct. The response to the question is complex, but balanced in that it demonstrates that Japan was affected in many ways. Mark: 8/8.

Examination practice

Question 1:   5 minutes
Question 2:   10 minutes
Question 3:   10 minutes
Question 4:   35 minutes

Below are a series of exam-style questions for different topics within this chapter for you to practise. Paper 1 exams are one hour long, not including five minutes of reading time at the exam's start when only reading is permitted. You may wish to practise only specific questions, and if this is the case, allow the time per question shown on the left. For guidance on how to answer the different question types see pages 29–30 (question 1a), pages 124–8 (question 1b), pages 65–8 (question 2), pages 170–4 (question 3), pages 218–23 (question 4).

Paper I Sample A

These questions relate to the Great Depression and its effect on Germany. Sources can be found on the following pages.

- Source D (page 182)
- Source E (page 185)
- Source F (page 185)
- Source G (page 186)
- Source H (page 187)

1 a) What, according to Source D, were the reasons for the rise of Adolf Hitler and the National Socialists to power in Germany? *(3 marks)*

b) What is the message conveyed by Source G? *(2 marks)*

2 Compare and contrast Source E and Source F regarding the role of the economic crisis for the rise of the National Socialist, or Nazi, Party. *(6 marks)*

3 With reference to their origin and purpose, assess the value and limitations for historians studying the Great Depression of Source F and Source H. *(6 marks)*

4 Using these sources and your own knowledge, discuss the effect of the Great Depression on Germany. *(8 marks)*

Paper I Sample B

These questions relate to the Abyssinian Crisis and its impact on international diplomacy. Sources can be found on the following pages.

- Source R (page 201)
- Source Y (page 207)
- Source DD (page 213)
- Source V (page 204)
- Source BB (page 209)

1 a) What, according to Source BB, was the importance of the Abyssinian Crisis for international diplomacy? *(3 marks)*

b) What is the message of Source FF? *(2 marks)*

2 Compare and contrast Sources R and Y regarding the importance of Italy's invasion of Abyssinia. *(6 marks)*

3 With reference to their origin and purpose, assess the value and limitations for historians studying the Abyssinian Crisis of Sources R and BB. *(6 marks)*

4 Using these sources and your own knowledge, discuss the impact of the Abyssinian Crisis on international diplomacy up to the end of 1936. *(8 marks)*

Extended examination practice

Sample question 1s

For guidance on how to answer this type of question see pages 29–30.

Sources can be found on the following pages:

- Source A (page 179)
- Source B (page 180)
- Source E (page 185)
- Source F (page 185)
- Source I (page 190)

1 What, according to Source A, was the effect of the Great Depression on France?

2 According to Source B, what was the effect of high protective tariffs on British foreign policy?

3 According to Source E, which groups supported Hitler and the National Socialists?

4 Why, according to Source F, did the Nazi Party find political success?

5 According to Source I, how did the Japanese military assert its control over the Japanese government?

Visual sources

For guidance on how to answer this type of question see page 122.

Sources can be found on the following pages:

- Source G (page 186)
- Source L (page 193)
- Source S (page 202)
- Source T (page 203)
- Source W (page 205)

1 What is the message conveyed by Source G?

2 What message is conveyed by Source L?

3 What is the message conveyed by Source S?

4 What is the message conveyed by Source T?

5 What is the message conveyed by Source W?

Sample question 2s

For guidance on how to answer this type of question see pages 65–8.

Sources can be found on the following pages:

- Source B (page 180)
- Source E (page 185)
- Source F (page 185)
- Source N (page 197)
- Source O (page 199)
- Source P (page 199)
- Source Q (page 200)
- Source V (page 204)
- Source Y (page 207)

1 Compare and contrast the views expressed in Sources B and D about the importance of imperial preference for European powers.

2 Compare and contrast the views of Sources E and F regarding the increasing strength of the National Socialists in German politics in the early 1930s.

3 Compare and contrast the views of Sources N and O regarding the importance of the Manchurian Crisis for international relations.

4 Compare and contrast the views expressed by Sources P and Q regarding the importance of the Manchurian Crisis.

5 Compare and contrast the views expressed in Sources V and Y regarding the importance of the Abyssinian Crisis.

Sample question 3s

For guidance on how to answer this type of question see pages 170–4.

Sources can be found on the following pages:

- Source A (page 179)
- Source B (page 180)
- Source C (page 181)
- Source E (page 185)
- Source I (page 190)
- Source J (page 191)
- Source N (page 197)
- Source O (page 199)
- Source P (page 199)
- Source Q (page 200)

1 With reference to their origins and purpose, discuss the value and limitations of Sources A and B for historians studying the impact of the Great Depression on France.

2 With reference to their origins and purpose, discuss the value and limitations of Sources C and E for historians studying the effect of the Great Depression on national politics.

3 With reference to their origins and purpose, discuss the value and limitations of Sources I and J for historians studying the causes of the Manchurian Crisis.

4 With reference to their origins and purpose, discuss the value and limitations of Sources N and P for historians studying the importance of the Manchurian Crisis on international relations.

5 With reference to their origins and purpose, discuss the value and limitations of Sources O and Q for historians studying the effect of the Manchurian Crisis on collective security.

Sample question 4s

These questions use sources from earlier chapters to practise your skills in answering essay questions that require the integration of sources.

Chapter 1

Sources can be found on the following pages:

- Source D (page 14)
- Source F (page 20)
- Source H (page 22)
- Source E (page 17)
- Source G (page 21)

1 Using these sources and your own knowledge, discuss the importance of the demands of the Allies for the 1919 Paris Peace Conference.

Chapter 2

Sources can be found on the following pages:

- Source P (page 47)
- Source R (page 48)
- Source U (page 50)
- Source Q (page 48)
- Source T (page 50)

2 Using these sources and your own knowledge, explain how the Treaty of Trianon affected Austria.

Chapter 3

- Source B (page 75)
- Source N (page 88)
- Source P (page 89)
- Source L (page 85)
- Source O (page 89)

3 Using these sources and your own knowledge, discuss how Germany was affected by the Peace of Paris.

Chapter 4

- Source B (page 134)
- Source D (page 137)
- Source G (page 140)
- Source C (page 136)
- Source E (page 138)

4 Using these sources and your own knowledge, discuss to what extent the League of Nations was successful in international diplomacy from 1920 to 1925.

✓ Activities

1 In groups, create your own Paper 1 questions from sources found in Chapters 1–4 using the above examples in the examination practice section as templates. Pass your questions to another group to answer under IB exam-timed conditions.

2 History is about making arguments using supportive evidence. Divide into four groups. Each group should take one of the four statements below and come up with evidence in support of the statement.

a) The Manchurian Crisis moved the world closer to the Second World War.

b) The Manchurian Crisis had little to do with the Second World War because it occurred ten years before Japan attacked the USA in 1941.

c) The Manchurian Crisis actually strengthened the League of Nations, but ironically it was this new-found security within the League's collective security arrangements that led the world into the Second World War because of the Abyssinian Crisis.

d) The Manchurian Crisis actually provided the world with more and better security and without it having happened, the world would have entered the Second World War sooner.

Now using your evidence debate the following question in class:

To what extent did the Manchurian Crisis contribute to the failure of the League of Nations and collective security?

Timeline

November 1918	Germany becomes a republic
	Armistice ends fighting between Allies and Germany
	Soviet Republic of Bavaria in Germany proclaimed
January 1919	Paris Peace Conference begins
	Spartacist uprising in Germany crushed
	Czechoslovakia seizes Těšín from Poland
March 1919	Hungarian Soviet Republic proclaimed
	Communist rebellion in Berlin put down
	Kapp *Putsch* in Berlin put down
June 1919 September 1919	Treaty of Versailles dealing with Germany signed
	League of Nations created along with mandate system
	Treaty of St Germain-in-Laye dealing with Austria signed
	D'Annunzio proclaims independent Fiume
November 1919	Treaty of Neuilly-sur-Seine dealing with Bulgaria signed
June 1920	Treaty of Trianon dealing with Hungary signed
August 1920	Treaty of Trianon dealing with Ottoman Empire signed

March 1921	Upper Silesia plebiscite; mixed result
	War between Poland and Soviet Union ends
April 1921	German reparation sums announced
Nov. 1921– Feb. 1922	Washington Naval Conference results in three disarmament treaties
April 1922	Geneva Conference to discuss German reparations
	Treaty of Rapallo signed between Germany and the USSR
May 1922	Upper Silesia divided between Germany and Poland
October 1922	Mussolini becomes prime minister of Italy
	League of Nations loan to save Austrian economy
January 1923	France and Belgium occupy Ruhr after Germany ends reparations
	Lithuania seizes Memel
August 1923	Corfu incident between Italy and Germany
July 1923	Treaty of Lausanne dealing with Republic of Turkey signed
August 1924	London Conference activates Dawes Plan regarding German reparations
October 1925	League of Nations resolves crisis between Bulgaria and Greece

December 1925	Locarno Treaties guaranteeing western European borders signed	**July 1934**	Attempted Nazi coup in Austria fails
August 1928	Kellogg–Briand Pact signed renouncing war to solve problems	**March 1935**	Germany announces rearmament
1929	Soviet Union's first Five-Year Plan for economic development starts but backdated to 1928	**April 1935**	Stresa Conference to oppose Germany
October 1929	Wall Street Crash in the USA; beginning of Great Depression	**May 1935**	Franco-Soviet Treaty of Mutual Assistance
January 1930	Young Plan reduces German reparations	**June 1935**	Anglo-German Naval Treaty
	London Naval Conference begins	**October 1935**	Italy invades Abyssinia
September 1931	Japan invades Manchuria	**December 1935**	Second London Naval Conference begins
October 1932	Iraq becomes first and only League mandate to achieve independence	**March 1936**	Germany reoccupies Rhineland
January 1933	Adolf Hitler becomes German chancellor	**October 1936**	Rome–Berlin Axis announced
	Roosevelt begins as US president	**November 1936**	Anti-Comintern Pact signed between Germany and Japan
February 1933	Japan leaves League of Nations	**1932–4**	League's World Disarmament Conference meets in Geneva, Switzerland
January 1934	Polish–German Non-Aggression Pact signed		

Glossary

Allied Disarmament Commission   Organization established to monitor the German military to ensure compliance with the Treaty of Versailles.

Allied Powers   Britain, France, the USA, Italy and other countries which fought against Germany, Austria-Hungary, Bulgaria and the Ottoman Empire.

Amau Doctrine   Japanese government's declaration that China and Asia were Japan's area of interest and that other nations were not to interfere in the region.

Arbitration   Submitting international disputes to the League and agreeing beforehand to accept whatever decision was reached.

Armistice   Agreement to stop fighting.

Arms race   Competition between nations to be the most heavily armed.

Asia Minor   Western-most peninsula of Asia.

Austro-Hungarian Empire   A multinational empire which was administrated in two separate parts: Austria and the Kingdom of Hungary, with the Habsburg Emperor of Austria also being the King of Hungary. Its territory compromised all of modern-day Austria, Hungary, Czech Republic, Slovakia, Slovenia, Croatia, Bosnia-Herzegovina and parts of Poland, Romania, Italy, Serbia, Montenegro and Ukraine. It was formed in 1867 from the Austrian Empire and lasted until 1918.

Balfour Declaration   A communication to the Zionists by A.J. Balfour, the British Foreign Secretary, declaring British support for establishing a national home for Jews in Palestine.

Balkan Entente   Agreement between Yugoslavia, Greece, Turkey and Romania to abandon territorial claims against each other and to work together against any aggression, particularly by Bulgaria.

Benevolent neutrality   Not willing to be involved but also not criticizing.

Bolshevik   A group that followed the teachings of Karl Marx. It preached the violent overthrow of the existing social order and capitalism in order to establish the working class as the only social and economic class.

Buffer state   A country separating two other nations who are enemies.

Capital ships   Large warships such as battleships and cruisers that are heavily armoured and armed.

Central Powers   The wartime alliance of Germany, Austria, Turkey and Bulgaria.

Chancellor   Head of the German parliament and equivalent to prime minister.

Coalition government   When two or more political parties join together to form a parliamentary majority, allowing a cabinet to operate a government.

Collective security   An agreement between nations that an aggressive act towards one nation will be treated as an aggressive act towards all nations under the agreement.

Collectivization   The policy of forcing farmers to consolidate their fields, equipment, seed and animals into large, state-managed farms that were meant to improve production and crop yields.

Communism   A political and economic system in which all private ownership of property is abolished along with all economic and social class divisions, countries and governments; the only class that would exist in a communist system would be the former working class.

Conference of Ambassadors   Organization composed of ambassadors from France, Britain, Italy and Japan that formed in 1920 to continue the diplomacy of the Allied Powers after the First World War; it functioned primarily in the early 1920s to settle major disputes involving any of the four represented powers.

Conscription   Compulsory military service for a certain length of time.

Constitutional monarchy   A governmental system which features a monarch as head of state with powers limited by a constitution; usually government primarily by parliament which selects ministers who are approved by the monarch.

Cordon sanitaire A French expression that originally meant a barrier to stop disease and that came to mean in international politics the barrier of newly independent and highly nationalistic states that bordered the Soviet Union in Europe between the two world wars.

Coup   Overthrow of a government.

Covenant   Rules and constitution of the League of Nations.

Customs union   A free-trade area.

Dardenelles   Strait connecting the Mediterranean and Aegean Seas with the Black Sea, separating Europe from Asia Minor.

Deficit spending   When a government spends more money than it brings in through taxation, usually to stimulate a country's economy.

Demilitarized   To remove all weapons and troops.

Democrats   US political party that, in the early 1920s, believed good government could solve national and international problems.

Détente   A French term used to describe an easing of tensions between countries.

Diktat   Harsh penalty imposed on a defeated country.

Disarmament   Limiting weapons and militaries in order to reduce the possibility of war.

Dominions   Self-ruling parts of the British Empire such as Australia, Canada, New Zealand, Newfoundland and South Africa.

Embargo   A ban on trade in order to isolate a nation.

Federal government   Governmental system in which individual states have control over local affairs while the national government manages foreign policy, defence and other affairs that affect the nation as a whole.

Fourteen Points   A list of points drawn up by Woodrow Wilson on which the peace settlement at the end of the First World War was based.

Free city   A city with international supervision, belonging to no particular nation.

Freikorps Heavily armed paramilitary units of ex-soldiers who were generally German nationalists, hated communism and were willing to use extreme brutality to crush dissent.

Gold standard   A system by which the value of a currency is linked to gold. When the British pound came off the gold standard in September 1931 its value fell from $4.86 to $3.49.

Gold standard   When a specific amount of paper currency can be exchanged for a set amount of gold.

Great Depression   Period starting in 1929 of severe global economic crisis that resulted in millions of people unemployed, thousands of banks closing from lack of funds, and political crises.

Guerrilla attacks   Military attacks by small groups usually on a larger military force.

Hyperinflation   Rapid reduction in the value of a currency.

Imperial preference   A system of commerce created by lowering import taxes between areas of an empire, while increasing taxes on imports from countries outside the empire.

Imperial War Cabinet   A cabinet made up of prime ministers of the Dominions of the British Empire, also called the Commonwealth, such as Canada, Australia, New Zealand and South Africa.

Import quota   A maximum amount of imports of specific products allowed into a country.

Income tax   Tax on wages.

Indemnity   A financial penalty where one country owes another.

Inheritance taxes   Tax on money or property granted to someone on the death of another person.

Inviolability   Forbidden to cross.

Isolationism   Policy of avoiding alliances and international agreements.

Italian nationalists   In this period, people who wanted to expand the nation state of Italy to include all Italian-language speakers.

Kaiser   Emperor of Germany. Wilhelm II, 1888–1918, was the last German Emperor.

Kiaochow   Territory located on the Shandong peninsula in China that was leased to Germany for 99 years starting in 1898; seized by Japan in the First World War.

Land redistribution   In Russia the idea of granting land to peasants.

Lebensraum German for living space, loosely defined as parts of eastern Europe.

Little Entente   A coalition of Czechoslovakia, Romania and Yugoslavia who agreed to work together against any Hungarian attempts to reclaim lost lands which they now occupied.

Locarno spirit   The optimistic mood of reconciliation and compromise that swept through western Europe after the signing of the Locarno treaties.

Mandates   Lands administered by the League of Nations in theory but by Britain and France almost exclusively in reality.

Mandatories   Nations that administered mandates for the League of Nations.

Mandatory powers   Countries that were granted mandates to supervise.

Marks   German currency.

Mobilization   Preparing armed forces for war.

Moderate socialists   Political groups who were influenced by Marxist thought, did not believe in the use of violence, and wanted to work within parliamentary government to improve living conditions and standards through legislation.

Monroe Doctrine   US government policy from the early nineteenth century which stated that European countries were not to interfere with nations in North and South America.

Moratorium   A pause in activity.

Napoleonic Europe   Period starting about 1799 and ending in 1815 when Europe was dominated by France, ruled by Napoleon Bonaparte, with new countries formed, others abolished and still others absorbed into France.

Nation state   A state consisting of a culturally united population.

National Socialists   Abbreviated name for the National Socialist German Workers' Party or Nazi Party, an ultra-nationalist group.

Neutrality Acts   US laws in the 1930s that required the US government to remain isolated from world affairs so as not to be drawn into war.

New Economic Policy   Economic system in the Soviet Union between 1921 and 1928 in which farmers paid taxes in grain, surplus grain could be sold on the private market for profit, currency was re-introduced small businesses were allowed to return to private ownership and operation.

Open-door policy   US policy that expected all nations to allow all nations to freely trade with China.

Ottoman Empire   Large, nationally and religiously diverse empire ruled by Turks that included most of the Middle East and a small part of Europe, including the Dardenelles and Bosphorus straits that linked the Aegean and Mediterranean Seas with the Black Sea.

Papal States   Small states in central Italy ruled by the Pope until being annexed to Italy.

Pariah state   A nation with no friendly relations with other states.

Parliamentary government   A government responsible to and elected by parliament.

Partition   The breaking up of a larger state into smaller ones.

Passive resistance   Resisting by not participating in any way, usually by refusing to work, shop or be provoked.

Permanent Court of International Justice   Court established by League of Nations in 1922 to rule on aspects of international law.

Petroleum products   Products based on oil, including gasoline, rubber and diesel fuel.

Plebiscite   When all eligible voters of an area vote to accept or reject a specific issue.

Prometheism   Polish ideology that worked to create nation states within the Soviet Union which would then be allies with Poland against Soviet, or Russian, aggression.

Prussia   Large German state that was primarily responsible for forming the German Empire in 1871.

Putsch   A German word used to describe a revolt.

Rearmament   The rebuilding or re-equipping of an army.

Reparations   Payments made by a defeated country to the victor in order to pay for the victor's war expenses, damages, and as a penalty for losing.

Repatriate   To return someone to their country.

Republic   A form of government in which representatives are elected by a population to rule, usually in a parliamentary method of government.

Republican Party   US political party that, in the early 1920s, emphasized free trade and complete independence in foreign policy.

Rome–Berlin Axis   Treaty of friendship between Germany and Italy in 1936, signalling an end to Italy's diplomatic co-operation with Britain and France.

Ruhr   A heavily industrialized area in western Germany.

Sanctions   A ban on trade.

Satellite state   A state that is technically independent, but under some control by another state.

Schlieffen Plan   German plan for war against France and Russia. The plan was to defeat France within weeks, moving through Belgium and Luxembourg, avoiding the fortified border between France and Germany. After the defeat of France, the mass of the German army would move quickly east by rail to invade Russia.

Secret annex   Parts of an agreement that are not made public.

Self-determination   The idea that a nation can choose its own form of government and international status such as independence.

Semi-isolation   Unofficial US government policy in the nineteenth and early twentieth centuries where the USA did not form alliances with or interfere in the affairs of European powers while, at the same time, developing economic relationships with them.

Socialist   One who believes that a society should be as equitable as possible with few, if any, differences between society members in terms of economic or social standing.

Spanish influenza pandemic   This disease killed between 50 million and 100 million people world-wide from 1918 to 1920.

Stimson Doctrine   US policy to not recognize border changes to China, specifically China's separation from Manchuria.

Straits zone   An area of land linking the Aegean and Black Seas, including the Dardanelles and Bosphorus straits, as well as Constantinople and other towns and cities.

Suez Canal   An important shipping route linking the Mediterranean and Red Seas and therefore the Atlantic and Indian Oceans.

Trade barrier   A government policy to restrict trade with other countries usually by placing high taxes on foreign imports so that domestic goods can be sold more cheaply.

Treason   Working against one's country.

Treaty registration   League of Nations initiative that filed and published treaties between the First and Second World Wars so that details were public.

Triple Alliance   Military alliance established in 1881 between Germany, Austria-Hungary and Italy.

Ultra-nationalist   Extreme nationalist usually opposed to all forms of socialism or communism, believing their nationality superior to that of others.

Unrestricted submarine warfare   Policy of allowing submarines to attack any type of ship from an enemy nation without warning.

Wall Street Crash   A rapid decline of the US stockmarket, located on Wall Street in New York, in October 1929 which led to an economic crisis.

War Communism   Economic system by the Bolsheviks during the Russian Civil War in which all property and businesses were owned by the state, currency was abolished and strikes were forbidden.

War pensions   Payments made to wounded or retired men from the military who served in war, or their families.

Zionists   Supporters of Zionism, a group that wanted to establish a Jewish national state in Palestine.

Further reading

Works dealing with the interwar period in general

The Origins of the Second World War by A.J.P. Taylor. Penguin, 2001.
The most famous book by one of the world's most famous historians that continues to inspire and provoke controversy.

Versailles and After: 1919–1933 by Ruth Henig. Methuen, 1984.
A very short work that reviews the period 1919–33, summarizes events succinctly.

A Shattered Peace: Versailles 1919 and the Price We Pay Today by David A. Andelman. John Wiley, 2008.
A highly praised work that connects modern day events to the Paris Peace Conference, 1919.

The Origins of the Second World War in Europe by P.M.H. Bell. Pearson, 2007.
A highly useful and readable work that exhibits excellent scholarship on the interwar period.

The Road to War by Richard Overy and Andrew Wheatcroft. Penguin, 2000.
A work that expands on A.J.P. Taylor's earlier views.

From Sarajevo to Potsdam by A.J.P. Taylor. Thames & Hudson, 1966.
Reviews the interwar period through to the end of the Second World War.

The Causes of the Second World War by Anthony Crozier. Blackwell, 1997.
Contains interesting historiography regarding the outbreak of the Second World War.

The Origins of the Second World War by R.J. Overy. Longman, 2008.
Argues that the Second World War was the result of the decline of old empires and the rise of new ones.

The Making of the Second World War by Anthony Adamthwaite. Routledge, 1992.
Based on French, British, German and Soviet documents, publishing many for the first time.

The Lights that Failed: European International History 1919–1933 by Zara Steiner. Oxford University Press, 2005.
Argues that real political stability was achieved in Europe in the mid-1920s, only to be destroyed by the Great Depression.

Works regarding the Paris Peace Conference and its immediate affects

Paris 1919: Six Months that Changed the World by Margaret MacMillan. Random House, 2003.
A multiple award-winning work that very thoroughly covers the Paris Peace Conference.

Revolutions and Peace Treaties 1917–1921 by Gerhard Schulz. Methuen, 1972.
A work that covers the collapse of the Central Powers and creation of treaties in Paris, 1919.

Works concentrated on specific countries or regions

The Foreign Policy of France from 1914 to 1945 by Jacques Néré. Routledge, 2002.
A work that discusses French foreign policy in incredible detail.

The Politics of Backwardness in Hungary: 1825–1945 by Andrew C. Janos. Princeton, 1982.
A very thorough work that covers Hungary in the interwar period.

A History of Modern Hungary 1867–1994 by Jörg K. Hoensch. Longman, 1996.
A work that covers the interwar period of Hungary.

Admiral Nicholas Horthy: Memoirs by Nicholas Horthy. Simon Publications, 2000.
This is a reprint of Horthy's memoirs and contains a unique perspective of eastern European affairs of the period.

Czechoslovakia in a Nationalist and Fascist Europe 1918–1948 edited by Mark Cornwall and R.J.W. Evans, Proceedings of the British Academy, vol. 140. Oxford University Press, 2007.
Part of a series of works that reflect modern research on Czechoslovakia after the First World War.

Poland, 1918–1945: An Interpretive and Documentary History of the Second Republic by Peter D. Stachura. Routledge, 2004.
One of the most thorough histories of modern Poland.

Rumania, 1866–1947 by Keith Hitchins. Clarendon Press, 1994.
A work that details the creation and maintenance of Romania.

Yugoslavia in Crisis, 1934–1941 by J.B. Hoptner. Columbia University Press, 1963.
A highly focused work that reviews the Kingdom of Yugoslavia that was in political crisis.

Bulgaria by R.J. Crampton. Oxford University Press, 2007.
A detailed work that reviews Bulgarian history in the nineteenth and twentieth centuries.

Toward an Entangling Alliance: American Isolationism, Internationalism, and Europe 1901–1950 by Ronald Powaski. Greenwood Press, 1991.
This work explains how the USA was forced to abandon isolationism.

Italy: From Revolution to Republic, 1700 to the Present by Spencer Di Scala. Westview Press, 1998.
A thorough history of Italy, covering the interwar period in great detail.

Germany: A Short History by Donald Detwiler. Southern Illinois University Press, 1999.
A very general history of Germany since ancient times.

Years of Russia, the USSR, and the Collapse of Soviet Communism by David Evans and Jane Jenkins. Hodder Education, 2008.
Thoroughly reviews the interwar period with statistics, primary sources and historiography.

Eastern Europe in the Twentieth Century and After by R.J. Crampton. Routledge, 1997.
A political history of the entire region, including the interwar period.

A Modern History of Japan: From Tokugawa Times to the Present by Andrew Gordon. Oxford University Press, 2008.
Provides an academic and thorough review of Japan's history including the interwar period.

Works regarding disarmament

Britain and the Problem of International Disarmament, 1919–1934, by Carolyn J. Kitching. Routledge, 1999.
A work that argues that Britain did not provide leadership in disarmament as argued by earlier historians.

Arms Limitation and Disarmament: Restraints on War, 1899–1939 by B.J.C. McKercher. Praeger, 1992.
This work reviews disarmament successes and failures in the early twentieth century.

British and American Naval Power: Politics and Policy, 1900–1936 by Phillips Payson O'Brien. Praeger, 1998.
The most thorough modern work on naval disarmament in the early twentieth century.

Works on the League of Nations including successes and failures

The League of Nations: Its Life and Times 1920–46 by F.S. Northedge. Holmes & Meier, 1986.
The most recent, and very thorough, discussion of the League of Nations' history.

The Manchurian Crisis and Japanese Society, 1931–33 by Sandra Wilson.
Routledge, 2002.
Provides unique perspectives of the Manchurian Crisis on Japanese society, including farmers, women and business groups.

Works regarding mandates

Colonialism and Development: Britain and Its Tropical Colonies, 1850–1960 by Michael Havinden and David Meredith. Routledge, 1993.
A helpful work that includes details of British mandates.

The Creation of Iraq, 1914–1921 by Reeva Spector Simon. Columbia University Press, 2004.
A work that covers the establishment of British rule over Mandate Iraq.

Mandates under the League of Nations by Quincy Wright. University of Chicago Press, 1930.
An older work that provides a wealth of data on every League mandate in the 1920s.

Reshaping Palestine: From Muhammad Ali to the British Mandate, 1831–1922 by Martin Sicker. Praeger, 1999.
A very well-researched work that provides vast source material in its review of Palestine.

The Dependent Empire, 1900–1948: Colonies, Protectorates, and the Mandates, Vol. 7 by Frederick Madden and John Darwin. Greenwood Press, 1994.
A massive work that details European dealings with colonies and mandates.

The French Overseas Empire by Frederick Quinn. Praeger, 2000.
A work that uses primary material from French archives hitherto unpublished.

The Israel–Arab Reader by William Laqueur. Penguin, 2008.
Contains all-important documents related to the Palestine mandate.

The Great Depression and its impact on political systems

The Global Impact of the Great Depression, 1929–1939 by Dietmar Rothermund.
Routledge, 1996.
An invaluable work for studying the effect of the Great Depression on the world.

Hitler: A Study in Tyranny by Alan Bullock. Harper & Row, 1991.
A candid review of Hitler that focuses only on proven facts, not entering into speculation.

Documents on Nazism 1919–1945 by Jeremy Noakes and Geoffrey Pridham.
University of Exeter Press, 1995.
A work that provides critically important documentation on the Nazi era.

'Why the German Republic fell' by Bruno Heilig published in *Why the German Republic Fell and Other Lessons of War and Peace Upholding True Democracy through Economic Freedom*, edited by Arthur Madsen. The Hogarth Press, 1941.
A work found online that provides a unique perspective of a newspaper writer and editor of the time.

Lend Me Your Ears: Great Speeches in History by William Safire. W.W. Norton, 2004.
A work that contains many of the important speeches in history.

Internet and film sources

- A vast number of primary documents, including treaties, speeches, letters and so forth can be found at Fordham University's Modern Internet History Sourcebook: www.fordham.edu/halsall/mod/modsbook.asp
- All treaties and much primary material of the period can be found at Michael Duffy's Firstworldwar.com: www.firstworldwar.com
- Political cartoons of the period from Britain may be found at the University of Kent's website: www.cartoons.ac.uk
- Many out-of-print books and period journals and magazines may be located with Google books. Searches can be made for those works that provide a full view and can be saved in a personal library.
- British National Archives contain primary documents of all periods, but can be difficult to navigate given the sheer volume of data available: www. nationalarchives.gov.uk
- US National Archives also contain primary documents in vast quantities, but can also be difficult to navigate given the sheer volume of data available: www.archives.gov
- The BBC television documentary series *World at War* contains interwar period material in its first volumes.
- *The 50 Year War* by PBS and the BBC is an excellent review of conflict in Palestine, including the Palestine mandate period.

Internal assessment

The internal assessment is an historical investigation on a historical topic. Below is a list of possible topics on international relations 1918–36 that could warrant further investigation. They have been organized by theme.

Paris Peace Conference

1 To what extent were the aims of the Allied Powers at the Paris Peace Conference the same?
2 How important was France in the creation of modern Poland?
3 How successful was Britain in realizing its aims at the Paris Peace Conference?
4 Why did the USA refuse to accept a non-discrimination statement regarding race in the League of Nations' Covenant?
5 Was the Treaty of Trianon the harshest of the treaties created at the Paris Peace Conference?

League of Nations

1 How successful was the League of Nations in preventing war up to 1936?
2 How did the absence of Germany affect the operations of the League of Nations up to 1925?
3 Why did the USA fail to join the League of Nations?
4 To what extent did the British and French governments see the purpose of the League of Nations differently?
5 Did the League of Nations' mandates operate differently from traditional European colonies?

Disarmament

1 To what extent was France's failure to disarm the result of the need to create employment in the Great Depression?
2 What was the effect of US disarmament on the shipbuilding industry in the USA?
3 Was the London Naval Conference of 1930 successful in achieving its goals?
4 How important was the departure of Japan from naval disarmament treaties in 1935?
5 To what extent was the failure of the World Disarmament Conference in 1932 the result of French foreign policy?

Great Depression

1 How did the Great Depression affect US foreign policy in Central America?
2 How successful was the British system of imperial preference in dealing with the Great Depression?
3 Was there a correlation between the Great Depression and the growing popularity of the German Communist Party before 1933?
4 To what extent did the Great Depression affect French politics?
5 What was the impact of the Great Depression on Yugoslav trade with Italy?

Manchurian Crisis

1 What was the effect of the Manchurian Crisis on Chinese politics?
2 How independent was domestic and foreign policy of Manchukuo?
3 Did the acquisition of Manchuria alleviate the effects of the Great Depression in Japan?
4 Was the Japanese Emperor unwilling or unable to prevent the military takeover of the Japanese government in the 1930s?
5 To what extent was the Manchurian Crisis responsible for Japan leaving the London Naval Conference of 1935?

Abyssinian Crisis

1 To what extent was Italy's invasion of Abyssinia motivated by economics?
2 What was the effect of the Italian invasion on the Ethiopian Orthodox Church?
3 How successful was the Italian military in achieving its war aims in Abyssinia?
4 How successful was the League of Nations' trade embargo on Italy as a result of the Abyssinian Crisis?
5 What was the reaction of Africans outside Abyssinia to the Abyssinian Crisis?

Index

The publishers would also like to thank the following for permission to reproduce material in this book:

David Higham Associates for extracts from *The Origins of the Second World War* by A.J.P. Taylor, 1961. Random House, New York and John Murray, London for extracts from *Paris 1919: Six Months that Changed the World* by Margaret MacMillan, 2003.

Acknowledgements:

Ms R.W. Harris for extracts from *Mandates under the League of Nations* by Quincy Wright, University of Chicago Press, 1930. Holmes & Meier for extracts from *The League of Nations: Its Life and Times 1920–46* by F.S. Northedge, Holmes & Meier, London, 1986. Pearson Education Limited for extracts from *The Origins of the Second World War in Europe*, by P.M.H. Bell, Pearson, London, 1997. Routledge for extracts from *Poland, 1918–1945: An Interpretive and Documentary History of the Second Republic* by Peter D. Stachura, Routledge, New York, 2004.

Ammol Publications, *Encyclopedia of International Affairs* by J.C. Johari (ed.), 1997. *The Atlantic*, June 1920. Blackwell, *The Causes of the Second World War* by Anthony Crozier, 1997. Cambridge University Press, *Mussolini Unleashed 1939–1941: Politics and Strategy in Fascist Italy's Last War* by MacGregor Knox, 1982 and *Social Darwinism in European and American Thought, 1860–1945: Nature as Model and Nature as Threat* by Mike Hawkins, 1997. Clarendon Press, *Rumania, 1866–1947* by Keith Hitchins, 1994. Columbia University Press, *The Creation of Iraq, 1914–1921* by Reeva Spector Simon, 2004 and *Yugoslavia in Crisis, 1934–1941* by J.B. Hoptner, 1963. Congressional Quarterly Press, *The Middle East*, 2007. *Daedalus*, Vol. 126, 1996. Doubleday, Page, & Co., *Woodrow Wilson as I Know Him* by Joseph Patrick Tumulty, 1921. Harper & Row, *Hitler: A Study in Tyranny* by Alan Bullock, 1962. Harvard University Press, *Some Problems of the Peace Conference* by Charles Haskins and Robert Lord, 1920. Hodder Education, *Years of Russia, the USSR and the Collapse of Soviet Communism* by Paul Evans and Jane Jenkins, 2008. Hogarth Press, *Why the German Republic Fell and Other Lessons of War and Peace Upholding True Democracy through Economic Freedom* by Arthur Madsen (ed.), 1941. *The Independent*, Vol. 97, p. 394, March 22, 1919. *Insight on the News*, 'Great powers paid price for "peace": history shows that the pacifist movement of the 1930s ultimately helped to usher in the horror of World War II by allowing rogue nations to rise to power unabated' by Stephen Goode, *Insight on the News*, Vol. 19, 2003. Little, Brown & Co., *The European World: A History* by Jerome Blum *et al.*, 1970. Living Age Company, *The Living Age*, Vol. 301, 1919. Longman, *A History of Modern Hungary 1867–1994* by Jörg K. Hoensch, 1996. Macmillan & Co., *Austria 1918–1938: A Study in Failure* by Malcolm Bullock, 1939. Methuen & Co., *Revolutions and Peace Treaties 1917–1921* by Gerhard Schulz, 1972 and *Versailles and After: 1919–1933* by Ruth Henig, 1984. Modern Age Books, *You Might Like Socialism: A Way of Life for Modern Man* by Corliss Lamont, 1939. National Alumni, *Source Records of the Great War, Vol. VII*, Charles F. Horne (ed.), 1923. Naval & Military Press, *My War Memories 1914–1918* by General Erich Ludendorff, 2005. Nelson-Hall, *Haile Selassie I: Ethiopia's Lion of Judah* by Peter Schwab, 1979. New York Times Company, *The New York Times Current History*, Vol. 20, July 1919–October 1920 and *The New York Times*, 11 November 1918, Vol. LXVIII, No. 22,206. W.W. Norton, *Lend me Your Ears: Great Speeches in History* by William Safire, 1997. Ohio University Press, *Namibia's Liberation Struggle: The Two-Edged Sword* by Colin Leys and John S. Saul, 1995. Old Colony Trust Company, *The League of Nations*, 1919. Oxford University Press, *Bulgaria* by R.J. Crampton, 2007; *Czechoslovakia in a Nationalist and Fascist Europe 1918–1948* by Mark Cornwall and R.J.W. Evans (eds), 2007 and *Germany: A Self-Portrait* by Harlan R. Crippen (ed.), 1944. Pearson Education, *The Inter-War Crisis: 1919–1939* by R.J. Overy, 2007 and *The Origins of the Second World War* by R.J. Overy, 1998. Penguin Books, *The Road to War* by Richard Overy and Andrew Wheatcroft, 1999. *Popular Mechanics*, 'Manchuria: what is it all about?' by Uthai Vincent Wilcox, *Popular Mechanics*, February 1932, Vol. 57, Number 2. Praeger, *Arms Limitation and Disarmament: Restraints on War, 1899–1939* by B.J.C. McKercher, 1992; *British and American Naval Power: Politics and Policy, 1900–1936* by P.P. O'Brien, 1998 and *Reshaping Palestine: From Muhammad Ali to the British Mandate, 1831–1922* by Martin Sicker, 1999. Princeton University Press, *The Politics of Backwardness in Hungary: 1825–1945* by Andrew C. Janos, 1982. Routledge, *Britain and the Problem of International Disarmament, 1919–1934* by Carolyn J. Kitching, 1999; *Colonialism and Development: Britain and Its Tropical Colonies, 1850–1960* by Michael Havinden and David Meredith, 1993; *The Foreign Policy of France* by Jacques Néré, 2002; *The Global Impact of the Great Depression, 1929–1939* by Dietmar Rothermund, 1996; *The Making of the Second World War* by Anthony Adamthwaite, 1992 and *The Manchurian Crisis and Japanese Society, 1931–33* by Sandra Wilson, 2002. Simon & Schuster, *Diplomacy* by Henry Kissinger, 1995. Simon Publications, *Admiral Nicholas Horthy: Memoirs* by Nicholas Horthy, 2000. Springer, *Sir Gerald Fitzmaurice and the World Crisis: A Legal Adviser in the Foreign Office 1930–1945* by Anthony Carty, 2000. Thames & Hudson, *From Sarajevo to Potsdam* by A.J.P. Taylor, 1966. University of Exeter Press, *Documents on Nazism 1919–1945* by Jeremy Noakes and Geoffrey Pridham, 1995. US State Department, *Peace and War: United States Foreign Policy, 1931–1941*. Viking Press, *The World of Yesterday* by Stephan Zweig, 1943. John Wiley & Sons, *A Shattered Peace: Versailles 1919 and the Price We Pay Today* by David A. Andelman, 2008. *World Affairs*, Vol. 158, 1995.

Every effort has been made to trace all copyright holders, but if any have been inadvertently overlooked the Publishers will be pleased to make the necessary arrangements at the first opportunity.